The Spirit of an Activist

The Spirit of an

Activist

The Life and Work of I. DeQUINCEY NEWMAN

Edited by *Sadye L. M. Logan*

Foreword by Vernon E. Jordan Jr. Prologue by James E. Clyburn

THE UNIVERSITY OF SOUTH CAROLINA PRESS

Published by the University of South Carolina Press
Columbia, South Carolina 29208

www.uscpress.com

Manufactured in the United States of America

25 24 23 22 21 6 5 4 3 2

Library of Congress Cataloging-in-Publication Data
can be found at http://catalog.loc.gov/.

ISBN: 978-1-61117-327-7 (hardcover)
ISBN: 978-1-61117-328-4 (ebook)

To the memory of Anne Paulina Hinton Newman
and to the students from South Carolina State and Claflin Colleges
who took a stand for freedom and justice: 1956–1967
and to the students who gave their lives for freedom and justice
in South Carolina
and to all the civil and human right activists who took a stand for a
free and just South Carolina
and to all who took a stance for freedom and justice everywhere

Seer

for Isaiah DeQuincey Newman

How it must have burnt your heart,
Isaiah, seer of the Lord, to think that
saints would worship boxed up in
buildings, yet torn apart by race, divided,
mumbling prayers. How it pained you to say,
"I come from a people of unclean ways," how
it pained you. But with gentle dignity, you
Darlington County man, whispered a prayer,
then declared it all spiritual this injustice against
the Negro, this stance of racist Jim Crow. And man
you labored with patience, even temper and grace
to enact the alchemy of turning stony hearts into
pliant and giving flesh. Yes, Isaiah, senator who
cleared away the dust Jim Crow left, perhaps your
heart has found some peace now.

from Kwame Dawes, *Grace* (presented
by Historic Columbia Foundation)

Contents

List of Illustrations

Foreword

When I think of the Reverend I. DeQuincey Newman, verses from one of Longfellow's poems reverberate in my mind: "Lives of great men all remind us we can make our lives sublime. And departing leave behind us foot prints on the sands of time." I. DeQuincey Newman was, by any measure, a great man. We met for the first time at an NAACP convention in Philadelphia, Pennsylvania, in 1961. Roy Wilkins had just appointed me the Georgia field secretary for the state conference of NAACP branches. I reported directly to Mrs. Ruby Hurley, director of the Southeastern Regional Office of the NAACP. My counterparts in Alabama, Mississippi, North Carolina, South Carolina, and Florida also reported to Mrs. Hurley.

The basic job of an NAACP field director was to build the membership of local chapters. This required not only traveling throughout the state but also a great deal of courage, flexibility, creativity, and abundant energy. Field directors also helped the local communities organize events, participate in voter registration programs, create youth councils, respond whenever there were allegations of discrimination, and conduct mass meetings (see Vernon E. Jordan., Jr., with Annette Gordon-Reed, *Vernon Can Read! A Memoir*, 2001). Being a field director was dangerous, and the community leaders who got involved shared the risk of losing everything, including their lives. Usually, however, the designated NAACP contact was someone who was not dependent on the white community for his or her livelihood. It was usually the local undertaker, the county agent, a doctor, or a minister.

Some of my fellow field directors were twice my age. A recent law school graduate from Howard University, I was not yet twenty-six years old. I immediately experienced a strong feeling of family, commitment, and organization when I met my fellow field directors and the heads of other components of the organization. When introduced to I. DeQuincey Newman, I felt that I had struck it rich. I loved his deep voice and his laugh. DeQuincey's bowtie and derby hat set him apart as unique as well as demonstrated that he was a smart dresser. I also loved that he took his praying seriously. I was convinced that when DeQuincey prayed, God was truly listening.

DeQuincey combined his seriousness about his ministry with a great appreciation for life. This appreciation of life resonated with me. DeQuincey lacked hypocrisy, and I could identify with that and with him. As a newcomer to the organization, I asked many questions and occasionally challenged my supervisors, Mrs. Hurley and Gloster Current. DeQuincey was very supportive and encouraged my boss and the others to take heed and pay closer attention to the younger staff members.

I met DeQuincey again in Beaufort County, South Carolina, one month after the Philadelphia convention. The southeastern regional office was holding a retreat at the Penn Community Center on St. Helena Island. At that time the Penn Center was under the leadership and direction of the Quakers. While I was on retreat, an unforgettable experience involving DeQuincey occurred. The experience concerned an incident related to the quality and quantity of the meals served during the retreat.

The Quakers, in keeping with the will of simplicity, provided a sparse menu consisting of two meals a day: breakfast early in the morning and supper at 4:00. Three hours after supper everyone was hungry and wishing for something to eat. We took matters into our own hands. We piled into a station wagon in search of food. As the youngest, I was the designated driver. The only café for blacks in the town was closed, so we kept driving until we saw a blinking neon sign with the words "Steaks, Chips, and Fish." It was a truck stop.

I turned into the parking lot and, to Mrs. Hurley's chagrin, drove around to the back. In those days blacks did not go to truck stops to dine. The only way to get food was through the back door. When Ruby Hurley asked where I was going, I replied, "I have a friend in here. I am going to stop and have a word with him." Mrs. Hurley protested. She sputtered in an irate tone: "You cannot go to the back door. You are an NAACP official." NAACP policy was to enter establishments only through the front doors, if at all.

Even as Mrs. Hurley vehemently ordered me to halt and desist, I continued. The Reverend I. DeQuincey Newman lent his rich voice to the duet between Mrs. Hurley and me, stating, "Vernon, Ruby has given you an order." But I persisted.

I went inside the establishment in search of the chef, whom I found to be an imposing black man, beautifully attired in chef gear. I told him my name and whom I represented. He politely inquired about our meeting, which all of black Beaufort knew about. I also explained our need for nourishment.

Medgar Evers, the field secretary in Mississippi, entered the kitchen to remind me gently that I was violating NAACP policy. Shortly after that, the chef returned with a huge, flat bread box with T-bone steaks, salad, onion rings, french fries, and hot rolls. When I inquired about the cost, the chef replied that the white owner was treating us to dinner, unknowingly.

Needless to say, Ruby Hurley was outraged at my youthful stupidity. In the middle of her tirade, DeQuincey Newman broke the silence in his deep, deep voice with a wit to match and said, "Ruby, I don't know what Vernon has in the box, but it sure smells good." We had a great meal, joined by Mrs. Hurley, happily, who provided the spirits with dinner.

The real point here was the cool, calming influence of I. DeQuincey Newman—the ultimate negotiator and diplomat. He understood Ruby's point of view as well as the need to get dinner.

I. DeQuincey Newman was a mentor and role model to so many young people in South Carolina. I am proud to claim his mentorship, which lasted long after my departure from the NAACP. In preparing my address to a joint session of the South Carolina General Assembly in 1976, I consulted heavily with DeQuincey, who gave sound counsel and sat approvingly through my presentation.

I. DeQuincey Newman—preacher, social activist, advocate, legislator, and NAACP man through and through—has a special place in the history of South Carolina. He was a force for good, for justice, and for change. I am honored by this friendship.

This book is about leadership and courage and selflessness and one man's journey on the road to freedom.

Vernon E. Jordan, Jr.

Acknowledgments

As I viewed images in *Out-of-the-Box in Dixie: Photography of the South Carolina Events that Changed America* in preparation for writing this book, the faces of former classmates at South Carolina State College (now University) stared back at me. Only then I realized that the Reverend I. DeQuincey Newman had been instrumental in securing the release of me and many of my classmates from the Orangeburg county jail, "Pink Palace," where we were confined after being arrested for marching in protest against racial segregation in my native South Carolina. Until this realization, I thought that Reverend Newman's and my paths had never crossed.

This book project reconnects his and my lives and rekindles the memories of half a century. Two decades ago I learned that Newman had hoped such a book would be written. I learned of this request in one of my early meetings with his widow, Anne Pauline Hinton Newman. One of the first things I did after my appointment in 1999 as I. DeQuincey Newman Professor of Social Work at the University of South Carolina was to contact his family to introduce myself and inform them about my vision for the Newman endowed professorship. My vision was consistent with the written goals of the chair. The Newman professorship was established in 1994 in remembrance of Newman's dedication to peace and equal opportunity in South Carolina, the nation, and the world. The chair seeks to fulfill two purposes: 1) to honor Reverend Newman's memory, his enduring contributions to the cause of improved human relations, and his distinguished public service; and 2) to influence recruitment programs addressing the needs of oppressed and historically underrepresented groups, encourage institutional diversity, and develop curricula and teacher training programs that promote peaceful social change.

I am deeply appreciative for the support of two outstanding graduate assistants, Marlene Briones and Kendra P. DeLoach, who assisted in typing drafts, typing the endnotes, and undertaking important library research. Gloria Thomas Pillow, former professor of African American literature at Michigan State University and daughter of James Thomas, reviewed the transcript of the editor's interview of her father, a close associate of Newman. Because of her father's illness, she reviewed and commented on his transcribed and edited reflections. She also read and offered helpful counsel on the entire manuscript. Perhaps the most substantive and constructive feedback came from Kieran Taylor, professor of history and coordinator of the Citadel Oral History Program. He helped me to view the manuscript through the lens of a historian.

The late Anne Newman and Emily Newman, her daughter, are among the chief benefactors of the project. Mrs. Newman was a staunch supporter from the beginning to the end. She was always available to answer questions or simply to help in whatever way she thought would move the project along. She passed away before this book went to press, but she expressed pride and gratitude for the effort made to capture the life and work of her late husband.

Chronology

Events that Shaped Reverend I. DeQuincey Newman's Life (1911–85), the State of South Carolina, the Nation, and the World

	Social, Economic, and Political Context	*Newman's Life Trajectory*
1911	Former Civil War hero and Reconstruction politician Robert Smalls foiled a lynch mob by spreading rumors that Charleston would burn if jailed African Americans were harmed	Newman's birth to Milton C. Newman and Charlotte "Lottie" Elizabeth Morris
1912	Wilson elected president; Septima Poinsette Clark began teaching career on Johns Island, S.C.; Booker T. Washington High School opened in Columbia, S.C.	
1913	Black leaders met with President Wilson to protest segregation	
1916	Wilson reelected; James Weldon Johnson appointed field secretary of NAACP	
1917	NAACP chapter organized in Charleston and Columbia, S.C.; Russian Revolution; U.S. entered World War I	Death of Newman's mother, Charlotte Elizabeth Morris Newman (b. 1882)
1919	Charleston race riot; black convict burned alive	Newman's first encounter with racial hatred
1920	Prohibition began; white women gained voting rights; NAACP had its first significant victory convincing white Charleston leaders to hire blacks to teach in black public schools in city; Harding elected president; rebirth of Ku Klux Klan, which claimed 5 million members	
1921	Dr. H. D. Monteith created the Victory Savings Bank in Columbia, S.C.	
1922	Beginning of massive number of black people migrating from South Carolina; NAACP placed large ads in major newspapers to present facts about lynching	

	Social, Economic, and Political Context	*Newman's Life Trajectory*
1923	Coolidge elected president	
1925	Nathaniel J. Frederick founded the black newspaper *Palmetto Leader* in Columbia, S.C.	
1929	Stock market crash; Great Depression; Hoover elected president	Newman obtained his local preacher's license
1930		Newman graduated from high school at Claflin College in Orangeburg, S.C., and enrolled at Clark College in Atlanta, Ga.
1931	Scottsboro Boys, nine African American defendants, falsely accused in a rape case; all but one initially sentenced to death; case later viewed as one of the most significant legal fights of the twentieth century	Newman's appointment as a deacon
1933	Franklin Roosevelt elected president; jobless total reached 5 million people; New Deal began	
1934		Newman graduated from Clark College; continued studies at Gammon Theological Seminary, Atlanta, Ga.
1935	Social Security Act; National Labor Relations Act (Wagner Act); NAACP lawyers Charles Houston and Thurgood Marshall won legal battle to admit African American students to University of Maryland	Newman's appointment as an elder
1936	Jesse Owens broke a world record at the Olympics; Dr. Mary McLeod Bethune appointed by President Roosevelt to head National Youth Administration's Division of Negro Affairs	
1937		Newman married Anne Pauline Hinton; Newman graduated from Gammon Theological Seminary
1939	Founding meeting of the South Carolina NAACP State Conference of Branches headed by Rev. Alonzo W. Wright, president, and Maggie B. Robinson, secretary; World War II began; NAACP moved Marian Anderson concert to Lincoln Memorial after Daughters of Revolution barred her from performing at Constitution Hall	

	Social, Economic, and Political Context	Newman's Life Trajectory
1940		Newman began serving as pastor at Trinity United Methodist in Orangeburg, S.C.
1941	Rev. James M. Hinton elected president of the S.C. NAACP State Conference of Branches with Modjeska Monteith Simkins as secretary and Levi F. Byrd as treasurer; Rev. E. A. Adams was president of NAACP's Columbia Chapter; NAACP led effort to ensure that President F. Roosevelt ordered a nondiscriminatory policy in war-related industries and federal employment	
1942	Internment of 117,000 Japanese Americans, of whom 71,000 were native-born; Holocaust revealed	
1943	S.C. NAACP State Conference suit for equalization of South Carolina's teachers' salaries filed in federal court (*Duvall v. Charleston School Board*); end of legal involuntary servitude in South	Newman assumed leadership role in NAACP
1944	Roosevelt elected to fourth term; D-day; John McCray became editor of *Lighthouse and Informer*, a voice for the new radical movement; Supreme Court decision in *Smith v. Allwright* ended the white primary; black-led S.C. Progressive Democratic Party (PDP) organized; Osceola McKaine, black PDP candidate, ran against Gov. Olin Johnston for U.S. Senate; PDP challenged state Democratic Party delegation's seating at the National Democratic Convention	
1945	Harry S. Truman assumes presidency after the death of FDR; bombs dropped on Hiroshima and Nagasaki; S.C. NAACP sued to equalize teachers' salaries in Columbia (*Thompson v. Gibbs*); NAACP started national outcry when Congress refused to fund Roosevelt's Fair Employment Practices Commission (FEPC)	
1946	Case of *John H. Wrigten v. University of South Carolina* resulted in the establishment of the Law School of South Carolina State College in Orangeburg; George Elmore, secretary of Richland County PDP, successfully registered	

	Social, Economic, and Political Context	*Newman's Life Trajectory*
1946 cont.	to vote; NAACP won the *Morgan v. Virginia* case, by which the Supreme Court banned states from having laws that sanctioned segregated facilities on interstate travel trains and buses	
1947	NAACP filed suit in federal district court in Columbia, S.C., on behalf of George A. Elmore, who was denied a ballot in the Democratic primary in the previous request, and Judge Waring issued decision that eliminated white primary in South Carolina; India partitioned into India and Pakistan	
1948	Rev. James M. Hinton opposed the regional plan of education in Clarendon County, S.C.; Esau Jenkins, lowcountry civil rights activist, founded the Progressive Club, which encouraged African Americans in the lowcountry to register to vote; Truman reelected president; State of Israel established; NAACP pressured Truman to sign Executive Order banning discrimination by federal government; *Brown v. Baskins* case secured full voting rights in South Carolina	Newman became vice president of the NAACP State Conference of Branches
1949	NATO formed; Harry Briggs petitioned Clarendon County by the NAACP for total education equality	
1950	Korean War began; South Carolina district; *Briggs v. Elliott* suit filed to desegregate public schools in Clarendon County; Ralph Bunch become first black person to receive Nobel Peace Prize for his work as a United Nations mediator	Newman served as district superintendent of Sumter District United Methodist Church until 1956
1951	Harry T. Moore was first NAACP official killed in the civil rights struggle on December 25, when a bomb was placed beneath the floor under his bed; his wife, Harriette, died nine days later	
1952	South Carolina voluntarily repealed the poll tax	
1953	Pres. Eisenhower announced cease-fire in Korea; Eloree, S.C., school board vowed to make wholesale purge of black schoolteachers who would not disown NAACP membership affiliation	

	Social, Economic, and Political Context	*Newman's Life Trajectory*
1954	Sarah Mae Flemming took a front seat on a segregated bus in South Carolina, was humiliated by the bus driver, and filed a suit against the bus company that resulted in the court striking down segregation of city buses; *Brown v. Board of Education of Topeka;* Esau Jenkins influenced building of the first high school for blacks on Johns and Wadmalaw Islands, S.C.	
1955	Rosa Parks arrested in Montgomery, Ala., for taking a front seat on a bus in a then-segregated city, noted as a catalyst for the largest grassroots civil rights movement spearheaded through collective efforts of NAACP, SCLC, and other black organizations; Osceola McKaine, PDP activist, died	Birth of Newman's daughter, Emily Morris
1956	S.C. legislature passed law stipulating no city or state employee could be affiliated with any civil rights organization	Newman began serving as pastor of Wesley Methodist Church, Charleston, S.C. (1956–58)
1957	Eisenhower sent troops to Little Rock Central High School in Arkansas; S.C. NAACP lost more than fifty of eighty-four branches; James T. McCain, founding member and president of Sumter, S.C., NAACP, worked to organize CORE in South Carolina; passage of Civil Rights Bill.	
1958		Newman elected president of the S.C. NAACP State Conference of Branches; served as pastor at Silver Hill United Methodist Church, Spartanburg, S.C.
1959	Alaska and Hawaii granted statehood; S.C. NAACP sued for $5 million by Davis Lee, a black publisher; Fidel Castro became premier of Cuba	
1960	Four black students began lunch counter sit-ins in Greensboro, N.C., which led to more than sixty stores officially desegregating their counters	Newman became field director of S.C. NAACP
1961	Kennedy elected president; Bay of Pigs invasion; Berlin wall built; Alan Shepard became first American in space	Newman led a "wade-in" at Myrtle Beach State Park, which was off-limits to blacks; S.C. NAACP members

	Social, Economic, and Political Context	*Newman's Life Trajectory*
1961 cont.		implemented ICC ruling to integrate bus terminals; black parents sought to integrate schools in Darlington, Beaufort, and Charleston, S.C.; suit filed to desegregate Sesquicentennial, Myrtle Beach, and all other state parks
1962	Cuban missile crisis; S.C. legislature voted to fly Confederate Naval Jack over capitol dome to mark one-hundredth anniversary of the Confederate secession	Newman led fact-finding initiative to establish Francis Burns United Methodist Church, Columbia, S.C.
1963	Medgar Evers, civil rights activist, assassinated in front of his house in Jackson, Miss.; John F. Kennedy assassinated; Lyndon B. Johnson became president; march on Washington; Harvey Gantt became first African American to enroll in Clemson University; James Solomon, Henri Monteith, and Robert Anderson enrolled in University of South Carolina; NAACP pushed for passage of the Equal Employment Opportunity Act	
1964	Twenty-fourth Amendment ratified, prohibiting poll taxes; Johnson ordered bombing of North Vietnam; Civil Rights Act of 1964 passed; President Johnson's War on Poverty and Great Society; Medicare and Medicaid programs started; Economic Opportunity Act and Food Stamp Act passed; Dr. Martin Luther King, Jr., awarded Nobel Peace Prize; S.C. NAACP cited in *New York Times* for successful voter registration efforts; "Operation Breadbasket," an equal job opportunity program, launched; Kenneth Kaunder, president of Zambia (former chairman of the Frontline State and a leader of the organization of African Unity Party) visited the front line of the S.C. civil rights movement; Supreme Court ended eight-year effort of Alabama officials to ban NAACP activities	
1965	Voting Rights Act passed; Watts riots; S.C. attorney Matthew Perry elected to NAACP National Board of Directors; Rev. J. Herbert Nelson of Orangeburg became S.C. NAACP president; fifteen hundred citizens marched on	

	Social, Economic, and Political Context	*Newman's Life Trajectory*
1965 cont.	S.C. state capitol protesting slow implementation of Economic Opportunity Act in South Carolina; NAACP "Battle for the Ballot" program launched in Barnwell and Allendale, S.C.	
1967	Urban riots in Cleveland, Newark, and Detroit; S.C. State College students boycotted classrooms over lack of confidence in the college president, B. C. Turner, to lead; NAACP and black community organized a petition calling for President Turner's removal; President Turner announced resignation	
1968	Martin Luther King, Jr., and Robert Kennedy assassinated; Soviet Union invaded Czechoslovakia; Orangeburg Massacre took place, killing three students—Samuel Hammond, Delano Middleton, and Henry Smith—and wounding twenty-four more; NAACP intervened to represent slain and injured students at S.C. State College; President Johnson signed civil rights bill banning discrimination in housing	Newman served as delegate to National Democratic Convention; *(Anne Pauline) Newman v. Piggy Park Enterprises:* first federal case in which equal accommodation was mandated by the courts; Newman initiated poverty tour of South Carolina's most impoverished areas, which was a precursor to the S.C. Food Stamp Program; conference to organize the poor conducted under Newman's leadership; Newman became director of the Progressive Development Corporation
1969	Nixon elected president; Neil Armstrong landed on the moon; NAACP opposed Clement F. Haynesworth's nomination to U.S. Supreme Court; Rev. Matthew McCollom elected president of NAACP; Isaac "Ike" Williams, former NAACP state youth director and longtime NAACP activist, named Newman's successor as field director of S.C. NAACP; Calvin Wright led the fight for African Americans to use swimming area of the Edisto River in Orangeburg, S.C.; Mrs. Coretta Scott King participated in the historic 113-day Charleston Hospital Workers Strike	Newman resigned as field director of S.C. NAACP after ten years; Newman appointed as executive president of Statewide Home Foundation
1970	I. S. Leevy Johnson, James Felder, and Herbert Fielding were first African Americans elected to S.C. House in General Assembly in 1902; NAACP sponsored youth task force to work	Newman established relationship with and visited several African countries (Liberia, Kenya, Zambia, and Rhodesia);

	Social, Economic, and Political Context	*Newman's Life Trajectory*
1970 cont.	in Barnwell, Spartanburg, and Columbia, S.C.; Cleveland Sellers, former national program secretary for SNCC, sentenced to one year in prison and fined $250 after being "convicted" of participating in the Orangeburg Massacre on the campus of S.C. State College, during which three black students were killed	Newman appointed to the State Study Committee on Aging
1971	James Clyburn became first minority adviser to a S.C. governor, John C. West; 308 female workers at the Medical University of South Carolina hospital went on strike; NAACP-sponsored voter registration drives netted seventy-seven hundred new eighteen-year-olds in Charleston and Richland Counties, S.C.; NAACP successfully opposed nomination and appointment of former congressman Albert Watson to U.S. Military Court of Appeals; NAACP launched statewide campaign to upgrade black professionals in the State Department of Education and local school districts; NAACP attacked discrimination at the C. F. Sauer Plant in Greenville, S.C., and the B. F. Goodrich Company in Camden, S.C.	Newman appointed as commissioner of the State Housing Authority
1972	Reapportionment suit issued against S.C. Senate; Nixon went to China; NAACP assisted Greater Columbia Community Relations Council in development of All American Plan, designed to recruit and hire "minorities" in retail and commercial businesses in the Columbia area	Newman served as delegate to National Democratic Convention
1973	Watergate hearings; NAACP opposed reenactment of death penalty law	
1974	James Clyburn headed S.C. Affairs Commission (until 1992); S.C. General Assembly rewrote election laws, under pressure from federal courts to end at-large election of legislators from counties and create single-member districts, enabling election of ten additional African Americans to S.C. House of Representatives; Nixon resigned; Ford became president; NAACP assisted in effort to modernize criminal justice system; NAACP challenged practices of expulsion and suspension of black students in public schools	

	Social, Economic, and Political Context	*Newman's Life Trajectory*
1975	Vietnam War ended; Helsinki agreement; African American legislators in the S.C. House formed the Legislative Black Caucus, chaired by Ernest Finney, Jr., to promote cooperative legislative actions	Newman became director of the Governor's Office of Rural Development; Newman appointed secretary of the State Board of Health and Environmental Control
1976	Bicentennial celebrated; Vernon Gordan addressed joint session of the S.C. Assembly; record high unemployment, economic recession; S.C. State College president Dr. M. Maceo Nance, Jr., awarded doctorate from the University of South Carolina, a first for a black recipient; attorney Matthew J. Perry, chief legal counsel for S.C. NAACP, named to U.S. Military Court of Appeals; attorney Ernest A. Finney, Jr., NAACP counsel and former Sumter branch president, elected as first black circuit judge in South Carolina since Reconstruction	
1977	Carter elected president; Alex Haley's *Roots* viewed by over 120 million viewers; Greenville dentist Dr. W. F. Gibson chosen to succeed Rev. M. D. McCollom as NAACP president	
1978	Camp David agreement; Ronald McNair, a native of Lake City, S.C., was one of three black men chosen by NASA	Newman served as President Carter's personal representative to Solomon Islands independence celebrations
1979	Soviet invasion of Afghanistan; England's Margaret Thatcher became the West's first woman prime minister; principal plaintiffs in *Brown v. Board of Education* cases met during the twenty-fifth celebration of the case's decision held in Columbia, S.C.; Septima Poinsette Clark awarded Living the Legacy Award by President Carter; NAACP initiated first bill ever signed by a governor that allowed voter registration in high schools	Newman awarded Order of the Palmetto
1980		Newman served as delegate to the National Democratic Convention
1981	Reagan elected president; Sandra Day O'Connor appointed to Supreme Court; NAACP presented plans for reapportionment of South Carolina's congressional lines;	Newman became co-owner of WDPN-FM radio station

	Social, Economic, and Political Context	Newman's Life Trajectory
1981 cont.	NAACP met with State Budget and Control Board to discuss lack of blacks in state government; NAACP established Fair Share Program with major corporations across the country and also led effort to extend Voting Rights Act for another twenty-five years	
1982	South Carolina Roundtable was formed to develop issues pertinent to blacks; S.C. NAACP president Dr. W. F. Gibson elected chairman of the Forum, consisting of black leaders across the state; Equal Rights Amendments failed ratification; NAACP registered more than 850,000 voters, and through its protest and support of the Supreme Court prevented President Reagan from giving tax breaks to racially segregated Bob Jones University	Newman elected to the S.C. Senate, the first black person elected to that body since Reconstruction
1983	NAACP field director's position abolished; S.C. NAACP held appreciation dinner for outgoing field director Isaac Williams	Newman resigned and organized the Middleton-Rosemond United Methodist Church, whose name changed in 1985 to I. DeQuincey Newman United Methodist Church
1984	Dr. William Gibson became chair of the National NAACP Board of Directors upon the death of Kelly Alexander; Geraldine Ferraro ran for U.S. vice president; Reagan reelected president; S.C. NAACP intervened on the side of the Justice Department in Senate reapportionment suit; Dr. Benjamin E. Mays, preacher, scholar, civil rights activist, presidential adviser, and sixth president of Morehouse College, died at eighty-nine; Nelson B. Rivers III became fourth executive secretary of the NAACP	
1985	Levi F. Byrd, founder and treasurer emeritus of the S.C. NAACP, died; Hampton County, S.C., victorious in landmark Supreme Court suit involving voting rights; Reagan began his second term; arms talk between United States and Soviet Union; Ernest Finney, Jr., became first African American associate justice on state supreme court since Reconstruction; Gorbachev became leader of U.S.S.R; NAACP led massive antiapartheid rally in New York	Newman's death

	Social, Economic, and Political Context	*Newman's Life Trajectory*
1999		Newman acknowledged by the *State* newspaper as one of one hundred memorable South Carolinians who raised questions and provided answers
2001		I. DeQuincey Newman Institute for Peace and Social Justice established at University of South Carolina College of Social Work.
2012		Historic marker unveiled for civil rights leader, Reverend I. DeQuincey Newman

Prologue

It is quite an honor for me to write the prologue to this book honoring the life and legacy of I. DeQuincey Newman. As the first South Carolinian and the second African American to rise to the third ranking position in the United States House of Representatives, I am acutely aware of how important it is to have strong shoulders to stand upon. Reverend Newman was one of those who provided some pretty broad shoulders for those in my generation.

His assistance came in many forms. Sometimes it was private counsel, and at other times it was a stirring public sermon. I. D. believed that it was important to lead by precept and example. He never asked us to go where he would not go or to do anything he would not do. It was a practice that I and many others admired. At most times it was deliberate and well-intended, while at other times it was his mere presence that motivated us.

There is one memory of Reverend Newman that stands out for me. It is a great example of the "precepts and examples" rule, as well as why sometimes it is necessary to find exceptions to the practiced rule. I often repeat this story, because it was a tremendous life lesson for me, and it speaks volumes of the man I greatly admired.

Reverend Newman urged a group of us to travel to Columbia in March 1961 from South Carolina State College's campus in order to participate in an NAACP-sponsored rally and march to the South Carolina State House. My roommate, Clarence "Duke" Missouri, and I were among those who responded. Our plan was to attend the rally but not participate in the march because it would probably lead to arrests, and we had had our fill of jail.

So we got dressed in our Sunday best and drove to Columbia, fully intending to see the marchers off from Washington Street's Zion Baptist Church and then return to Orangeburg. However, when we arrived, Reverend Newman took one look at our attire and intuitively knew our intentions. He knew how to manipulate a situation to achieve his desired outcome and quickly led Duke and me to a group of students who had responded to the call from the campus of our alma mater, Mather Academy in Camden. He told us that the students wanted us to lead them in the march. Our egos got the better of us and we agreed, but we told the students that when the order was given to turn around, we would follow the order to avoid arrest. They agreed.

When Chief J. P. Strom, head of the State Law Enforcement Division, called me by name and told me to turn around before we reached the capitol grounds, I turned to acquiesce and lead the students back to the church. However, Rev. David Carter from Newberry launched into a tirade about how no one would turn us around, and emotions being what they were, the Mather Academy students got caught up in the rhetoric and pushed Duke and me forward in their determined march to reach the capitol. The next thing we all knew, we were being marched off to jail.

After several hours spent on army cots on the firing range in the basement of the Columbia City Jail, a nervous Mather student approached me and asked when we would be getting out. I assured him that Reverend Newman was out collecting the bail and that we should be released soon. The student left seemingly reassured but returned a while later and asked, "Clyburn, who did you say was out collecting the bail money?" I replied, "Reverend Newman." The teenager quietly inquired whether Reverend Newman was the little man with the goatee, and I answered affirmatively. He then responded, "Well, he's back in that corner over there." Consequently we spent three days in jail waiting for someone to bail us out, and I never wore that three-piece olive green suit again.

That is when I learned a real lesson about each of us having a role to play. It was expected that Reverend Newman's role was to organize and secure bail for those of us jailed in our exploits. Yet he felt passionately about our efforts and the need to lead by example. I learned that day that we all have roles to play, and the success of our efforts depends in large measure on our knowing our roles and playing those roles effectively. I knew even back then that my most effective role during our marches and demonstrations was as a negotiator. Thanks to Reverend Newman, to this day I try never to forget my role.

Reverend Newman epitomized that philosophy, and he became not only an effective negotiator with South Carolina's elected leaders but in many instances also their friend and confidant. Eventually he was elected to the senate himself, becoming the first African American since post-Reconstruction to do so. Some have criticized Reverend Newman's efforts to become part of the system that he once fought so doggedly against, but he knew that the only way to change the system is from the inside.

Reverend Newman was a towering giant of his time. It was not self-promotion and ego that propelled Reverend Newman to lead the charge for civil rights. Instead it was his sense of humanity and the divinely given right of equality in which he believed so passionately. His heart was always in the ministry, and his faith was the abiding foundation that raised him to extraordinary heights.

Reverend Newman was a dear friend and dependable mentor. He paved the way that has enabled me to become the first African American to represent South Carolina in Congress since the late nineteenth century. I am eternally grateful for his leadership and friendship, and I commend Dr. Sadye Logan for carrying on his legacy, occupying the endowed chair that bears his name at the University of South Carolina. Dr. Logan's dedication to this project is just another manifestation of the tenacity that Reverend Newman instilled in those of us who follow in his footsteps.

Congressman James E. Clyburn

Introduction

This book has been a journey of discoveries about Reverend Isaiah DeQuincey Newman, his family, his colleagues, the history of the state of South Carolina, as well as about the one doing the discovering. It is intended that readers will also experience a journey of discoveries—that they too will leave this experience more informed and motivated in continuing to work for the creation of a more just and equal society. It is further intended that this book serve to move I. DeQuincey Newman's contributions to building a more just and equal society beyond a mere footnote in our history books. Ultimately this book will serve as a primary source of data for serious students interested in a more in-depth analysis of human and civil rights, activism, and advocacy. More important is that it also spark an interest in the young and curious who have never heard of people in the civil rights struggle such as Esau Jenkins (Johns Island), Septima Poinsette Clark (Charleston), Harry Briggs and Joseph A. DeLaine (Clarendon County), Levy G. Byrd (Cheraw), John H. McCray (Lincolnville), Modjeska Simkins (Columbia), James T. McCain (Sumter), and many more. Each of these agents of change is deserving of a singular place of recognition in the civil rights movement. However, all in some ways focused on education, whether public schools for general education or citizenship schools for adult citizenship education. Education was used as a primary strategy to uplift and free black Americans from bondage. One might say that John H. McCray (1910–87), editor of the *Lighthouse and Informer* (1938–54), taught through his journalistic skills. The motto of his paper was "Shedding Light for a Growing Race."

Modjeska Simkins (1899–1972), like John McCray, was a formidable agent of change. She was fearless in her leadership role in the local and state

National Association for the Advancement of Colored People (NAACP). Black women were not the acknowledged leaders in the civil rights movement. This was also true for Modjeska Simkins, who was considered along with John McCray and James M. Hinton (1891–1970), NAACP state president, as the most important black leaders in South Carolina.

Newman recognized in the waning influence of these three leaders that the NAACP leadership baton had been passed to him whether intentional or not. No one seemed able to explain fully the lull that came over the activist NAACP and its three prominent and outspoken leaders of the 1930s and 1940s. Much of the demise, however, was attributed to the repressive racial atmosphere of the mid-1950s. It was purported that after the *Brown v. Board of Education* decision Hinton, the once charismatic head of the state NAACP, had lost the touch and somehow failed to move the NAACP forward in the wake of the *Brown* decision. According to Simkins, who was secretary of the NAACP state conference from 1940 to 1957, it appeared that outside pressures from the white establishment along with harassment by agitators who attacked his home with a barrage of gunfire were at the core of Hinton's stagnant leadership.[1]

On the other hand, a red-baiting campaign was levied against Simkins by South Carolina political machinery and the racist *Charleston News and Courier* newspaper. McCray, the third visible and vocal leader in the South Carolina NAACP, was the first of the three to experience the wrath of the South Carolina white power structure. In 1949 McCray covered the rape trial and subsequent execution of a twenty-four-year-old black man and reported that the alleged rape of the white teenage girl was in fact consensual sex. A white reporter, independent of McCray, made the same accusation. Both men were charged with criminal libel. The white reporter was never brought to trial, but McCray was convicted and eventually served sixty days on a chain gang. It was said that McCray's "aggressive style" often placed him at odds with the white power structure.[2] By 1958 Hinton had formally resigned as NAACP state president. Simkins was not nominated for the eighteenth time as NAACP conference secretary, and McCray's fragile financial situation was exacerbated by his sixty-day stint on the chain gang, leading to the eventual demise of his newspaper, the mouthpiece for the civil rights movement and justice issues. The white establishment used its usual tactics to silence or effectively diminish these black activist voices: imprisonment, character assassination, or the terrorist-style attack with a barrage of gunfire directed at the individual or the individual's place of residence. Taken together these events led to the closing of an extraordinary period of black activism in South Carolina and the ongoing struggle under Newman's leadership for black empowerment and justice.

Newman may be thought of as the opposite of McCray in terms of temperament and leadership style, but he had a resolve for persistence and toughness. Under Newman's leadership, the primary strategy for change was nonviolent direct action as a means to political negotiation. At the core of this approach was the NAACP Legal Committee that Newman initiated as soon as he took office. He invited Matthew J. Perry (1921–2011) to serve as the committee chair and attorney for legal defense. Newman effectively used South Carolina's highly valued conservative strongholds, its political and legal systems, against it. This process was not without conflict and intergenerational bias. Newman found it necessary to navigate between the older entrenched black conservatives and the younger, more militant activists. Newman through this strategy, however, brought about change in public life in South Carolina that is now taken for granted. Examples of such change ranged from being able to drink water from any water fountain, trying on clothing in department stores before purchase, eating in any restaurant, attending the school of one's choice, employment opportunities beyond day labor or domestic work, and utilizing public accommodations such as parks, beaches, and hotels to running for and being elected to public office.

The time is long overdue to honor and pay tribute to the memory and contributions of I. DeQuincey Newman, a humanitarian and distinguished statesman who worked tirelessly to leave the world and South Carolina better than he found them.

Although this book is essentially biographical, it required a diverse mix of narratives and voices to capture Newman's rich and varied contributions to transforming South Carolina's rigid and unjust racial structure. This volume attempts to capture the essence and spirit of an activist who always put others first. Therefore this book is also about the disproportionate numbers of poor families and children still in existence, those suffering from poor physical and mental health, those incarcerated, the frail elderly, the students and others who participated in sit-ins and marched, and some who gave their lives. In this regard, significant contributions to this volume were made not only by politicians, historians, members of the clergy, educators, members of the judicial system, and icons of the civil rights movement but also by the narratives told in the words of everyday people, capturing the day-to-day experiences of I. DeQuincey Newman.

Many of the narratives contributed here were produced from audio and visual recordings of the Newman Oral History Project, conducted by the editor of this volume from the summer of 2005 to fall 2007. The recordings are archived at the Newman Institute Archival and Resource Room at the University of South Carolina College of Social Work. The narrators are Gloria Blackwell (Rackley), Donald L. Fowler, Robert E. McNair, Jerome Noble, Matthew J. Perry, Jr., Harrison Rearden, Richard W. Riley, Alex Sanders, William "Bill" Saunders, Hiram Spain, Jr., James S. Thomas, Isaac W. Williams, and Esther Nell Knuckles Glymph Witherspoon. The contributors served as extensions of the narratives. The contributors include Millicent Brown, Josephine A. McRant, Wim Roefs, Wallace Brown, Sr., G. Robert Cook, Carrie Crawford Washington, Karen Ross Grant, and Tanya S. Brice. Anne Pauline Hinton Newman and her daughter, Emily Morris Newman, were totally committed to the completion of this project and were equal to other contributors in their contributions to this volume. They provided tireless support, lent otherwise unavailable family photographs, and also participated in the Newman Oral History Project through taped and visually recorded interviews. Taken together, these contributors provide a rich and diverse perspective on I. DeQuincey Newman's life and legacy.

Unlike black men in the struggle for justice and peace, black women were generally not acknowledged as key actors in South Carolina or elsewhere. They were relegated to the background. Therefore it is not surprising that only two female voices are among the narratives in this book, interestlingly signaling the beginning as well as the ending of the thirteen narratives. An ongoing reframing of the civil rights movement from a feminist perspective continues to provide substantive evidence of the presence and contribution of black men and women.

Notes

1. Woods, "Modjeska Simkins," 115–16.
2. Herb Frazier, "McCray, John Henry."

Isaiah DeQuincey Newman

The Servant Leader

Sadye L. M. Logan

Blacks have battered down walls of segregation in many instances and while we are not yet as a people, on the inside of the political arena, we are not altogether on the outside either.

I. DeQuincey Newman

Isaiah DeQuincey Newman's life embodied many contradictions. He described himself as a country preacher, though he graduated from an esteemed theological seminary. He was an intellectual and so to speak, "walked with kings, but never lost the common touch." Like most educated African Americans of his generation or earlier, he was taught that it was his duty and mission in life to uplift his less fortunate brothers and sisters.

This essay serves as an introductory framework for this book, an exploration and tribute to the life and work of I. DeQuincey. It explore Newman's life as a servant-leader who was as comfortable making the case for equality and justice in the streets as he was behind the scenes forging unity among South Carolina's black and white leaders. His ability to work seamlessly in multiple ways over a lifetime is important in appreciating and understanding what it means to be in the struggle for a just and equal society. This is relevant in that Newman's life and work are a microcosm of the civil rights movement covering this incredible arc of the twentieth century. He was a key player during the early 1940s through the 1970s in much of the state's dramatic racial and political history. He effectively used the political and legal systems to change the quality of life of all Americans but especially African Americans,

Newman's mother, Charlotte "Lottie" Elizabeth Morris, daughter of Rebecca Tiller King Morris and Robert Dempsey Morris, Jr. Courtesy of the Newman family.

including where we lived; where and how we participated in recreation activities; how we ate, slept, and studied; and how we interacted with each other.

The Person

The Reverend Isaiah DeQuincey Newman was born on April 17, 1911, to Reverend Melton C. and Charlotte Morris Newman. He was often referred to by friends and colleagues as South Carolina's twentieth-century patriarch of the civil rights movement. He was described as courtly and courteous. His voice was resonant, deliberate, and measured.[1] His mother died of tuberculosis two weeks short of his sixth birthday, leaving him and three older sisters at home.[2] While his sisters stayed with their father, Newman was raised in the home of his maternal grandmother in Hartsville, South Carolina. During one of his visits to his father's home in Kingstree, he witnessed an event that left an indelible impression on his consciousness and spurred his commitment to working for a just society. Newman was eight years old when he witnessed the Ku Klux Klan (KKK), a white supremacist group, set fire late one night to a caboose that was serving as a lockup for a recently arrested African American man. The Newman family lived near the convict camp where prisoners who worked on the chain gang were kept. Newman remembered lying in bed listening to the man in the caboose screaming, "Help, Help, Help!" as he burned to death. Newman recalled, "I ran into my father's room and asked, 'Pa ain't you going over and help the man?' My father said, 'Go back to bed boy.' And I was insistent. I shook him, I said, 'Pa, go and help the man.' But he didn't."[3] Although Newman's father understood the violent racial climate of South Carolina and the Klan's mission to terrorize black people, this response was troubling to an eight-year-old child. Newman later said of this incident, "I tell you I put that in my memory bank. I kept that in my heart for a long time and I held it against my father. There was a man being burned alive, and my father wouldn't turn a hand to help him. Of course, I learned since then had he gone to give help, he would have been shot down, just killed."[4]

Newman as a young man in his late twenties with younger siblings, from left to right: King William Milton II, Omega Franklin, Isaiah DeQuincey, Ernest Wilber, Ernestine Wilma. Courtesy of the Newman family.

Newman's father and daughter. Courtesy of the Newman family.

Newman's father later married Serena Louise Hamilton, daughter of Reverend G. J. and Mrs. Emma Childs Hamilton of Charleston, South Carolina. Serena and Milton Newman were the parents of eleven children. Although he lived in the home of his maternal grandparents, I. DeQuincey had ongoing contact with his father and all of his siblings, including the eleven children born from his father's second marriage. Both his mother and his stepmother were schoolteachers. His father was an itinerant Methodist preacher whose early preaching took the family to numerous small towns in South Carolina, including Anderson, Greenville, Hartsville, and Kingstree.[5] Newman promised his mother on her deathbed that he would become a minister like his father. At the age of eighteen he obtained his local preacher's license on August 23, 1929, from the Florence District Conference at the South Carolina

Newman and his mother. Courtesy of the Newman family.

Annual Conference. Like teaching, pastoring in the black community, especially for black men, was viewed as a noble and respectable profession.

As a youngster growing up in rural South Carolina, Newman was perceived by his family and teachers as being unique and possessing unusual intellectual abilities. However, he was also like most other boys growing up in the rural areas of the state. He enjoyed swimming and hanging out with a few close friends. Given the racial climate and the quality of life for most black South Carolinians, especially black children living in rural South Carolina, swimming generally occurred in local creeks or rivers. One hot summer day, three years after witnessing the horrific death of a convict being burned to death by the KKK, Newman played hooky from Sunday school and went swimming in the local creek with a few of his friends. What was intended to be great fun ended in the tragic drowning death of one of Newman's friends.[6] Newman felt guilty about playing hooky from Sunday school but especially guilty and saddened that he was not able to save his friend from drowning.

Newman's father, Meloncy (Melton) Charles Soniat du Fossat Newman. Courtesy of the Newman family.

While still in the latency period of development, a vulnerable time in a child's life, Newman had experienced three tragedies: his mother's death, the burning death of an inmate, and the drowning of a boyhood friend.

Despite several traumatic experiences in the first twelve years of his life, it could be said that Newman grew up under privileged conditions in rural South Carolina. According to Newman's daughter, Emily, her father's maternal grandmother, Rebecca Tiller King, was perceived in her community as white, and his maternal grandfather, Robert Dempsey Morris, Jr., was of mixed race. Being of mixed-race parentage and possessing white or light skin have been considered advantages for some in the black community in South Carolina.[7] Newman's maternal grandparents owned a grits mill and two plantations, New Hope and Clyde. His maternal grandfather was a free person and a lawyer before the Civil War and, in economic terms, was considered affluent until the 1940s.[8] The efforts of Newman's maternal great-grandfather,

Newman's maternal grandmother, Rebecca Tiller King Morris, daughter of Livinia Tiller King and Nathan King. Courtesy of the Newman family.

Robert Morris, Sr., in the 1848 case *Roberts v. City of Boston* helped to "set in motion a jurisprudence of opposition to segregated public education" that culminated 105 years later in *Brown v. Board of Education*."[9]

Although many books were not readily available during Newman's growing-up years, he enjoyed reading as a child and carried this joy for reading into his adult life. At age eighteen his intelligence quotient was measured at 160.[10] The Newman family held a vision of hope and progress that was fueled tenaciously by the pursuit of higher education. Despite this hopeful vision, I. DeQuincey was cautioned by his parents, as all black children were, "to be careful around white folks." He said, "We were taught to tiptoe, to be on guard."[11]Newman attended the public schools of Williamsburg County and completed high school at Claflin College (now Claflin University) in Orangeburg, South Carolina. The inferior education program for African Americans, especially in rural areas, usually meant that schooling ended at the third or fourth grade. Only a rare few African American families were financially able to enroll their children in the private schools established for African American children or colleges in Orangeburg, Charleston, or Columbia. Upon graduating from Claflin high school at the age of nineteen, Newman enrolled at Clark College in Atlanta, Georgia.[12] Newman graduated from Clark College in 1934 with a bachelor of arts degree in English literature. He continued his studies in Atlanta at Gammon School of Theology, a premier resource for black church scholars. Newman graduated from Gammon in 1937 with a bachelor of divinity degree and with the ability to read and write five foreign languages: French, German, Greek, Hebrew, and Latin.[13]

When Newman was in his late twenties and completing his studies for the ministry at Gammon, another life-changing event occurred that further moved him toward a life as advocate for a more just and equal society. While he was a student pastor practice-preaching in Red Oak, Georgia, on a visit to one of his sick parishioners, a sharecropper on a plantation, he attempted to persuade the plantation owner to have the sharecropper taken to the local hospital for medical care. He recalled the incident:

> My congregation was sharecroppers on a nearby plantation. They lived in peonage, in dirt-floor shacks; the kids wore burlap sack dresses and no shoes. One day, I went to visit a man in the congregation who was so sick, filthy, and unkempt that blowflies were starting to light on him. On my way out from the plantation, I was met with the owner of the plantation. He was carrying a shotgun and told me there would

be dire consequences if I ever set foot on his property again. I tried to convince him to put the man in a hospital, but he ran me off the place. That night, a friend and I snuck back after midnight. We bundled the man up in blankets and drove him to the hospital, where he eventually got well. Then we arranged for him to go to Philadelphia, where some of his grown children were living. That experience was such that there was no possible way I could avoid extending my ministry into the civil rights field.[14]

Pursuing His Commitment to Civil Rights

Prior to his graduation from Gammon, on December 10, 1933, Newman was appointed as deacon of the United Methodist Church and elder on December 8, 1935. Elders, in a priestly function, connect people to God, while deacons, in a servant leadership function, connect people of God to services in the world.[15] The duties and responsibilities reflected in these roles keep pastors transient in the Methodist circuit system. Newman's graduation from Gammon in 1937 marked the conclusion of his formal religious training. He returned to South Carolina with a job as a Methodist minister and a wife, the attractive, intelligent, well-respected eighteen-year-old Anne Pauline Hinton Newman. It appeared that she respected his opinion on certain matters that were important to her. She shared with the author that it was he who persuaded her to study teaching instead of nursing because he thought teaching was a more noble profession. She therefore went on to earn a bachelor's degree in elementary education from Claflin College in 1948 but said that she never truly enjoyed teaching despite doing so for nearly twenty-five years. The blue-eyed daughter of a white father and a biracial mother, Hinton was often mistaken as white.[16] While her white skin could be a source of confusion, her ability to pass also served the Newmans well in their civil rights work that brought them in contact with Columbia white merchants.

According to Newman, his first weekly salary as a Methodist minister was "sixty cents, a quart of canned peaches, a quart of whippoorwill peas, and a piece of hog jowl."[17] He and his wife lived in Hartsville with his father. He took the job as principal at a small school in Pasley, South Carolina. Between 1938 and 1950 he was assigned to churches in various towns in South Carolina, including Orangeburg, Bethune, York, Wellford, Kingstree, Spartanburg, Charleston, and Camden.[18] Twelve years of pastoring all over the state brought Newman in contact with the masses as well as the established black leadership structure in the churches and in the political arena. He continued

Newman's future bride, Anne Pauline Hinton. Courtesy of the Newman family.

to move forward in the religious and political arenas. From 1950 to 1956 he was United Methodist Church district superintendent in Sumter, South Carolina. From 1956 to 1958 he served as pastor of Wesley Methodist Church in Charleston, South Carolina. From 1958 to 1960 he served as pastor at Silver Hill United Methodist Church in Spartanburg, South Carolina (see "Making the Impossible Possible").[19] One year prior to his appointment as Sumter District United Methodist Church superintendent, the Newmans became parents to a daughter, Emily Morris.

As a minister Newman was a natural leader of the African American communities in which he lived. It is commonly recognized that the black church served as the social, civil, political, and spiritual hub of the black community.[20] Newman viewed the black church as the only institution that was owned and controlled by blacks. In an interview he said, "The man in the pulpit was the spokesman and easily identified as a leader. He was the leader of a flock, which gets together on certain occasions. He was accepted as the leader of the community because of his visibility and opportunities to mold opinion."[21] Newman asserted that the African American clergy had freedom of expression.[22] Assuming a visible activist leadership role was less complicated for independent business professionals in the African American community such as doctors, lawyers, morticians, or some educators. Available scholarship further suggests that while those black entrepreneurs who were especially dependent primarily on black clienteles had more freedom, black teachers in the public school system were vulnerable. The fear of losing or being fired from their jobs forced many supporters of "the cause" to do so anonymously. As discussed in "Making the Impossible Possible," the role of the black clergy has taken many forms during the struggle for justice and black empowerment. Some scholars found them to be a negligible or even counterproductive force during the 1960s, while others have treated the black ministry more favorably.[23]

From the start, Newman's church was fused with his political commitments to racial equality and social justice. Along with other high-profile African Americans, Newman was a Republican Party activist beginning in the 1930s. African Americans were loyal to the Republican Party of the President Lincoln era because of ties connected to the Civil War, Reconstruction, and the New Deal. However, with the establishment of the white Democratic Party, the South Carolina Democratic Party wrestled political control from the state's Republican Party and established its dominance. Given that South Carolina had remained a predominately black state since 1820, the Democratic Party was acutely aware of the potential political power of the African American population. It was a common practice of white politicians to gain votes by appealing to whites' fear of black leadership and denying blacks the right to participate in the political process. Black Carolinians directed organized resistance toward the white Democratic Party from its inception until the party was forced to abandon its racist platform in the mid-twentieth century. The exclusion of blacks from the white Democratic Party was successfully challenged in 1947 when the National Association for the Advancement of Colored People (NAACP) filed suit in federal court to open the Democratic Party primaries to its black voters.[24] The suit was sparked by a 1944 Supreme Court ruling outlawing laws in Texas that barred blacks from voting in that state's Democratic primaries. The ruling reverberated through the former Confederate states that upheld the same principles and practices.

The attorneys representing the suit were Thurgood Marshall (who later became a justice in the U.S. Supreme Court) and Harold Boulware of Columbia, South Carolina. The attorneys for the Democratic Party argued that the party was a private club and had a right to exclude whomever it chose as well as to require a pledge from its voters to support "the principle of racial segregation."[25] U.S. District Judge J. Waties Waring of Charleston ruled that it was illegal for the Democratic Party, in the conduct of elections, to make any racial or religious discrimination.[26] Judge Waring's ruling was met with outrage and bitter recrimination by the all-white Democratic Party. The backlash among other events was so strong that Judge Waring was increasingly isolated from most of his fellow white South Carolinians and became more outspoken in his opposition to segregation and white supremacy.[27] Although African Americans began enrolling and voting after the ruling, white South Carolinians found other creative ways to discourage black participation. This resistance persisted until the 1965 Voting Rights Act, which removed literary tests and brought federal supervision of voter registration to South Carolina for the first time. It took South Carolina African Americans ninety-seven years to return civil rights to the place they had been during Reconstruction.

Newman recalled being present in 1944 for the first organizing convention of the Progressive Democratic Party (PDP) and was elected fourth vice president.[28] By 1948 when the South Carolina State NAACP Conference of Branches under the leadership of its charismatic, outspoken president Reverend James Hinton resolved to wage an all-out war on racial oppression and discrimination, Newman was the pastor at Orangeburg Trinity Methodist Church. The church was used during Newman's pastorate as a safe place for protest meetings and became an icon of the civil rights movement. Newman was active in opening the church as a space for civil rights organizing efforts. He was also a PDP activist and president of the Orangeburg chapter of the NAACP. He served as vice president of the NAACP conference from 1948 to 1958 and was inspired by strong NAACP supporters such as John McCray, activist and publisher of the *Lighthouse and Informer*, and Osceola McKaine, a highly regarded activist for diverse justice issues (see the time line in the appendix for more information on McCray and McKaine). After ten years as vice president of the NAACP conference, Newman was elected in 1958 as president of the NAACP conference. The time would soon come when he would take up the role of the "supersalesman" that then conference president James A. Hinton thought was needed "to convert" or convince black people to become members of the NAACP.

Newman was a natural activist. His spirit of activism extended as far back as his days as a student at Claflin.[29] His involvement in the NAACP served as the foundation for the various leadership roles he assumed in the

African American and white communities. In 1939, when the South Carolina NAACP was formed, Modjeska Simkins was one of the founders, and she was secretary of the state conference from 1941 to 1957. It was no small feat at this juncture in society that a black woman was in a powerful leadership role of a major black organization. Simkins was a "mover and shaker." She became a leading figure in the state conference of the NAACP.[30] Her fire and passion as a leader were often viewed as caustic and abrasive and placed her in an adversarial position with the white political establishment.[31] Apparently there was some acrimony on Simkins's part as a result of the NAACP moving away from her and toward Newman and his appointment as president of the state conference and later as NAACP field director.[32] It was reported that the NAACP distanced itself from Simkins due to reports alleging that she was connected with organizations that served as Communist "fronts" as well as being supportive of friends who were avowed Communists. It was insinuated that her ouster and Newman's rise within the NAACP left a bitter taste.[33]

Newman's associates believed that his respect for Simkins's leadership and unwavering fight for justice and equality were genuine. Newman, no less an adversary to the white establishment than Simkins, who was a more in-your-face leader, had a different style and philosophy as a strategist in working to change the racist structure of the old South. Newman, a leader who angered more slowly, used his wit, intelligence, philosophy, morality, and practicality in dealing with the white political establishment. Both leaders were effective in their fight against South Carolina's racist power structure. However, it is important to note an observation by Simkins's biographer Barbara Woods. In acknowledging Simkins's uniqueness as a female freedom fighter, Woods said, "I've often thought that a black male could not have gotten away with what Modjeska Simkins did."[34] Simkins spoke her mind without censure. She ran for public office well into her eighties and used her press credentials to crash political meetings whenever she felt inclined to do so.[35]

When Newman became field director in 1960, the state and the country were transitioning from a more quiet approach, to combating injustices through the legal system, to a more assertive, confrontational, demonstrative approach. Despite the marches and sit-ins during the decade of the 1960s, the NAACP of the earlier decades (the late 1930s, 1940s, and early 1950s) was considered more militant and was hated by the white establishment.[36] The Orangeburg chapter where Newman served as president was dynamic. It not only boycotted businesses owned by the white Citizens' Council, a group formed to prevent implementation of the *Brown* decision to desegregate public schools, but also initiated a boycott of national brand-name products that were purchased in large quantities by the black community. The boycott would have an immediate economic impact on the local white businesses in the community. Robert H. Jennings, Jr., then the mayor (1953–54) of Orangeburg, was a leading member of the Citizens' Council and owner of Orangeburg Fuel and Ice, the local Coca-Cola bottling company, and the Palmetto Bakery, one of the largest bread suppliers in the state. Businesses such as Standard Oil; Ford Motor Company; Lance Company, maker of "Nabs"; Curtis Company, maker of the popular "Baby Ruth" candy bars; and Lays, the maker of potato chips and popcorn, were boycotted by protesters, as were other products such as Coca-Cola and Sunbeam Bread. George Bell Timmerman, Jr., was governor (1955–59), and Ernest Frederick "Fritz" Hollings was lieutenant governor. Timmerman took office when the U.S. Supreme Court had unanimously issued its landmark *Brown v. Board of Education* decision. Timmerman resolutely opposed integration, as had James Byrnes (1950–54), his predecessor as governor. The 1956 session of the legislature was called "Segregation Session" because of its hostile stance on civil rights, including the introduction of legislation barring NAACP members from public employment.[37]

Hollings was governor (1959–63) for the first three years of Newman's role as NAACP field director. Hollings, a segregationist, described a meeting with Newman and other black leaders to discuss the state's role in eliminating racial segregation and discrimination. According to Hollings,

> I stated as firmly as possible, I was the governor of the Negro people as well as the White people. I know they didn't believe it, but I was going to be their governor whether they believed it or liked it. I also wanted them to understand that with all their feelings about second-class citizenship and civil rights, that their recourse was in the courts and I couldn't, *ipso facto*, change the law in South Carolina. . . . And I intoned, I was going to make damn certain they weren't going to have little children used as pawns and getting hurt at the lunch counters. I wasn't going to put up with them firing up the students to take over the town of Orangeburg. I know I can't control private property, I said, looking at Newman, but I can control the sidewalks and I am only going to allow fourteen people in to shop and when they come out, I will allow another fourteen in—no more! I am going to maintain the public peace and public safety. Newman said he had talked to a New York lawyer and that I couldn't do this. I told him to tell the New York lawyer I was going to do it. Tell him to come down and interfere and

> I will lock him up. And I can tell you further—tell Earl Warren [chief justice of the US Supreme Court] that if he came to Rock Hill and I will lock him up, too.[38]

Hollings concluded that his posturing did not appease or convince the group about his stance on civil rights. They left this meeting dissatisfied. This interchange served to signal for the group that this was the tip of the iceberg and that the task ahead would be extremely difficult. It is important to note that Chief Justice Warren was no friend to white segregationists. His ruling struck down the doctrine of "separate but equal" in public education and at least theoretically placed the law on the side of the black people's struggle for civil rights.

The protest work that had begun in Orangeburg during the mid-1950s was later expanded under Newman's leadership and gained traction in Orangeburg with massive student involvement at S.C. State and Claflin Colleges and attention from the local and national media. For example, three years into his role as field director of the state NAACP, on June 5, 1963, Newman published a list of nine demands that addressed racial segregation and discrimination, especially in the public arenas and in state government, equal employment opportunities, and involvement in voter registration (see the conclusion, "Newman's Vision of a 'Just' South Carolina"). In addition he announced eight cities—Charleston, Columbia, Florence, Greenville, Orangeburg, Rock Hill, Spartanburg, and Sumter—targeted for massive demonstrations unless progress was made in ending the discrimination in public accommodations, in the political arena, and in the education system.[39]

As reflected in Governor Hollings's response above, Columbia responded slowly and inadequately to Newman's demands; Charleston witnessed rioting before exhibiting any willingness to move forward; and Florence, Greenville, Rock Hill, and Spartanburg reached some consensus without riots.[40] In Orangeburg, where the white establishment continued its refusal to desegregate public facilities, demonstrators were met with water hoses in winter and summer months and arrested by the local police. The black citizenry was threatened with economic sanctions and vigilante-like violence.

Newman refocused his strategies on politics and the courts. However, he continued to include marches, wade-ins, sit-ins, and voter registration. Voter registration continued to be a critical part of Newman's work. He never lost sight of the power and importance of the vote in the creation of a more just and equal nation for black Americans. Newman never wavered. He kept the pressure up for change.

At the time Newman took up the leadership of the South Carolina NAACP, James T. McCain, a former NAACP member, launched the Congress of Racial Equality (CORE), an interracial, radical group. McCain's intent was to spearhead a CORE membership drive in South Carolina. CORE's early focus was on educational activities and nonviolent direct action, such as sit-ins. These strategies served as means of integrating public facilities and fighting racial segregation and discrimination. McCain's efforts in the 1960s to organize CORE paralleled Newman's efforts to reenergize the NAACP. Newman's and McCain's efforts to register black South Carolinians increased the voter registration rolls to over thirty-seven thousand voters.[41]

The fluctuation in growth and development went back to 1943 when the NAACP emerged as a force to be reckoned with in South Carolina. At the time approximately 3,000 African Americans out of a population of 814,164 were registered to vote. Although African Americans constituted 42.8 percent of the population, only 0.8 percent of voting-age African Americans were on the voter-registration rolls.[42] It was the intent of the white power structure to keep black voters off the voter registration rolls. In the period between 1943 and 1946 there was an increase in black registered voters from approximately 3,000 to 50,000 largely due to the collective efforts of the NAACP, the PDP, the Congress of Industrial Organizations–Political Action Committee (CIO–PAC), and the Southern Conference for Human Welfare.[43] In 1948 the South Carolina State Conference of the NAACP Branches, at Newman's suggestion, hired Eugene Alonzo Randolph Montgomery as its executive secretary to lead its organizing and promotional activities. Montgomery's extraordinary organizing efforts raised the NAACP membership rolls to 14,237 at the end of 1948. Within the ranks of the organization, it was common knowledge that the unofficial membership rolls were much higher. The organization's honor code was not to publicize the names of those members who were vulnerable to retribution from the white community.[44] Between1955 and 1957 a renewed wave of repression was gripping the country as a result of the recent *Brown v. Board of Education* ruling, the politically motivated red-baiting campaign against high-profiled or activist citizenry, and the heated racial and political controversy over the 1957 Civil Rights Bill. This growing racial tension within the larger society was directly impacting the NAACP membership rolls. During this time the number of NAACP branches in South Carolina decreased from eighty-four to thirty-one. The membership was at an all-time low of approximately 2,200.[45]

The work to organize the NAACP's field office as well as to tackle the state's entrenched response to desegregation and its racist ideology pertaining to people of color, especially African Americans, was a daunting task. Anne Newman was her husband's greatest supporter throughout this transformative period of the nation, the state, and their life together.[46] Anne said that she agreed to accept the position of secretary to the NAACP because no one else wanted the job. She knew that Newman could not effectively perform his duties as field director without a dependable, competent secretary. Given that she looked white, Anne was able to transact the business of the NAACP effectively without reprisals or other forms of rejections that would have been directed toward her husband.[47] She spoke of how it was possible for her to buy office supplies and other essential items necessary to carry out the day-to-day operations of the field office. Anne's job also entailed sensitive and serious planning, negotiations, and maintenance of open communication between the various NAACP branches as well as with the New York headquarters.

Throughout his life Newman played a pivotal role in South Carolina's political and troubling racial history. On the political front, Newman served as a delegate to the National Democratic Conventions in 1968, 1972, and 1980. He was also president of the Columbia Ward Nineteen Democratic Club and chairperson of the state black caucus. He also became a trusted negotiator and sometime confidant to state leaders such as Governor and then Senator Ernest Hollings (1959–63 and 1966–98, respectively) and Governors Robert McNair (1965–71) and John West (1971–75).[48] Being a trusted confidant included meeting privately with state leaders. He brought a necessary style of statesmanship and diplomacy to a deeply divided, tense, and volatile politics. Viewed from the outside, these secret meetings supported Newman's detractors' image of him as an accommodationist. Some went as far as to describe him as an "Uncle Tom."[49] In the face of such criticism, it is important to ponder the following questions: How much courage does it take to criticize? Is it more important to keep pushing back with intelligent foresight or to be murdered or incarcerated because of thoughtless militancy?

South Carolina governor Robert McNair remarked about these clandestine meetings this way: "He [Newman] walked a tightrope. He maintained his credibility with his own people, many who were more militant than he. But he also kept the communications open with the white leadership."[50] Newman's private discussions about the state's political and racial conflicts with state leaders were sometimes misconstrued as orchestrated by some members of the white establishment as well as the black community and not designed to truly effect real change.[51] It appeared that some members of the state leaders' inner circle did not recognize that resolving the deeply entrenched racial conflicts of the state required a multidimensional approach. Newman described his role this way: "I don't want to stick a pin in anybody's balloon, but [in] my being a party to things—however privileged—there was some method to it . . . I have never passed up an opportunity to open the door a little wider if I thought for a moment that I could use my position as Executive Assistant to Dr. [Archie] Ellis, or working for Governor [John] West or Governor [Robert] McNair or Governor [James] Edwards, or Governor [Richard] Riley. I would have been content being a shepherd of a flock as a minister, but being quietly the insider, I was in a better position to serve the ultimate purpose of improving the political, social and economic status of black people in the State."[52]

Newman and other leaders not only agreed to disagree with state leaders but also stood firm in realizing the goals of the movement. It is of critical importance to view Newman's activist role in the context of his mission to change the entrenched racial climate and the political landscape of South Carolina. His protégé Isaac "Ike" Williams, who succeeded him as NAACP field director, described Newman as a consummate strategist as field director for the NAACP— a gentle giant, with extraordinary insight, and tremendous willpower and shrewdness.[53] Williams spoke of Newman leading hundreds of marches and demonstrations during the 1960s, starting and ending with prayers in church. He recalled a 1963 march in Charleston that began at St. Luke's Church. "He was incredibly eloquent," Williams said. "He talked about dignity and freedom. He could sooth and arouse a crowd at the same time. The entire congregation left that church after this talk and followed him into the streets."[54] Newman's belief in nonviolent protest as the most effective means of achieving the goals of the NAACP was consistent with the state's eventual wish to preserve its image as one of the southern states that moved to desegregate its public accommodations with dignity and without violence.

Newman in the Struggle

Despite South Carolinians' wishes in the face of the federal mandate to dismantle their segregated school system, they worked to maintain the myth of nonviolence and the illusion of cooperation with federal mandates. The Jim Crow laws of public accommodations, the white supremacist electoral process, and continuing racist discriminatory practices served to maintain serious and destructive racial conflict within the state. Newman was arrested up to twelve times during civil rights demonstrations at segregated lunch counters, state parks, and schools.[55] In describing these potentially violent encounters Newman said, "Many of them were touch-and-go. But it was the same as soldiers in battle. You're scared but you feel it's something that has to be done. The strength comes from somewhere, and psychologically you're prepared for the worse."[56] Given that it was never a secret where demonstrations would be held, assurance was given from the highest level in the governor's office that the South Carolina Law Enforcement Division (SLED) would be available to protect demonstrators and property. However, this was not always the case.[57] In 1961 Newman was nearly lynched by an angry white mob in Horry County. He was leading a "wade-in" at Myrtle Beach State Park, which was then off-limits to blacks. Newman was arrested and escorted by the local sheriff in his car to the county line with the angry mob in pursuit. Newman was no stranger to death and tragedy. He also knew of others in the struggle who had been violently attacked and/or harassed with death threats by local white Citizens' Councils to the point of leaving the state. However, this was the first time that he was threatened with lynching by a mob of white angry people. He found himself running to save his life. He said of the event, "I drove 120 miles per hour from Marion County to Florence County. I out distanced them finally, but I didn't slow up until I got to Lake City." This near-death experience left an indelible mark on Newman's psyche. He described it this way: "I was so frightened that I couldn't talk for two days. I was literally struck dumb."[58] Despite this horrific experience Newman persevered.

Ike Williams recalled a poignant experience as Newman's mentee on June 12, 1963, when he was only seventeen years old. He and Newman had been out attending rallies across the state and returned home late that night. It was also the night that they heard the news that Medgar Evers (1925–63), Newman's friend and NAACP fellow field director in Mississippi, had been assassinated. Evers was returning home from an NAACP meeting when a member of the KKK shot him in his driveway and killed him instantly. Williams described the location of Newman's residence as situated in a manner where something similar could happen to Newman on a late-night return from a meeting or some similar event. Williams shared that he had never seen the vulnerability and concern in Newman that he experienced that night as they approached his home, which was surrounded by wooded areas on the back and across the street. What resonated with Williams was Newman's request that if anything should ever happen to him he wanted Williams to see that Anne and Emily were taken care of. Williams said that this level of trust to him was simply beyond comprehension, especially given that he was only seventeen years of age. However, he solemnly agreed to do as Newman requested.

Newman spoke of not being harmed physically or otherwise during his tenure as a civil rights activist. The incident of being chased by an angry mob, however, was indicative of the psychological harm inflicted when one's life is on the line for justice. Yet there was no public mention or acknowledgment of the threat against his life by angry whites or his fear for the safety of his family. In Newman's mind what he did as a leader and activist was something that had to be done. He said, "I pride myself on being a realist, and I knew how far white officeholders would go. So I would push only so far and then regroup and make another strike."[59] Other activists in the struggle questioned the effectiveness of Newman's strategy and whether a more strident, aggressive approach was needed. Student activists were also finding their voices and were asserting themselves in the movement.

Tragedy and Betrayal

The 1968 racial crisis in Orangeburg was a reflection of students' dissatisfaction with the status quo and entrenched racial injustices. This crisis came toward the end of Newman's term as NAACP field director. This period was also a time when groups made up of younger, more militant leaders, such as the Student Non-Violent Coordinating Committee (SNCC), did not believe in maintaining "the peaceful and quiet" status with the hopes that the white establishment would eventually acquiesce.[60] The students at the local universities were fed up with the slow pace of integration and wanted to see some visible changes regarding usage of public accommodations in the Orangeburg area as well as in the leadership of their institutions. Instead of acquiescing as they were encouraged to do, the students at South Carolina State College in Orangeburg pushed back hard. Their dissatisfaction with the leadership of South Carolina State's president Benner Turner and their consequent 1967 boycott of classes successfully ended his career.[61] Leading up to Turner's resignation, staff writer Paul Clancy of the *State* newspaper and columnist Hugh Gibson of the *Charleston News and Courier* speculated about the future of the all-black South Carolina State College. According to Clancy, "They (the students) had felt that bringing white instructors to the campus would eventually bring white students to the campus. Having a desegregated student body at Orangeburg would make state leaders think more about the quality of education being served up (at) the school."[62] Gibson, on the other hand, stated that "S.C. State is an anachronism under today's civil rights laws. Almost certainly, the time is not far distant when Washington will compel what South Carolina could now do with good grace voluntarily."[63] In Gibson's view, the time was ripe for "end(ing) S.C. State's days as a Negro college and disperse students and faculty among other state-supported or private colleges and universities."[64] The student boycott of classes culminating in their college president's resignation was the tip of the iceberg for the conflict that culminated in the horrible tragedy of a year later.

The conservative newspapers in Columbia (the *State*) and Orangeburg (the *Times and Democrat*) were equally vociferous in their opinions of the events leading up to the tragedy in Orangeburg. The *State*'s editor at the time, William D. Workman, Jr., and the white-owned *Times and Democrat* sided with South Carolina State College president B. C. Turner during the student-led boycott. According to the *State* editorial, "Immaturity is asserting itself as students seek to dictate what shall and shall not be done by the college's administration, not only with respect to retention of faculty but to reinstatement of student agitators. . . . We cannot predict to what extent a student body will go . . . (but) we can predict that South Carolinians, regardless of race, will not permit public institutions of higher learning in this state to degenerate into academic anarchy."[65] In a similar vein the *Times and Democrat* wrote, "The time has come for the administration to take a firm hand. If the students are foolish enough—and their leaders must be immature and adolescent—to go through with their march to Columbia, it might be a good idea to find the College closed to them on their return."[66]

As the situation in Orangeburg continued to percolate, the *State*, in an April 1967 editorial, raised the now-classic questions regarding black and white race relations. Noting that B. C. Turner was black and two of South Carolina State College's trustees were black, the *State* editorial asked, "What DOES the Negro community want?" and "Who speaks for the Negro community, assuming there is any single group?" Newman in his role as state NAACP field director responded to the questions and apparent confusion about ferment in the black community by addressing the problem of race relations in the South and most particularly for the state of South Carolina. He said, "There was ferment when he (B.C. Turner) was elected over other Negroes who had already proven their ability. They were turned down by the then all-White board in favor of Dr. Turner because they were identified with the Negro aspiration for equality of opportunity. Dr. Turner was not so identified." He continued, "The pattern of race relations designed by white South Carolinians . . . takes for granted that it [the power structure] can appoint a leader for the Negro community without first entering into dialogue with the community concerning proposed appointments."[67]

The tension and resistance on the part of the white establishment to desegregate Orangeburg erupted into what was later described as the "Orangeburg

The steering committee of the Orangeburg freedom movement, left to right: Reverend Matthew W. McCollom, James E. Sulton, Dr. Harlowe E. Caldwell, Constance Baker-Motley, John E. Brunson, Lincoln Jenkins, Gloria Blackwell (Rackley), J. Arthur Brown, and Dr. Charles E. Thomas. Photograph by and courtesy of Cecil J. Williams.

Massacre." When the owner of a white-owned bowling alley refused to admit African Americans, the students at South Carolina State College began a protest. The governor sent in the Highway Patrol and the National Guard as the protest escalated. While there was some agreement on the actual events, interpretations of what happened differ. One certain fact is that a seventeen-year-old high school student from the local African American high school and two eighteen-year-old students from South Carolina State College were shot and killed.[68] Some referred to Governor McNair's decision to dispatch 250 National Guardsmen and additional Highway Patrolmen to Orangeburg the night of February 8, 1968, as the biggest mistake of his political career.[69] South Carolina's governmental response was an overreaction to the student protest in Orangeburg. The governor's obvious earlier patience in negotiating with black student dissidents had apparently run its course.

The fallout of the decision to use brutal law enforcement tactics against the students still reverberates in South Carolina. This reverberation is currently reflected in South Carolina's ambivalence about what words best capture that horrific event: "shooting deaths of three students"; the "killing of three students"; or the "massacre of three students." Some white South Carolinians, especially those who had close working relationships with the governor, objected to the term "massacre," which suggests that the killing was of a number of usually helpless or unresisting human beings under circumstances of atrocity or cruelty. The horror underlying the killing of the three young men was the fact that they were shot in their backs! Given that this atrocity occurred on Governor McNair's watch, blame was attributed to his leadership. Nearly three decades later Ike Williams, a fiery student dissident in Orangeburg during the 1960s student protests, remembered a governor with a sense of fairness and goodwill. Williams spoke of discussing the Orangeburg "shootings" with the governor and wanted the people of South Carolina to know that Governor McNair "is a man whose entire life has been dedicated to the well-being of all and it would be neither fair nor accurate for his tenure in high office to be remembered in history solely for an event that was fatally out of character with everything else he did."

There is no denying that the killing of the three young students in Orangeburg on that fateful night in February 1968 left an indelible mark on the consciences of the state and the nation. This ugly side of racism shocked even an experienced veteran of racial protest such as Newman. Weeks prior to the killings, Newman had traveled to Orangeburg for a strategy meeting with NAACP officials and student leaders near the campus. Unsuccessful attempts were made to contact Governor McNair, whom the group wanted to intervene personally. Although Newman had been a key contact for the governor in resolving tension between the governor and the black community, he was not consulted by McNair during this week of crisis. During the time of the killings, Newman was in Cincinnati, Ohio, attending a meeting of the National Conference of Negro Methodists. However, given the condition on the ground in Orangeburg, Newman was asked to return to the state by state NAACP officials.

Could this tragedy have been averted? This is a critical question for all to contemplate and vow not to ever let happen again. Further, it is not surprising that Governor John West (1971–75), the governor following McNair, said that he wanted his legacy to be remembered as that of improved race relations.[70]

Newman, however, like South Carolina State College president M. Maceo Nance, Jr., believed that if Orangeburg's leading black citizens had had the courage to step forward and if legal action had been brought against the owner of the local bowling alley, along with the full enforcement of the Civil Rights Act of 1964 by federal and state authorities, the bloody confrontation on February 8, 1968, on South Carolina State College's campus could have been averted.[71] It was Newman's belief that swift court action could have diverted attention from the point of contention—a local bowling alley near South Carolina State and Claflin Colleges that denied access to African Americans. However, according to Newman, a tragedy was not averted because the leading African American citizens of Orangeburg did not want their names listed as plaintiffs in an action against the bowling alley owner for fear of what the white power structure might think. Ike Williams thought that poor communication was at the heart of the tragedy. There were in his estimation many levels of leadership on and off the S.C. state campus, which resulted in instability and a breakdown in the system that had been negotiated during the student unrest a year earlier.

Newman thought that the governor made himself absent in this time of crisis. Newman's disappointment and outrage with the lack of constructive response from the governor's office is captured in these words: "The fact that such a thing could happen and did happen is an indication that despite all that might be considered progress in terms of interracial cooperation, beneath the surface South Carolina is just about in the same boat as Alabama and Mississippi. The perpetrators of the tragedy and those who have covered up for them have rendered a great disservice to sometimes heroic efforts that have been made in the area of race relations and interracial cooperation."[72] This tragedy marked a low point in Newman's fight for a just South Carolina. To Newman, as a nonviolent activist, the killings affirmed that South Carolina was literally and figuratively a part of the racial violence that swept the nation. It also reminded Newman that what had been accomplished during his decade of work regarding racial justice was just a small part of what was needed. He later stated that it was the Orangeburg tragedy that accelerated his departure as field director of the NAACP ("The NAACP Years" provides details).[73]

To many African Americans, including Newman, this tragedy was a betrayal of the unspoken pact between blacks and whites to work things out without overt violence.[74] Newman described the event as leaving an indelible mark on the civil rights movement in South Carolina. His general disappointment was apparent in a speech in which he reflected on a controversial position taken by Governor McNair with respect to the black community's displeasure with the embattled president of South Carolina State College, among other issues.[75] The stance taken by the governor totally disregarded not only the trust that Newman had in his leadership, but also the support from the black community that McNair had garnered through Newman's active intercession. With no attempt to disguise his disappointment, Newman

Newman on a 1969 tour of impoverished and depressed areas in the state. Photograph by Bill Barley. Courtesy of SCPC.

said that "the Negro bloc vote in the Second Congressional District alone turned 97 percent for McNair in the last election (1966). We have been kicked in the teeth."[76]

Poverty, Hunger, and Economic Opportunities

With the ending of his position in 1969 as NAACP field director for the state of South Carolina, Newman turned his activist spirit toward state government. From 1975 to 1981 he served as director of the Governor's Office of Rural Development. Newman worked to combat poverty and hunger in the state's depressed and rural areas. He saw this position as a means to fill a void that was not addressed by the civil rights demonstrations.

During the 1960s and 1970s Senator Hollings was interested in hunger as a national problem. He spoke of his myopia toward the problem in his home state lifting and allowing him to see hunger face-to-face. In addition to the senator's close encounter with poverty, he had what he described as a dramatic awakening when visiting the worst of slums in one of Charleston's African American communities. Adults at night after work were attending education programs to better themselves. This shattered Hollings's long-held belief that "They like poverty," "They are lazy," and "They don't like to work."[77] Newman's focus on poverty brought him in contact again with the now Senator Hollings. In 1968, still reeling from what he described as "ghetto poverty at its worst," the senator received a telephone call from Newman, who had heard of his tour in Charleston. Inspired by the outcome of that tour, Newman invited Hollings to look at poverty in Columbia. Columbia had recently been voted an "All-American" city for the second time. Hollings was initially annoyed when Newman arrived for the poverty tour with a delegation, including radio, TV, and newspaper reporters with equipment necessary for broadcasting the tour. This encounter reminded Hollings of others with Newman when he was governor. Of that time Hollings observed, "The Reverend Mr. Newman was always in the public press, always in the news, his name always on a petition or in a letter; complaining about the state of the Negroes. He was the antagonist; he never seemed daunted; he was always pursuing; he was what in those days we called trouble. When I became governor (1959–1963), I realized that we were bound to have many confrontations—and tangle we did. It seemed that at every news conference I was asked to comment on some charge or blast he had made. Yet, it wasn't until he came with a large group one day to the reception room of the governor's office that I recognized his brilliance."[78] Somehow Hollings's observation belies a degree of näiveté. It appears that he did not realize that Newman was discharging his responsibilities as a civil rights activist or that Newman's job and the goal of the NAACP were to change the racist structures of South Carolina by any means necessary, short of violence.

Recognizing Hollings's annoyance with the presence of reporters and cameras recording this encounter, Newman assured him that some people would never come to the slums and that it was therefore necessary to take images of them to the people. Hollings agreed that Newman was right and that no one would believe the degree of poverty they witnessed that day on the outskirts of the "All-American" capital city.

Newman's focus on poverty and hunger in rural South Carolina brought hope and self-help to communities that were neglected or forgotten by state government. Newman saw his work as director of rural development as laying a foundation for more meaningful interventions to reduce the level of poverty in the state. "Change," he said, "doesn't take place and is not initiated among people who are getting along well, but among those who are not getting along well. Fortunately for us, there has been a liberal element among the 'haves' that have provided leadership to the less articulate people, and without whom we would not be nearly as far along as we are. It's the poor themselves—the 'have-nots' themselves—who really have to bear the brunt of the efforts to bring about needed changes. So, the War on Poverty, with its involvement of the poor in policy-making positions on the local level, has made a monumental achievement in producing local—good local—leadership among the poor" (for more detail, see "A Vision for Change").[79] Because he and Newman were focusing on economic opportunities, Senator Hollings interpreted this to mean that he and Newman were now working on the same side of the streets.

Legacy

The Reverend I. DeQuincey Newman was often referred to as a consensus and bridge builder in his role as a civil rights activist. He was aware that he was also not always viewed in a positive light by both black and white Carolinians.[80] Despite covert criticism of his approach to bringing about change, his style of activism moved black Americans out of the shadows of patronage to becoming respected players in the political arena. Newman had a long vision. He never separated civil rights from the larger objectives of black self-help and empowerment. He believed in blacks exercising greater control over their own lives. He once described himself as an activist in the tradition of John the Baptist, someone committed to changing hearts and minds.[81] He was also a champion for greater equality in the distribution of social opportunity and economic justice.

Clearly, Newman believed that it was the role of a Christian to challenge a society that was not serving God through working to uplift the masses. He saw his role as a minister and politician as that of creating and maintaining choices for people to improve their lives. He summed up his work in the civil rights movement as successful in eliminating legal segregation, while recognizing that one cannot legally do away with prejudices. He said, "[Black people] have battered down walls of segregation in many instances and while we are not yet, as a people, on the inside of the political arena, we are not altogether on the outside either. We have our foot in the door and a long way to go."[82] "I sometimes get the feeling," he said, " that we didn't get as much accomplished as we thought we had in terms of adjusting the white power structure to the black presence . . . I am sometimes led to believe that we've got to start all over again."[83] He was aware that the legal and legislative triumphs did not mark the end of the struggle for racial and economic equality in South Carolina.

Given Newman's pivotal role in South Carolina's emergence as a more racially inclusive society, he is absent from past[84] and current[85] research on this period. Idus A. Newby, for example, viewed black activism under Newman's leadership as largely ineffective and resulting from white moderation (see "Leadership in Black and White").[86]

Contemporary scholars, social observers, and news reporters saw the need to transform what is referred to as the traditional telling and popular understanding of the civil rights movement. The intent, according to Peter F. Lau, is not to focus on the primary leaders, major organizations, key events, and national institutions but rather to recover the "hidden history" of the movement, a movement of ordinary African Americans struggling for an expansive vision of freedom, not merely for an end to Jim Crow and the possession of formal civil rights.[87] It seems incredulous to ignore one aspect of a movement in order to accentuate the other when in fact it is all an interconnected continuous flow. The so-called "hidden history" cannot and should not be separated from the "highlighted history"—each had an important and necessary role to play, and one could not exist without the other. The approach of diminishing the highlighted history of the movement to acknowledge the hidden history gives the appearance of pitting one against the other. I contend that it would be unconscionable to pit one against the other, especially if it is solely for the sake of scholarship or what might be thought of as balanced reporting. In this highlighting of Newman's role as an activist for racial equality, the intention is to acknowledge all of the change agents who went before him as well as those who stood with him.

Available data suggest that Newman's accomplishments were numerous. When he retired in 1969 as field director of the NAACP, he was widely known for fighting tirelessly to eliminate legal segregation in the state, for the dignity and respect of black Carolinians, for environmental protection, for national awareness to the state of hunger and poverty in South Carolina, and ultimately for political, economic, and social justice. From 1972 to 1974 he assumed the position of special assistant to R. Archie Ellis, commissioner of the Department of Social Services. Newman's appointment followed months of criticism at the department by the South Carolina Council on Human Relations and welfare rights organizations alleging that recipients had been embarrassed by condescending local welfare office staff and that public assistance payments were too low. Newman's job was to rectify that situation and give assurance that the civil rights of welfare recipients were not being violated.[88] Criticism was directed at Newman because of his appointment as an executive in state government. Some believed that such an appointment was diametrically opposed to his role as an activist for human and civil rights. He countered such criticism by stating, "If there are some who say I am no longer a civil rights leader, I would say that I've done far more . . . I've gotten far more accomplished by being in here than I would have being out there in the streets."[89] Newman believed that his work served to improve the political, social, and economic status of black people in the state. Some observers of the time describe this in terms of numerical and leadership gains in state government. Yet others are even more specific and speak of the appointment of blacks to the state law enforcement agency and to numerous boards and commissions. Also included was the integration of technical education in the state long before the integration of the schools and universities.

Newman retired from full-time ministry in 1973 but continued to work as a supply minister, or someone who was assigned in the absence of a permanent minister, until 1982. However, he served as director of the Governor's Office of Rural Development (1975–81) (see "A Vision for Change"). He assumed this position at a time when most people his age were turning toward retirement. Some wondered if this appointment was an effort to marginalize a black freedom fighter. Newman, however, knew that his entire life was destined for the purpose of dismantling the walls of racism and oppressive life-altering conditions. The overwhelming poverty he witnessed in his travels across rural South Carolina was not different from the same style of peonage that he witnessed in Red Oak, Georgia, as a practicing pastor. He felt compelled to continue the struggle regardless of the context or the form it took. Prior to the establishment of the Office of Rural Development, the state's response to poverty and hunger was simply to ignore it by drawing a line—civic leaders built fences—around the slum areas or displacing families by tearing down unfit housing and not rebuilding it.[90] The Office of Rural Development was established to strengthen institutional responses to the needs of the poor and to provide state technical assistance and strategies to strengthen the planning capabilities of multicounty regional institutions in order to increase rural residents' participation in public affairs and community and rural development. Newman worked to develop employment, health care, grassroots citizen involvement, and water and sewer services for the rural poor of the state. The rural development projects included life skills education, after-school and day-care programs, a crab-trap project, a chair-making training project, and the Good Hope Farmer's Cooperatives (for more detail, see "A Vision for Change").[91] The chair-making training project was successful and provided a marketable income for the men involved in the making and sale of the chairs. The cooperatives helped farmers in at least five counties find buyers for their sweet potatoes, one of the crops they were harvesting. Despite his extensive involvement at the local, state, and national levels, it is important to note that Newman's concerns about apartheid and injustice extended

Newman, Mrs. A. P. H. Newman, and James Clyburn. Courtesy of the Newman family.

beyond the boundaries of South Carolina and the United States (see "Making the Impossible Possible").

Newman always prepared someone to take his place as he completed one mission after another. For example, he was replaced by Harrison Rearden as executive assistant to the state social service commissioner, by Wallace Brown, Sr., as director of the Office of Rural Development, by Isaac Williams as field director of the state NAACP, and by Kay Patterson, (1985–2007) as state senator. Patterson was also a candidate for the senate seat that Newman was elected to in 1985. Newman served as mentor to a long list of mentees including Congressman James E. Clyburn, attorney Vernon E. Jordan, Dr. Hiram Spain, Karen Grant, and Jerome Noble. He mentored by example and offered wise counsel when requested. All of his mentees confirmed that Newman mentored by example. He offered counsel to his mentees only when requested. His mentees described him as an example of a person who not only talked the talk but also practiced what he preached.

Newman was also the first black senator to serve in the South Carolina Senate since Reconstruction. On October 25, 1983, he was elected in a special election to fill a senate seat for the Chester-Fairfield-Richland District vacated by Alex Sanders, who resigned to become a judge on the new state appeals court. Newman thought of this election as an opportunity to serve as a role model for the kind of person who should be elected as a statesman. He thought that this position called for "someone of maturity . . . someone who is not seeking office to satisfy his ego, someone who doesn't have anything to gain in material values."[89] For many African Americans, Newman's election to the South Carolina Senate after nearly a decade as a freedom fighter was an extraordinary event. Although many viewed it as a made-for-movie type climax to his work in the trenches as a foot soldier for justice, there were many who did not. There were some whose sentiments were captured in the reflection of Newman's protégé Isaac "Ike" Williams. According to Williams, "Sometimes there are roles for kings and roles for kingmakers . . . and every kingmaker can't be king." Williams thought that Newman's finest work was in his role as kingmaker but not as a senator.[92] Reverend McKinley Bowman, Newman's longtime friend and partner in the struggle for over forty years, put it this way: "When we started to talk about the Senate to get that done, there were four or five of us that had ambitions. We met in a meeting behind closed doors and agreed that would be his." Bowman continued, "Being the leader in the kind of office that he had, you don't get compliments for that, you get a cussing out."[93] Modjeska Simkins, a former NAACP colleague of Newman, believed that "the state's power structure cheated blacks when the cancer-stricken Newman was elected to the South Carolina legislature in 1983."[94] On his first day in the senate, Newman remarked, "October 25th (the day of his election) was the convergent point for the right man in the place at the time. I am thankful that providence determined that I was the right man."[95] Also in 1983 he shared with several close associates a mystical vision that came to him, in which he was instructed to design and organize a new church that focused exclusively on the needs of its members and the community.[96] Newman was instrumental in the planning and building of a church that was named after two bishops, Middleton-Rosemond United Methodist Church of Columbia, South Carolina. Immediately upon his death in 1985, the church governing body changed the church's name to I. DeQuincey Newman United Methodist Church.[97]

Despite the nay-saying, Newman was reelected in 1985, but he resigned his seat in the same year on July 31 because of ill health.[98] He was a heavy smoker and was often photographed at protest events smoking a cigarette. The excessive smoking led to lung cancer and emphysema. Anne, his wife, lived and worked in close proximity with him. She too suffered in later life from emphysema and found it necessary to use an oxygen machine to support her breathing. The resurgence of Newman's cancer in 1985 was extremely

Portrait of Newman in the senate chambers of the state capitol. Courtesy of the Newman family.

Newman greeting well-wishers and supporters at his senatorial swearing-in ceremony, left to right: Newman, Bishop Jack Meadows, and Governor Richard Riley. Courtesy of the Newman family.

Newman's swearing-in ceremony, with Anne Newman holding the Bible. Courtesy of the Newman family.

stressful for the family. Both Anne and their daughter, Emily, thought that recovery this time was not a possibility. Newman seemingly accepted his condition as an act of providence. He continued to be available and responsive to members of his congregation. After his resignation from the senate, he continued to get enjoyment from reading, Scrabble playing, and raising organically grown vegetables. He enjoyed not only eating his own homegrown vegetables but also sharing them with others.[99]

In one of his last interviews Newman shared that he would like to be remembered as "one having the good judgment in the period of racial transition in the state, who had a hand in keeping things in balance."[100] On October 21, 1985, the Reverend I. DeQuincey Newman died at age seventy-four from lung cancer and emphysema. According to close friends and longtime colleagues, it appeared that he kept things in balance to the end. Of this occasion U.S. District Judge Matthew Perry, a friend for more than thirty-five years and who visited Newman the day before his passing, said, "I talked to him at his bedside. He knew that the end was in sight. He had accepted his fate."

Perry concluded that an air of calm understanding remained with Newman to the very end.[101]

Newman was eulogized by family, friends, and colleagues. His longtime friend and coworker Matthew Perry said, "I think he was one of the most forceful and intelligent persons in the forefront of the civil rights movement in the entire century. He will be remembered as the man who certainly created the awareness with all South Carolinians with whom he had contact concerning the basic worth of a human no matter what the color of their [*sic*] skin." In a similar vein, Richard Riley lamented, "Few people have demonstrated during their lifetime that they cared about the good of all South Carolinians, and translated those thoughts into actions, more than I. DeQuincey Newman. Our great feelings of loss and personal grief are mixed with the certain knowledge that our lives have been blessed by his presence. The history books will record his greatness, the hearts and minds of those he touched will record his humanity."[102]

Summary and Conclusion

I. DeQuincey Newman, as reflected in this account of his life, was a tireless servant of the people. He extolled the dignity and worth of the individual and always maintained personal humility and hopefulness. Overall his life's work suggests ongoing development and refinement of those racialized areas of life that create oppressive conditions and all forms of injustices.

One might surmise that a great deal of progress was made during Newman's tenure as a civil rights activist with respect to justice and equality. In illustrating the changes, Newman noted that in comparison to the past and the days of his youth, "the difference is vast." For example, he said, "while a person now has fear for his job security and while he entertains fear of not being accepted for certain types of employment, 20 to 25 years ago, he would not even have contemplated or aspired for an untraditional type of job because he knew full well he would not even get it. Nowadays, there is not present as much of threat of bodily harm and other forms of reprisal as were the case from 15 years ago on back."[103] However, as Newman moved toward retirement from state government in the early 1980s, he shared a prophetic vision of the country's future. He expressed misgivings about the nation's increasing conservative mood. He believed that the new wave of conservatism engulfing the country would result in "a crisis of such proportion that it will just about destroy this country—not physically—but it will destroy this country spiritually because it will have the effect of demoralizing the citizenry." He continued to clarify his meaning. He said, "When you have been in a forward movement for so long, and you suddenly shift into reverse there is a grinding of the gears. Some of the cogs in the gear mechanism become stripped, and after that, there is immobilization."[104]

Both South Carolina and the United States of America have made progress in the racial and political areas; however, unjust policy and practice issues are still reflected in the areas of affirmative action; racial justice for all groups of color, especially the growing immigrant populations; poor quality education for groups of color; discrimination in housing, employment, physical and mental health care, public welfare, and criminal justice; poverty; and political activity. Newman was particularly interested in improving the quality of life in these areas for citizens in the rural areas and for the elderly. Essentially the quality-of-life issues that Reverend Newman advocated intersected with all areas of life. His life's work focuses our attention not only on the role and responsibility of all citizens but also on the government. He supported self-help economics and empowerment practices.

Newman's life and accomplishments serve as a model for anyone interested in political, economic, and social justice. He was compassionate, dignified, and free of anger. The interests of others motivated his actions. He valued the basic rights of a human being regardless of his/her ethnic background. He cared about the good of all South Carolinians and translated those thoughts into action. His lifetime goal was to create a more just and equitable society. In this regard he explained, "We've achieved a modicum of political integration and to a lesser extent economic integration, but there is not much evidence of social integration."[105] He attributed any barrier to accomplishments in these areas as simply "a matter of the heart."

I. DeQuincey Newman was a transformer. He used his positive outlook, intelligence, and humor to dismantle the structures of segregation and discrimination in South Carolina. As a civil rights activist, he believed—not unlike Levi G. Byrd, Martin Luther King, Jr., Medgar Evers, Roy Wilkins, Esau Jenkins, Modjeska Simkins, Septima Poinsette Clark, Joseph Armstrong DeLaine, James T. McCain, and many others—that a combination of agitation, protest politics, and the political process used to effect change was more effective than armed resistance.

As a servant leader, Newman never focused on personal gain; rather he considered each struggle an opportunity to benefit African American and poor South Carolinians. He remained connected to his humanity by reminding himself that one should never take oneself too seriously and that people will remember you not for what you did for them but for what you did *to* them.[106] Newman's leadership represented a selfless model in the ongoing fight for black empowerment, self-determination, and equality. He was a great humanitarian who touched the hearts and minds of everyone he encountered. He fought to ensure a society free of oppression and prejudices.

Notes

1. Page, "New Role for Newman."

2. Emily Morris Newman, interview by Sadye Logan, oral history of Isaiah DeQuincey Newman's life and legacy, Newman Institute, Columbia, S.C., July 21, 2006.

3. Stucker, "Did You Know"; *Will the Circle Be Unbroken.*

4. Ibid.

5. Anne Pauline Newman, interview by Logan, summer 2006.

6. Emily Morris Newman, interview by Logan, summer 2006.

7. Ibid. Lighter-skinned African Americans in the Brown Fellowship Society (1790–1945) considered themselves superior to darker-skinned African Americans. Although still considered inferior by the white population, South Carolina's mulattos, octoroons (persons with one-eighth black ancestry), and quadroons (persons with one-quarter black ancestry) were often given their freedom while darker-skinned individuals remained in slavery. Officially the stated purpose (of the society) was to provide respectable funerals for society members, support widows, and educate surviving children. Determined not to upset the white community, the society did nothing to help slaves (indeed some lighter-skinned members were slave-owners themselves) and were careful about whom they admitted to their ranks, which consisted of no more than fifty men at a time. Typically only free lighter-skinned African Americans (with relatively affluent jobs) were allowed to join, but sometimes darker-skinned individuals who had naturally straight hair were permitted as well. All who joined were considered prosperous, and a few were wealthy.

8. Emily Morris Newman, interview by Logan, summer 2006.

9. John Clay Smith, Jr., *Emancipation.*

10. Emily Morris Newman, interview by Logan, summer 2006.

11. Stucker, "Did You Know," 10.

12. Emily Morris Newman, interview by Logan, 2006.

13. Ibid.

14. Stucker, "Did You Know," 9. Living in peonage was a common practice in the Deep South. Sharecroppers were pressured to pay debts or taxes through peonage. Peonage developed in the South after the abolition of slavery in 1865. An employer paid fines imposed for a petty crime based on Black Codes and Jim Crow laws, in exchange for work by the sentenced person. When agricultural laborers and tenants were advanced cash and supplies, any attempt to leave was interpreted as having obtained credit under false pretenses, which under state law was a criminal offense. Peonage is interpreted in the Constitution (Title 18, U.S.C., Section 1581) as holding a person in debt servitude.

15. *The United Methodist Book of Discipline* (Nashville: United Methodist Publishing House, 2008.

16. Anne Pauline Newman, interview by Logan, 2006. Additional information about Anne Pauline Hinton Newman can be found in the following sources: Sadye Logan, "How Anne Newman Changed Our Lives," (Columbia, S.C.) *State*, February 22, 2009, http://www.thestate.com/editoral-colums/v-print/story/692552.html (accessed June 9, 2009); Logan, "In Their Own Voices."

17. Stucker, "Did You Know."

18. Anne Pauline Newman, interview by Logan, 2006.

19. Ibid.

20. Billingsley, *Mighty Like a River.*

21. Brinson, "The Reverend Mr. Newman."

22. Ibid.

23. Lincoln and Mamiya, *The Black Church*; Payne, *I've Got the Rights of Freedom.*

24. Fowler, "Democratic Party."

25. Orlando, *Southern Politics.*

26. Egerton, "The End of the South."

27. Yarbrough, *A Passion for Justice*; "New Role for Newman: He Works within the Establishment for Civil Rights," (Columbia, S.C.) *State*, October 15, 1972, A4.

28. Richards, "Progressive Democratic Party." African American leaders in South Carolina were members of the Republican Party in 1960. For example, onetime House of Representatives member and successful businessman Earl Middleton, of Orangeburg, was a Republican.

29. Emily Morris Newman, interview by Logan, summer 2006.

30. Woods, "Modjeska Simkins," 115–16.

31. Wickenberg, "Simkins Leaves Legacy."

32. Ibid.

33. Ibid.; Woods, "Modjeska Simkins."

34. Wickenberg, "Simkins Leaves Legacy," A5.

35. Ibid.

36. Grose, *South Carolina at the Brink.*

37. Brown, "Civil Rights Activism"; Lee, "Timmerman."

38. Hollings, *The Case against Hunger*, 26.

39. Brown, "Civil Rights Activism."

40. Grose, *South Carolina at the Brink.*

41. Brinson, "Quiet Man Helped."

42. "Report and Recommendation on Membership and Staff," NAACP Papers (1957), Manuscript Division , Library of Congress, Washington, D.C., III: A-37.

43. Ibid., A-37.

44. Anne Pauline Newman, interview by Logan, fall 2006.

45. Grose, *South Carolina at the Brink.*

46. Anne Pauline Newman, interview by Logan, fall 2006.

47. Ibid.

48. Grose, 1981, cited in Grose, *Activist Spirit Still Burns in Rev. Newman.*

49. Ibid.

50. Fladung, "Senator I. DeQuincey Newman Dies."

51. Grose, *Activist Spirit Still Burns in Rev. Newman*, 113.

52. Ibid.

53. Ike Williams, interview by Logan, summer 2006.

54. Ibid.

55. Brinson, "The Reverend Mr. Newman."

56. Ibid.

57. Stucker, "Did You Know," 11.

58. Ibid.; S. Suitts, G. King, and V. Grosvenor, *Will the Circle Be Unbroken*, 1979.

59. Wolley, "Newman"; Hollings, *The Case against Hunger.*

60. Sellers, with Terrell, *The River of No Return.*

61. Hugh Gibson, editorial, (Charleston, S.C.) *News and Courier*, April 9, 1967.

62. Paul Clancy, editorial, "Bombs, Blossoms," (Columbia, S.C.) *State*, April 23, 1967, A2A.

63. Gibson, editorial, "Unrest Still Grips State." (Charleston, S.C.) *News and Courier*, April 9, 1967.

64. Ibid.

65. William D. Workman, Jr., editorial, (Columbia, S.C.) *State*, March 23, 1967.

66. "Enough Is Enough Kids," *Orangeburg Times and Democrat*, March 9, 1967.

67. I. DeQuincey Newman, editorial, "NAACP and State College, (Columbia, S.C.) *State*, April 23, 1967, 12 A (Columbia, S.C.) *State*, December 20, 1983, 26.

68. Bass and Nelson, "Newman Says More Blacks Will Win SC Senate Seats," in *The Orangeburg Massacre*, p. 20

69. Ibid.

70. Hartsook, "West, John Carl," 1014.

71. Bass and Nelson, *The Orangeburg Massacre.*

72. Ibid.

73. Ibid.; Grose, 1981.

74. Bass and Nelson, *The Orangeburg Massacre.*

75. Grose, 1981.

76. Grose, *South Carolina at the Brink*, 190.

77. Hollings, *The Case against Hunger*, 25–26.

78. Ibid.

79. Grose, *Activist Spirit Still Burns in Rev. Newman*, 1981.

80. Newby, *Black Carolinians.*

81. Kern, "S.C. Mourns."

82. Newman Says More Blacks Will Win SC Senate," 16-A. Charleston, S.C. *News and Courier*, December 20, 1983.

83. Grose, *Activist Spirit Still Burns in Newman,* 1981.

84. Newby, *Black Carolinians.*

85. Moore and Burton, *Toward the Meeting of the Waters.*

86. Newby, *Black Carolinians.*

87. Lau, *Democracy Rising.*

88. Page, "New Role for Newman"; Karen Ross Grant, interview by Logan, 2006; Cook, interview by Logan, fall 2006.

89. Grose, *Activist Spirit Still Burns in Newman,* 1981.

90. Hollings, *The Case against Hunger.*

91. Page, "New Role for Newman"; Karen Ross Grant, interview by Logan, 2006; Cook, interview by Logan, fall 2006.

92. Ike Williams, interview by Logan, summer 2006.

93. Fladung, "Senator I. DeQuincey Newman Dies."

94. Wickenberg, "Simkins Leaves Legacy," A5.

95. Fladung, "Senator I. DeQuincey Newman Dies."

96. Stucker, "Did You Know," 11.

97. Karen Ross Grant, interview by Logan, 2006.

98. Carey Hopkins, personal communication, March 5, 2001. Mr. Hopkins was Senator Newman's campaign manager.

99. Page, "New Role for Newman."

100. Stucker, "Did You Know," 11.

101. Fladung, "Senator I. DeQuincey Newman Dies."

102. Kern, "S.C. Mourns," A5.

103. Emily Morris Newman, interview by Logan, 2006.

104. Grose, *Activist Spirit Still Burns in Newman,* 1981, A5.

105. Brinson, "The Reverend Mr. Newman."

106. Emily Morris Newman, interview by Logan, fall 2006.

Making the Impossible Possible

Building Alliance between Religion and Politics

Sadye L. M. Logan and Josephine A. McRant

A desire presupposes the possibility of action to achieve it;
action presupposes a goal which is worth achieving.

Ayn Rand, *Atlas Shrugged*

The United States Supreme Court, the highest court of the nation, interpreted the First Amendment to the Constitution of the United States to mean that church and state shall remain separate. Simply stated, the state shall not have the influence either to prohibit or to promote a person's religious belief. There have been numerous debates over this interpretation in every level of the court, including the very court that first handed down this interpretation. What these debates could never address, however, was how to draw a line between church and state in the heart of a man such as Isaiah DeQuincey Newman. His unwavering lifelong commitment to church and state is what made him unique. This lifelong commitment, however, was centered in a leadership principle based on faith and courage. He was called to serve.

A Call to Serve

Newman began preaching in 1929 at the age of eighteen and was very aware of the continuing problems of racial discrimination and other forms of oppression experienced by African Americans and other people of color in the community and in his congregation. He approached these problems from a social and political perspective but within the context of his Christian principles. His life reflected an innate compassion and a burning desire to help others. Newman knew from an early age that he would be a preacher. In explaining his call to preach, Newman said, "In a manner of speaking, I have been a preacher all my life—not formally—but it was always there, and I knew the day would come, it was just a matter of a lapse of time."[1] In years to come, Newman's life unfolded in a manner that illustrated his knowing commitment to serve others (see "Isaiah DeQuincey Newman" and "The NAACP Years").

Newman began his formal religious life in Atlanta, Georgia, as a seminary student and was formally connected to the Atlanta Conference. He transferred from the Atlanta Conference to the South Carolina Conference at the time of his graduation from Gammon Theological Seminary in 1937. In the South Carolina Conference, he continued his preaching and teaching, which he based on the principle that although people's lives are different, their hearts are the same—a sameness that suggests a commitment and responsibility to the oppressed and disfranchised among us. In a sermon titled "God and the Day's Work" in the early 1940s at the Saint James Methodist Church, he instructed his membership on the importance of serving others through working for God. He believed in practicing what he preached. In this lecture he taught the importance of choosing an occupation and serving God in and through one's job. He said that a Christian must "select his job carefully and prayerfully" and "choose a vocation that does not conflict with his Christian principles."[2]

Newman never let anything prevent him from an opportunity to serve and apply his Christian principles—principles, in most cases, that were linked to some form of politics. In explaining this stance, he said, "I have been persuaded for a long time that one of the surest ways for effective social change is at the ballot box [and in] the quality of candidates we choose for public office. And, for that reason, I have spent a great deal of time urging voter registration, maximizing voter turnout on election day and disseminating information regarding the various stands that candidates for office have taken on issues. So, much of my ministry has been geared to activities down where the rubber meets the road, so to speak. The application of the principles of Christianity to everyday living [does] not exclud[e] the political life of the State."[3] His activist ministry included his role as a leader in the Orangeburg and South Carolina branches of the NAACP (see "Isaiah DeQuincey Newman" and "The NAACP Years"). This much-traveled road led him through

Newman as pastor, Trinity United Methodist Church, Orangeburg, S.C. Courtesy of the Newman family.

over half a century of service as a minister and as a builder of alliances between the state's political, social, and religious communities.

Between 1938 and 1950 Newman served in four different churches, one of which was Trinity Baptist Church in Orangeburg, South Carolina. By this time his sermons had become more sophisticated and far removed from what he once phrased as being "tolerated" by his congregations. However, Newman's teachings and demonstration of Christian responsibilities extended beyond the walls of the church to the broader community, including the national and international levels (see "Isaiah DeQuincey Newman" and "The NAACP Years"). Newman worked hard to demonstrate in his life what he preached from the pulpit. He was an activist but a humble man.

Following his tenure at Trinity United Methodist Church in Orangeburg, Newman was assigned as the district superintendent for the United Methodist Church of Sumter District from 1950 to 1956. After this assignment Newman became the pastor at Wesley Methodist Church (1956–58) in Charleston, South Carolina. Reverend H. V. Manning, Newman's predecessor at Wesley, introduced Newman to his new congregation in October 1956. In his introduction Reverend Manning said, "In the times in which we live,

Newman as pastor, Wesley Methodist Church, Charleston, S.C. Courtesy of the Newman family.

Methodism in Charleston needs a person who is sensitive to the social and community problems. Here again, your pastor has distinguished himself. He has been very active in civic affairs not only in the state of South Carolina, but in other sections of the nation."[4] Reverend Manning, who left Wesley for an appointment as president of Claflin College, was of course making reference to the tension-charged racial atmosphere resulting from the court-ordered desegregation of public schools.

Politics, the Black Church, and Civil Rights

Newman's style of ministry had its roots in the civil rights movement—called the most important recent example of a political movement in which religious forces played a tremendous role.[5] As was evident under Newman's leadership, though many churchgoing black people supported his involvement in civil rights, many also did not believe that the church should be at the forefront of the movement. The continuum of belief ranged from those who believed that the "business of religion is religion" to those who believed that the black churches should be at the center of political action. Research on the impact and role of black churches in the lives of its members has produced several typologies.[6] The seminal work on the black church by Charles Eric Lincoln and Lawrence H. Mamiya, both scholars of religion, provides a sliding-scale topology or a dialectical model of church and pastor characteristics that includes activism. They used the polarities of priestly and prophetic functions to capture church activism. Priestly functions concern maintenance and the spiritual life of its members. Prophetic functions involve the church in political action and community change.

Other scholars describe the black church within the context of the civil rights movement and other forms of political and social activism, including personal empowerment. They have identified three types of black clergy and parishioners according to their beliefs or attitudes: traditionalists, moderates, and militants. Traditionalists, for example, held the view that churches should be about religion and spiritual things and stay out of political involvement. Moderates, despite believing that religion should be deeply concerned with spiritual and worldly matters, preferred to work for change gradually and without causing any disturbances. Militants believed that they were called through faith to direct political action, including direct action if that were necessary to promote positive change. Although the tension between these three groups lessened over time, it never completely disappeared.[7] Newman's type of activism fit more closely within the militants' belief structure and the prophetic functions. His supporters fit all three categories. Some were overtly available to the struggle; others were covertly available but provided financial support; and others wanted nothing to do with the cause. Not unlike Martin Luther King, Jr., Newman believed that the way to lasting peace and justice was through cooperation and nonviolent confrontation. His approach was nonviolent civil disobedience. According to King, there are four steps in this approach:

careful collection of the facts to verify that injustice does exist;
negotiation—always to be carried out before merely confrontational methods are used;
self-purification—a necessary prelude to civil disobedience so that participants are clear about their own motives and strong enough within themselves not to return violence for violence;
direct action—marches, sit-ins, protests.[8]

Newman effectively used direct action as a form of political action, the purpose being to force a community or group to address an issue that members have refused to confront or negotiate. King went on to say that people should obey just laws but that God also calls people to engage in civil disobedience against unjust laws. He differentiates just and unjust laws as follows:

a just law squares with the law of God;
a just law is equally binding on all, while one that is unjust is made to apply to a minority, who had no part in bringing it into being, by the majority;
a just law may be unjust in its application.

During the years between 1960 and 1969 Newman's leadership role in his church ministry changed. He assumed leadership responsibility for the state NAACP as field director. During that time he was not assigned as a church pastor; however, the church provided an ideal venue for addressing many of the ills in places across the state. In South Carolina his pioneering works with the NAACP gave him many opportunities to see the inside of jails and wrestle with the prophetic aspects of his religious beliefs (see "Isaiah DeQuincey Newman" and "The NAACP Years"). Newman and many others such as Gloria Blackwell Rackley, Charles Thomas, Jr., Matthew Perry, J. Herbert Nelson, J. Arthur Brow, and the student activists Jim Clyburn, Isaac Williams, MacArthur Goodwin (a Claflin College student leader), Leonard Glover (a Benedict College student who demonstrated against segregated businesses in Columbia), Fred Moore (expelled from South Carolina State because of involvement in NAACP activities), and Thomas Gaither (a Claflin College student described as the "travelingest student"[9] in the United States because of his nationwide appearances on behalf of the student-engaged activities) made enormous sacrifices as they engaged in attaining political and human rights for others. They were often arrested for holding sit-ins and rallies at places where black people were not allowed before, and sometimes during, integration.

In many cases Newman appealed to the masses as both a minister and an advocate for human rights and was the only hope for relief from racial oppression. One such instance was reflected in a letter to Reverend Newman from a black man who had been arrested and charged with armed robbery. He stated that during the arrest, the arresting officers searched his room without a warrant; they shot him in the neck and gave him no medical attention. Further, the officers would not allow him to make a phone call. He summed up the situation: "All of my rights were violated and I want to do something about it. So, I am pleading for your help in every way that I can. This is the only hope that I have."[10]

The World as His Church

As a part of Newman's leadership efforts at Trinity United Methodist Church (Orangeburg), he worked to establish a church mission in South Africa. This mission was concerned with issues similar to those confronting his congregation in South Carolina. On his travels to South Africa, Newman observed the religious and social oppressions of apartheid. Such oppression and repression went against everything he believed in as a Christian and advocate for human rights. He was compelled to assert his efforts to help eradicate such ills not only in Africa but also at home. He led efforts to make financial contributions to help relieve some of the poverty that was a fallout from apartheid. Unlike the black ministry of the early twentieth century, Newman utilized the church to bring blacks together to organize coalitions and to garner strength to fight the injustices of racism and other discriminatory practices. In contrast, the earlier district conferences and the annual conventions denounced the symptoms of racial oppression but not the system.[11] According to Idus A. Newby, the black churches at the turn of the twentieth century "limited their social concerns to matters related to personal regeneration. Prohibition and education were [the] primary focus of concern."[12] Newby goes on to say that even when significant social issues were discussed, little if anything was done about them, either because people felt disempowered or because the two major denominations (Methodists and Baptists), not unlike the society, generally equated systemic problems with individual degeneracy. Newman, however, as early as the 1940s in one of his many sermons challenged members of the congregation to exercise their political rights as citizens. He urged them to register to vote to remove elected officials who were not upholding their responsibilities sufficiently: "June 5th, 6th and 7th should witness every Negro who can qualify making their way to the place of registration so that they can help to vote out of office, those who keep them in economic and political servitude. In failing to do this, all the fine and pious things we say regarding our men in service, will be only the rendering of lip service, which will signify nothing."[13]

Racism and the Methodist Church

It is commonly recognized that the black church has provided more than a place of worship for its community. The extent to which the historic black church provided unity beyond class boundaries, though, is questionable, especially in the Deep South. In the early stages Methodism was introduced to both slaves and free men. However, many colonists resented this approach to religion and expressed their resentment through violent and hostile acts against the preachers and black people in the congregations. Many of the church members believed that slavery was right and good and had some beneficial effects on the slaves. Slavery was therefore dismissed as a political issue and not an immoral institution. In this regard, the church's response was to separate and segregate its black worshipers to pews in the back corners of the churches or to separate meetinghouses.[14] Eventually the disrespect and unkind treatment by the white worshipers forced the former slaves to form independent churches. This initiative gave birth to the black Methodist Church and to black self-help and the functioning of the black church as a revolutionary unit during slavery. For example, in 1822 the African Methodist Episcopal Church (A.M.E.) in Charleston, South Carolina, was banned as subversive after disclosure of Denmark Vesey's slave revolt conspiracy. It was alleged that many of the four thousand members of the church in Charleston were involved in the 1822 slave insurrection.[15]

The United Methodist Church traces its roots to the Methodist movement of John Wesley in England in the 1700s.[16] Formation of the United Methodist Church was created nationally on April 23, 1968, when the Methodist Church merged with the Evangelical United Brethren Church.[17] The appendix captures the chronology of events leading to the merger. Few people were aware of a significant event that occurred in 1939, when the Methodist Episcopal Church, the Methodist Episcopal Church South, and the Methodist Protestant Church merged to form the Methodist Church. This year also marked the beginning of the Methodist Church's constitutionally segregated, racially based central jurisdiction. Given that the "Southern churches did not want the inclusiveness shown to African Americans by the Northern churches," the church's law-making assembly, the General Conference, created the Central Jurisdiction. The Central Jurisdiction served as the compromise for segregating the church's African American members into a nongeographical unit.[18] This created a church within a church and thereby denied full entry of African Americans into the newly formed United Methodist Church. Nonblack churches were broken down by geographical boundaries. Within the structure of the Central Jurisdiction, black leadership could serve only black congregations.

Many regarded this as a shameful period of church history. This was a difficult time for black people within Methodism.[19] According to James Thomas, a bishop in the United Methodist Church (see narrative section), who helped to dismantle the Central Jurisdiction, blacks stayed in the church under these conditions because they saw the church to be as much theirs as anyone else's. He believed that a story yet to be told is the work that occurred among a group of concerned black members of the Central Jurisdiction and a few white churchgoers in the South and many in the North to transform the conscience of the church against segregation.[20] This fight to change the conscience of the church began as early as 1948 when a committee was formed at the Central Jurisdiction Conference to study ways of eliminating the Central Jurisdiction. In 1952 the General Conference established the Board of Social and Economic Relations for the purpose of addressing social and economic disparities within the General Conference. In 1955 Newman in his role as chair of the South Carolina board memorialized the General Conference as follows:

> Whereas, the General Conference in 1952 declared that, "Segregation has no place in the Methodist Church," and whereas, the general agencies of the Church operates under the mandates of the General Conference, and whereas, it is known and widely publicized that the Publishing House practices racial segregation in its plant in Nashville, and racial discrimination in its general employment practices. Therefore, be it resolved that the South Carolina Conference now in session in Trinity Church, Camden, South Carolina, October 15, 1955, memorialize the 1956 session of the General Conference to investigate these practices and order their discontinuance. We further memorialize the General Conference to establish an executive or administrative position with policy-making power and employ a Negro for the same.[21]

Despite the board's pronouncement in 1955 to the General Conference that segregation had no place in the Methodist Church and the dissolution of the Central Jurisdiction in 1968, changes in the structure and operations of the church were slow and stressful. The decision to transition into a unified Methodist Church was not popular with everyone, especially among the southern churches. The black South Carolina Conference was persistent. Newman also chaired the committee of "Concerned Clergy and Laity of the South Carolina Conference of the United Methodist Church." In a memorandum dated August 5, 1969, he addressed his concerns about the direction the merger was going. The memo was addressed to the ministerial and lay members of the South Carolina Conference, United Methodist Church. He was notifying the committee of an impending August 17, 1969, meeting to address major problems that were threatening the merger. Newman's memorandum read as follows: "Brothers and sisters we have problems—big problems. They stem from the racism that was so apparent at the last session of our Annual Conference." He proceeded to outline the problems: "Attempt to suppress freedom of speech . . . lack of respect prevailing atmosphere of hostility, mistrust . . . abuse of power . . . abuse and subversion of appointive powers and prerogatives . . . we have a split conference." Newman urged the attendance of everyone and warned members of the committee that "this is no time for craven vacillation nor weak-kneed indecision." Newman, as always, was focused first on their Christian responsibility and asked, "How can we reconcile the world to Christ if we cannot achieve reconciliation among ourselves?"[22]

Perhaps at the forefront of Newman's thinking was a January 6, 1969, article in the *State* entitled "Negroes Allegedly Are Turned Away from Church Doors."[23] In addition, in the agreement of the black and white Methodist Churches to unite, Newman recognized that there was still much to overcome before the two churches could come together as a unified body. He was concerned not only about those black members who were fearful of "rocking the boat," or in other words demanding the abolishment of a segregated church, but also with the lagged time of the South Carolina Conference in creating the unity between the two churches. During this tense time of the merger, the South Carolina Conference in 1970 appointed six members to a conference committee to work out racial differences and bring the two churches together in the smoothest manner possible. Rhett Jackson, chair of the committee to unite the South Carolina conferences, said that he and Matthew McCollom, an African American minister (Orangeburg) and current state president of the NAACP, traveled the state to explain reasons for the proposed merger. According to Jackson, "We had a lot of resistance from (white) members in churches from Columbia to Charleston."[24] The 1971 merger proposal from Jackson's committee was defeated. Bishop Paul Harder appointed a new committee to prepare a revised proposal. Reverend Eben Taylor, a former district superintendent of the South Carolina Annual Conference and a high school friend of Jackson, was a part of the second successful committee. The second committee crafted a successful proposal that resulted in a 1972 merger of the black and white Methodist Churches.

The overall merger process was hindered by such racist thinking as reflected in churches in Mississippi. According to Eben Taylor, "Many of the Mississippi pastors said that they would refuse to take orders from black superintendents, so they designed a system wherein the conferences would be divided into four districts with senior and junior superintendents. The senior superintendents would all be white."[25] The Mississippi proposal, however, was declared unconstitutional and had to be revised. Today the merger is viewed as a success. In the words of Taylor, "The United Methodist church is full of heroes."[26] Many lay and clergy people such as Bishop James S. Thomas, Reverend Matthew McCollom, Reverend Denny Gleaton, Esther Witherspoon, and Bishop Lance Webb made sacrifices to abolish the racially based Central Jurisdiction. The twenty-nine-year struggle within the Methodist Church was a microcosm of the tumultuous civil rights struggle in the larger U.S. society. Many strongly believed that the changing racial climate in the church was directly influenced by the changing climate in the broader society. Newman demonstrated the same kind of strength and bravery to help in dismantling the Central Jurisdiction and end segregation in the United Methodist Church as he did in dismantling segregation and injustice in the broader society.

Builder of Churches

During his lifetime Newman founded two churches in addition to establishing a church mission in South Africa. The first was Francis Burns United Methodist Church in north Columbia, South Carolina. Newman and a group of about ten men conceived the need for a United Methodist church in the north section of Columbia to serve the predominantly black population. The conference authorized a fact-finding survey, which was conducted on December 30, 1960. With the support of other churches, Francis Burns United Methodist was officially established on March 30, 1972. This church was founded during the time when Newman was conference missionary secretary and field director for the NAACP. The early worship services were held at the home of the Newmans on Chappelle Street in Columbia, South Carolina. The church was named after the first missionary African American bishop of the Methodist Episcopal Church, who was ordained in 1858.[27]

Newman was diagnosed with lung cancer in 1982. Although his health was failing, he founded another church. The impetus to do so was based on what he described as a premonition from God. After extensive testing, he opted not to have surgery and accepted the possibility of imminent death. He shared his thoughts about his decision in a letter to Bishop Roy C. Clark of the South Carolina United Methodist Church Conference. "At this juncture," Newman wrote, "I found consolation in the knowledge and belief that if refusing surgery meant the ultimate consequences, I was alright, because I was at peace with God, my fellowman and myself. I did opt for radiation therapy, and keeping my own counsel, I also opted for the spiritual 'radiation' that is available to those who trust the Lord."[28] He outlined in this letter specifics of the vision:

> About the middle of the afternoon, while sitting on the side of my hospital bed contemplating the future, or the lack of one, I noticed a white looking light that began to emanate from the walls and ceiling of my room. The light increased in a brightness and whiteness until the walls and ceiling became one massive light, brighter and whiter, I believe, than a 1500 watt florescent light. Then a voice spoke to me saying, "Come go with me." I answered, "Alright, sir." In the twinkling of an eye, I was transported spiritually from my hospital room to the Meadowlake Estates housing development. I was elevated high enough above to see everything beneath. The voice said, "take a good look." I looked at all the houses and up and down all the streets. The voice asked, "do you see a church?" I answered "no Sir." Whereupon the voice asked, "what are you going to do about it?"[29]

Newman explained in his letter that he did not know what to make of this "mystical experience." He thought that had this experience occurred in an earlier period in his life, when he was younger and in better health, it might have been clearer what the Holy Spirit was directing him to do. The fact that he was now seventy years old, retired, and diagnosed with lung cancer made him doubt that he was being directed to establish a new church. "I asked myself," he said, "would the Lord see fit to impress into a special assignment someone with such huge physical deficits?"[30]

During the course of the next six weeks, Newman completed radiation therapy and had more tests. On September 7, 1982, he was cancer free. After consulting his wife, Bishop Clark, Jack Meadors, Reverend Stokes, and a few other trustworthy confidants, Newman began implementing the vision to start a church in the Meadowlake community. Within two weeks he had signed up approximately twenty-four persons to participant in the new church project. The group of twenty-four held their first church service in the Carpenters and Millwrights Trade Union Hall at 7420 North Main Street.

The new church was completed, given the name of Middleton Rosemond, and had its official beginning on April 1, 1984. The church was named after two investiture services were held at College Place United Methodist Church in Columbia. Newman was the first pastor of the new church; Reverend Luonne Rouse succeeded him in 1983 when symptom of his cancer returned. After his transition, in 1985 the congregation renamed the church I. DeQuincey Newman United Methodist for its founder.

Christian Values and Politics

For Reverend Newman, the relationship between Christian values and the work he did was inseparable. According to Bishop Frederick C. James, Newman worked a lifetime "building an alliance between the claims of religion and the climate of politics." He goes on to say, "Most politics can be defined as an engagement in the art, science, and practice of government as it affects the lives and posterity of human beings."[31]

One might surmise that Newman's final mission of claiming a seat in the South Carolina Senate was a final integration of his Christian values and politics in action. His life mission was the creation of a just and peaceful society. In Newman's way of thinking, his seat in the South Carolina Senate was another way to continue to open doors for others. He made his decision to run for the senate seat after consulting with longtime friends and confidants such as Reverend William McKinley Bowman, H. P. Stevenson, and Congressman William Jennings Bryan Dorn. Newman also talked with justice-elect Alex Sanders of the South Carolina Court of Appeals, who previously held the vacated seat Newman was seeking to fill. There were opposing Republican candidates, but Newman was more acutely aware of strong opposition from some of the black community. Some felt that he was too old to run for such an important office and that a younger person would be better able to withstand the rigorous campaign battle. Others believed that Newman was not "black enough" and would dilute the effectiveness of his race.[32]

In spite of the opposition, Newman had faith in his ability to win. He had been involved in politics most of his life. Newman felt that he would not be a senator only for District Seven; he would represent the entire state of South Carolina as well as open the door for other blacks to be elected to the senate. "He had no skeletons in his closet and had the ability to negotiate."[33] As a candidate for the South Carolina Senate, District Seven, Seat One, he represented three counties: Richland, Fairfield, and Kershaw. His constituents in these counties were predominately white. His platform reflected his Christian principles. He wanted to be an instrument for "fostering interracial goodwill, conciliation and reconciliation and thus contribute to the rooting out of the cancerous tumors of white and black racism from society."[34] He also wanted to deal with the issue of reapportionment to establish equal representation of the races, restore and beautify neglected rural areas, promote industrial development to generate jobs, and support state funding to increase the patient care and education provided by Richland Memorial Hospital.[35]

At the age of seventy-three, with most of his life behind him, Newman set out on the campaign trail. The vigor and passion he demonstrated in his lifelong pursuits for social justice were evident in his final mission to change the pages of history in South Carolina. He recruited Carey Hopkins, a longtime neighbor, as his campaign manager. Hopkins said in an interview that like Newman, he came face-to-face with naysayers who believed that he could not win the election. He said they received overwhelming support from organizations such as the Fireman's Unit: "They looked at Newman's long-standing history of his work for not just blacks, but all races. Many of them (firemen) knew him already." Some of his strong supporters were Perry Palmer, a local funeral-home owner, and Miriam Evans, deputy director of the Columbia Urban League and a community activist. Hopkins said that Newman also received strong support from students from local colleges and universities such as Benedict College and the University of South Carolina.

Newman defeated Republican John Camp, receiving 17,868 votes to Camp's 15,111 in a special election on October 23, 1983. Newman's election victory made history as he became the first black senator elected to the South Carolina Senate since Reconstruction.[36]

The Ultimate Alliance—Preacher and Senator

Newman completed the balance of his term that ended in June 1984. During the early part of his term in the senate, he continued to preach at Middleton-Rosemond United Methodist Church. When his congregation became confused by his many titles, he emphatically stated that his parishioners were to call him "Reverend," not "Senator." He said God called him to be a preacher first, and that was his most important title.

Newman's health was declining steadily, but he carried on with his two roles, demonstrating the ultimate balance between church and state. He attended to his senate responsibilities during the week and his ministerial role in the evenings and on weekends. Even when gravely ill, he did not neglect these duties. For example, one of his young parishioners who was ill and in the hospital remembered an experience of Newman putting others' needs first. Although at the time Newman was gravely ill, she recalled receiving a visit from him and his wife. This visit held a special significance for the young parishioner. She was deeply touched by his personal sacrifice.

Due to his failing health, on May 28, 1984, Newman issued a press release stating that he did not plan to run for reelection for a full senate term in 1984. He was also unable to continue his ministerial duties and responsibilities.

The Final Mission

Newman died at the age of seventy-four on October 21, 1985. Funeral services for Newman were held in Columbia, South Carolina, at Shandon United Methodist Church on October 23, 1985. Just as Newman built alliances between blacks and whites, Christians and non-Christians, the common and the uncommon, and politicians and citizens during his lifetime, he brought this same inclusiveness at the time of his death. The crowd swelled within the walls of the church and billowed into the streets for a chance to bid farewell to their preacher, senator, and friend. The South Carolina Senate held a memorial service in its chambers on November 26, 1985. A prayer by George E. Meetze, senate chaplain, summed up the sentiments of everyone whose lives the late I. DeQuincey Newman had affected: "We thank thee for the life and labors of Thy servant, Isaiah DeQuincey Newman; for his goodly heritage, his godly parents, his home and early training. We thank thee for the nobility of his manhood, the integrity of his person, the sharpness of his mind and the spaciousness of his spirit; for his steadfastness under provocation, for his gifts of reconciliation, for his transparent spirituality, his patience under suffering. We thank thee for the spiritual basis he shared of and in our common life. We thank thee that he heard Him and followed Him who said, 'If ye would be great be ye servant of all.'"[37]

Notes

1. *Will the Circle Be Unbroken.*
2. Grose, "Activist Spirit."
3. I. D. Newman, "God and the Days' Work," sermon to his congregation, University of South Carolina Political Collections, 1940.
4. Stucker, "Did You Know."
5. Fowler et al., *Religion and Politics.*
6. Johnstone, "Negro Preachers Take Sides"; I. D. Newman, "If Thou Be a Great People . . . ," sermon to Trinity Methodist Church, Orangeburg, S.C., June 24, 1945; Newby, *Black Carolinians;* Franklin Frazier, *The Negro Church*; Lincoln and Mamiya, *The Black Church.*
7. Corbett and Corbett, *Politics and Religion.*
8. "Letter from Birmingham Jail," 1963. African Studies Center, University of Pennsylvania.
9. Williams, *Out of the Box*, 194
10. I. D. Newman, "If Thou Be a Great People."
11. Newby, *Black Carolinians.*
12. Ibid., 159.

13. H. V. Manning's introduction of I. D. Newman to new congregation, Wesley Methodist Church, Charleston, S.C., October 21, 1956.

14. Gregg, *History of the AME Church.*

15. Nantambu, "Role of the Black Church."

16. Richey, Rowe, and Schmidt, eds., *The Methodist Experience.*

17. Ibid.

18. James S. Thomas, "In Remembering Central Jurisdiction: The Story That Needs to Be Told," in Jan Snider, ed. *Remembering Central Jurisdiction: The Story Needs to Be Told* (Nashville: United Methodist News Service, 2005), 1; James S. Thomas, *Methodism's Racial Dilemma: The Story of the Central Jurisdiction* (Nashville: Abingdon Press, 1992).

19. Kirk, *Desegregation of the Methodist Church*; Thomas, "In Remembering Central Jurisdiction."

20. Thomas, "In Remembering Central Jurisdiction."

21. *The Journal of the South Carolina Conference: 1954.*

22. Jake Davis, Letter to Reverend Newman appealing for help, November 11, 1969.

23. I. D. Newman, sermon to Trinity United Methodist Church, Orangeburg, S.C., early 1940s.

24. Peck, "Many White Methodists."

25. Ibid.

26. Ibid.

27. I. D. Newman, "Memorandum to the Concerned Clergy and Laity," August 5, 1969, Newman Papers, University of South Carolina Political Collections, Columbia.

28. Letter to Bishop Roy C. Clark, South Carolina United Methodist Church Conference, Newman papers, University of South Carolina Political Collections, Columbia, S.C.; Bishop Frederick C. James, quote from a draft paper, December 14, 2006. University of South Carolina, College of Social Work, Newman Institute.

29. "Negroes Allegedly Are Turned Away from Church Doors," (Columbia, S.C.) *State*, January 6, 1969.

30. Bishop James, quote from a draft paper, December 14, 2006.

31. I. DeQuincey Newman, 1984.

32. Curry, *Passionate Journey*, 55.

33. I. D. Newman, letter to Bishop Roy C. Clark, April 28, 1983. University of South Carolina Political Collections.

34. Newman Papers, University of South Carolina Political Collection, Columbia.

35. Bishop James, quote from a draft paper, December 14, 2006; ibid.

36. Carey Hopkins, telephone interview, March 5, 2006; Newman Papers, University of South Carolina Political Collection, Columbia.

37. Meetze, invocation, 1985.

The NAACP Years

Newman as South Carolina Field Director

Millicent E. Brown

Leadership and learning are indispensable to each other.

John F. Kennedy, speech prepared for delivery in Dallas
the day of his assassination, November 22, 1963

Newman assumed a leadership role in the NAACP beginning in 1943. During that time (1940–46) the NAACP experienced an increase in black registered voters. The period of his leadership, the 1950s through the 1960s, was one of revitalization of commitment and was a legacy of rich activism and courage.

Inside the NAACP

Rarely are the internal policies and bureaucratic mechanisms of the NAACP described in civil rights accounts. Rather historians focus on its legal and governmental challenges without sharing the intricacies of the operations of its many chapters. Close examination of the extensive records, archived at the Library of Congress in Washington, D.C., and contained in 114 linear feet of storage boxes, makes it possible for meaningful scrutiny of day-to-day operations that can make the seriousness and dangers of their historical, nationwide confrontations almost secondary by comparison. There is an eerie attention to record-keeping detail that demonstrates part of an ability to keep a "well-oiled" national organization functional. Of possible surprise to those not familiar with these records are personnel and financial accounts revealing another side of this organization and countless employees.[1] Newman's

Newman and Roy Wilkins. Courtesy of the Newman family.

employment letter dated December 2, 1959, was sent to his North Converse Street address in Spartanburg, where he, his wife, Anne, and their one child, Emily, then resided. The duties of that contract had been discussed a few days earlier with Roy Wilkins, executive secretary (1955–77), who wrote the official agreement marking January 1, 1960, as Newman's start date. As a field director, Newman was directly supervised by the longtime director of branches, Gloster B. Current (1946–78). Newman, in relinquishing his role as itinerant pastor and Methodist minister after thirty-one years of service from the pulpit, would work closely with Ruby Hurley, the southeastern regional coordinator in the Atlanta office. A one-year probationary period was stipulated, after which an evaluation would be made as to whether the following responsibilities had been met: "You will be expected to assume responsibility for the direction and conduct of state-wide membership and fund-raising campaigns, organization and revitalization of branches, youth councils, and college chapters, conducting such investigations as may be required by the national and regional offices or state officers and further, keeping the national and regional offices as well as the state conference advised of your activities."[2]

Immediately Newman's schedule and correspondence reflected his dedication to these duties. The first month's summary of activities submitted to his new employees included speaking at a prayer pilgrimage in Greenville, editing the monthly newsletter, packing and moving to Columbia from Spartanburg, conferring with the state conference president in Sumter, meeting with executive board members of the South Carolina Council on Human Relations to map out cooperative strategies, speaking at Greenville and Spartanburg Ministerial Alliance meetings, and attending the Statewide Conference of Religious Leaders held at both Benedict and Allen Colleges in Columbia, South Carolina. Such detailed recaps of his work are exhausting to read, much less fathom, given the daily, weekly, and monthly demands of this position.

Newman's commitment to the full-time field director post made him entirely dependent on a small, fixed salary, carrying none of the obvious advantages of pastoring a church. Especially the lack of a parsonage put pressure on the family to find suitable housing, in a more urban area. The Newmans moved to their first Columbia, South Carolina, residence, from which all NAACP organizational business was conducted. The plans to construct their own home were begun shortly after their arrival in Columbia, and a Federal Housing Administration (FHA) loan provided much of the necessary funding. By the fall of 1960 Newman was forced to request an additional loan of twelve hundred dollars from the national office of the NAACP, as purchase of the lot and closing costs had depleted the family's savings. The money was sorely needed for bridging the gap "between the money I borrowed from FHA and the actual cost of construction, and also, to be prepared to purchase several articles of kitchen ware and some other household furnishings."[3]

While Gloster B. Current, Newman's direct supervisor, had approved the idea, the response from Roy Wilkins's assistant, John A. Morsell, expressed the executive secretary's concern over Newman's ability to pay the loan back in the promised fifty-dollar monthly installments. While assuring Newman that no interest would be charged by the national office, Wilkins wanted details of the size of the FHA loan and the repayment rate before a check could be sent. Later correspondence between Morsell and Newman indicates that the money was in fact sent and the new field director's salary lessened by twenty-five dollars per bimonthly pay period until the loan was satisfied. In customary fashion, Newman wrote to the home office thanking them, describing it as "a good shower of rain following a July drought."[4]

Another example of financial stress and formality with which all concerns were handled, the finalizing of Anne Newman's salary, is recorded in separate private memos to Current. Newman's wife of twenty-three years had served as secretary for the state conference for three or four years prior to her husband's elevation to field director. A condition of his employment had been the retention of Anne Newman as office secretary for a monthly stipend of one hundred dollars. Following a series of "reminders" about missed payments, Current requested Wilkins to get the finance department to send payments automatically and directly to Mrs. Newman, as "sometimes this department forgets to make a request for the voucher."[5] A review of the ongoing letters and communications, including mimeographed copies that numbered in the several hundreds per month, indicate how valued and necessary the office secretary's services were throughout the years of her service.

Youth Work

By the end of 1960 most "housekeeping" matters and accounting for the expected reports and record keeping had become routine. As the business of stepping up the state's actions in breaking through segregated barriers to schools and public arenas accelerated, more and more of Newman's social activism led to dramatic intrigues, as his correspondence reflects. As indicated in his employment letter, activation or creation of youth councils and collegiate chapters across the state was demanded as high-school- and college-aged black youths identified more with "the movement." To this end Newman received approval from New York to hire Julie Wright, a Claflin College graduate, to organize youths during the summer of 1960. His original request was for two students, but the home office was willing to provide only one fifty-dollar-per-week, eight-week commitment from June 27 to August 19.[6] Newman's suggestion that her travel expenses also be paid by national was rejected and countered with the demand that the state assume the responsibility for student board, food, and travel. In keeping with regular NAACP practices for traveling staff and volunteers, Julie Wright was housed in private homes across the state throughout the summer at a time when hotels were not only financially prohibitive but also racially segregated. She attempted to meet the proposed quota of one thousand youth memberships and the raising of five hundred dollars for the organization's Freedom Fund. It is assumed that the original target of two thousand members was dependent on two students being hired for the duration of the summer and that the goal was halved when only Wright came on board.

NAACP strategy session, left to right: MacArthur Goodwin, Claflin student leader; Newman; Dr. Gloria Blackwell (Rackley); and Grace Brooks, speech instructor, South Carolina State College. Photograph by and courtesy of Cecil J. Williams.

By the time the request for additional personnel was made, the four North Carolina Agricultural and Technical State University students belonging to the local NAACP youth group in Greensboro, North Carolina, had initiated the February 1, 1960, sit-in demonstrations at Woolworth's. This was followed by similar actions in cities throughout the South. Newman and his colleagues knew well the impact yet to be made by young demonstrators taking to the streets to protest for a more immediate resolution to the long-awaited demands for access to public accommodations in stores, parks, and theaters and at lunch counters. These direct-action confrontations were not immediately supported by the national office, but student members of NAACP branches in South Carolina had no difficulty gaining the support of Newman and NAACP branch presidents in South Carolina, including Reverend Matthew McCollom (Orangeburg), J. Arthur Brown (Charleston), and Billy Fleming (Manning), and countless other officials throughout the state who had earlier experiences, directly or indirectly, with mass mobilization. Students from South Carolina State and Claflin Colleges, especially, built on the experience of student protests of the 1950s and the economic boycott led by the businessman James Sulton, who was still a visible and forceful community voice.

Julie Wright's responsibilities included visiting and recruiting students at all of the black campuses of higher education in the state in addition to the ones in Orangeburg: Allen and Benedict Colleges in Columbia; Friendship Junior College in Rock Hill; Morris College in Sumter; and the two schools in Denmark, South Carolina, Voorhees College and Denmark Technical School. While the NAACP cannot take full credit for all the student activism over the next four years, it is through its ranks that the majority of youth organizers emerged until the middle of the decade. Those communities in which Newman, Wright, and energetic local branch presidents supported youth involvement offered opportunities for the honing of valuable organizing skills.

In Orangeburg student organizers with the Student Nonviolent Coordinating Committee (SNCC) tested the state NAACP's ability to close ranks and claim NAACP control over the growing student demands for more direct action. Correspondence between Newman and the national office reflects the concern that this "solidly NAACP-organized state" had with conceding the youth activities to other civil rights groups. It is, however, the presence of these other groups and their more confrontational strategies that provoked the NAACP leaders throughout the state to incorporate new attacks on segregation. While some states were more obvious in their division of tactics and philosophies according to which organization was spearheading the efforts, South Carolina's youths, organized under the NAACP banner, made it quite clear that they were ready to take nonviolent but decidedly direct stances, around which they hoped the elders would band. Newman, Reverend McCollom, the attorney Matthew J. Perry, Jr., J. Arthur Brown, and others around the state not only accepted the new energy but also continued to see the new movement as inseparable from their own. From 1960 through 1964, with the passage of the Civil Rights Bill, student-led protests and organized demonstrations sponsored by the NAACP were credited (or blamed) for the ongoing attempts to break through racial barriers.[7] Newman's commitment to youths and support for their willingness to be put on the front line of attacks from police, school administrators, merchants, and peers made him a welcomed person on the scene and in the jails. Ultimately the ability to keep the NAACP banner over the movement had a lot to do with the fact

Students from S.C. State and Claflin Colleges demonstrating in Orangeburg against segregation. Photograph by and courtesy of Cecil J. Williams.

that it was able to provide the organizational structure for raising bail bonds as hundreds upon hundreds of young people were arrested.

An aspect of South Carolina's youth movement that receives little mention in Charleston or Orangeburg, as well as in other communities throughout the South, is the intergenerational impact of NAACP leaders and their own family members. Reverend Newman's one child, Emily Newman, was with him at Columbia's Valley Park when a group of blacks was denied entry in the summer of 1960, giving grounds for the suit ultimately filed against all segregated facilities in South Carolina parks and playgrounds.[8] Emily Newman was arrested as a minor in the Charleston riot that followed a major nighttime demonstration at the *Post and Courier* newspaper building in 1962. In being willing to put their own children in harm's way, many of the leaders showed the courage of their convictions, which did much to cement the older generation to the activities of the youths. Moreover many of the original plaintiffs in the ongoing school desegregation battles between 1955 and

1963, when the state's public schools were finally integrated, were the children of NAACP leaders.

The 1963 entry of the NAACP youth leader and Newman protégé Harvey Gantt (Charleston, South Carolina) into Clemson University and Modjeska Simkins's niece, Henri Monteith (Columbia, South Carolina), into the University of South Carolina occurred as NAACP state president J. Arthur Brown's daughter, the author of this essay, and Charleston branch president Reverend B. J. Glover's daughter Oveta entered previously all-white public schools, demonstrating the close connection that young activists had through the experiences of their own family members and the personal influences of state figures such as Newman and the attorney and legal counsel Matthew J. Perry, Jr. NAACP branch president Charles Thomas's daughter Anne, one of the first to desegregate the Orangeburg schools in 1964, is but another example of the close intergenerational involvement existing in the earlier phase of the movement. The involvement of one's son or daughter was

Harvey Gantt greeting Newman at his home in Charleston, where they discussed Gantt's upcoming legal strategy to win admission to Clemson University in 1960. Photograph by and courtesy of Cecil J. Williams.

a deliberate indication of the personal nature the struggle demanded if others were to be convinced to sacrifice likewise for change, according to leaders interviewed.[9]

As Newman became a welcome and familiar face to young demonstrators across the state and direct action stepped up the urgency for complete elimination of segregated public facilities and resources, white politicians, merchants, and community leaders moved to one side of the issue or the other, with most in the camp resisting any "forced" accommodations to thousands of demanding youths. South Carolina's NAACP forces, after so many years of gradualism, joined the ranks of other civil rights organizations in accepting street protests, sit-ins, wade-ins, pray-ins, and play-ins as fair game for forcing federal, state, and local governments to take a stand against racial discrimination. Youthful exuberance created understandable conflicts with older leaders, however, when student leaders wanted to go into "unfamiliar territory" thought to be too far removed from eyewitnesses and possible police protection. Night marches, deemed unwise by the NAACP national office and others concerned about the ability to keep the demonstrations "safe," were another point of departure.

James Blake, a protégé of Newman who worked closely with leaders in Charleston as a high school student and then some years later as national NAACP youth director, recounted several arguments about tactics and logistics that bothered the elders but ultimately found students taking their moves into their own hands between 1962 and 1964. Student leaders had begun to work out their own communications with state law enforcement division officials such as Captain Pete Strom, to whom leaders and demonstrators turned for the protection of movement members.[10] Captain Strom's commitment to the maintenance of "order" and restraint on the part of his officers brought a degree of confidence throughout the period as he and a few other public officials professed themselves unwilling to provoke chaos even as official stands were taken in opposition to the demonstrations or desegregation goals. The quality of the relationship between law officials and movement participants was especially important as demonstrations increased across the state, and no two or three persons could be identified as the only "leaders" or "instigators."

Launching a Frontal Attack on Discrimination

On June 5, 1963, Reverend Newman made the announcement of a statewide attack on discrimination to be launched in the state's eight largest cities (see also "Newman's Vision of a 'Just' South Carolina").[11] As demonstrators were no longer relying on impromptu surprises at area stores, this round of protests was announced in several of the state's local newspapers in the form of a set of "goals" presented to Governor Donald S. Russell and to the mayors in Charleston, Columbia, Orangeburg, and Sumter. The promise of massive street demonstrations was not to be fulfilled. Yet even with small numbers of actual demonstrators, the NAACP launched this all-out effort with the intent to irritate the legal system into compliance.[12] Rather than a "jail, no bail" approach, bail bond was raised to get those arrested released as soon as possible. To popularize the issues further, ten student activists were hired for the summer of 1963 to work with Newman and Blake throughout the state, especially in Sumter and Orangeburg.[13] Columbia had desegregated its lunch counters since the previous year with no publicity or incident.[14] But as Newman intimated to Wilkins, the former was of the opinion that "we are headed for a crisis" in South Carolina.[15]

Although the state was slow to accept desegregation, Newman, like many others, could see that circumstances were changing in race relations, and he was preparing himself for a new day and a new role. At the same time that barriers to access were falling, he announced his intention to resign from his field director position in order to accept a full-time pastorate in the South Carolina Annual Conference of the Methodist Church. In his own words, Newman described an "insatiable urge to return to the itinerant ministry and to accept the opportunity to crusade again as a volunteer worker in the NAACP."[16] A plaque to be awarded to Newman from the national office was ordered, giving his dates of service as January 1, 1960, through September 30, 1963, and honoring him for "distinguished service in the cause of freedom and equality."[17] We know that the resignation did not actually happen, but it becomes obvious from the communications of the next two years that change was imminent and that the national office and its agenda of maintaining its position as *the* largest-membership civil rights organization were causing concern to the field director.

In a January 20, 1964, request to the NAACP national office from Newman for financial assistance to fund a voter registration campaign in South Carolina's third congressional district (Abbeville, Anderson, Edgefield, Greenwood, McCormick, Newberry, Oconee, Pickens, and Saluda Counties), Richland County (Columbia), and fourth congressional district (Greenville, Laurens, Spartanburg, and Union), Newman noted that funds were also available through the white house-supported Voter Education Project (VEP). The character and caliber of in-state leadership for such endeavors were different from those of years past, but emphasis on electoral politics was only increasing.

Newman distributing voting campaign literature. Photograph by and courtesy of Cecil J. Williams.

Newman's letter to Roy Wilkins in February 1964 announced his period of public and politically motivated fasting. Among the results he hoped to achieve were "a stronger spiritual undergirding" to fulfill the NAACP's aims and the means of "a more effective witness for Christ in the area of social concerns."[18] Such "individualistic ideas about attaining objectives of our movement" were deemed unwise by Gloster B. Current, director of branches, and "a drastic departure from Association policy." He instructed Newman that for any days spent in fasting, his salary would be adjusted.[19] Anne Newman did not see this event as having a negative impact on her husband's motivation to serve. According to her, the greatest pressure bearing on her husband, motivating his possible departure from the organization, was a growing disappointment with the state and local leadership. It seemed that too few were willing to continue taking the kinds of stances expected of activists or to put in the number of hours as offered in years past. There is no paper trail to document these concerns, but his widow adamantly defended the position that her husband was in no way turning away from the NAACP; rather he was at a loss for how to generate the kind of vitality he knew was needed to follow through on achieving the completed goals of black equality.[20] He was certainly not content with first-stage successes. By July 1964 Newman released a statewide call to action as field director in the name of peaceful transitioning into a new social order in South Carolina: "The NAACP as a pioneer in the areas of civil rights realizes that it has responsibilities for the orderly changeover from racial segregation to racial integration under the terms of the civil rights bill (1964)."

South Carolina now had an opportunity for creating new ways to assure fair access not only at the polls but also to statewide elected offices, which would require a redrawing of the state's existing legislative districts. Newman was disappointed by his inability to get national office support for a major new initiative voted on by the South Carolina Conference of Branches: to support a federal suit for legislative reapportionment, considered long overdue. As much as Newman and other state organization leaders wanted to take the lead in moving toward implementing the Civil Rights Bill, the national office suggested waiting for other groups to join in the effort. The national office did not want to risk a high level of visibility and unpopularity in the state. Subsequent reports of statewide activities indicate that Reverend I. DeQuincey Newman was not about to allow the national office's fears about the diminishing influence of the NAACP to stifle his lifelong commitment to enduring political and social change. In fact over the next five years a variety of initiatives demonstrated an expanding philosophy of outreach in response to the newer political and economic challenges brought in the aftermath of civil rights legislation of 1964 and 1965.

The Aftermath of Civil Rights Legislation

Longtime NAACP member Gloria Blackwell's (Rackley's) successful lawsuit against the Orangeburg Regional Hospital was decided on February 17, 1965. Filed originally in 1961 as a protest to being refused access to "White" waiting room facilities when bringing her daughter Jamelle into the emergency room, the case made its way into the federal court system by 1962 and marked a critical breakthrough in public access at long last. Blackwell (Rackley) had been fired from her teaching position in Orangeburg in 1963 as a result of participating in local and other statewide demonstrations, and she had been hired as "assistant field secretary" under Newman before gaining employment at Norfolk State University in Norfolk, Virginia. Dubbed an "integration order" by newspapers, the lawsuit led immediately to the scheduling of a march in Charleston, called by Newman and state president J. Arthur Brown, during which it was announced that that city would be filing a suit to desegregate the Medical College Hospital, as Orangeburg signaled "the beginning of the end of segregated tax supported facilities in South Carolina."[21] To that end, Newman's schedule in the latter part of the decade was every bit as ambitious as that during the first part. He reported 3,640 miles traveled tending to state conference business in just the first two months of 1965. Sixteen speaking engagements and eleven branch visitations filled his calendar in March and April of that year, representing the pace for much of the next two years, with emphasis on statewide implementation of the Civil Rights and Voting Rights Acts.

A close relationship developed between the State Conference of Branches and the U.S. Office of Economic Opportunity (OEO), with added emphasis on educating citizens about the new Anti-Poverty Act. By April 1965 youth members statewide were meeting in Union, South Carolina, to hear from Dr. Anna Belle Sherman of OEO and "youth involvement in the War on Poverty." In addition Newman joined five other plaintiffs in filing for "injunctive relief" to prohibit the State Department of Education, school superintendents, and school board officials in Charleston, Columbia, Orangeburg, Sumter, Rock Hill, and Spartanburg from offering "Tuition Grants" to segregated private schools. The resistance to school desegregation was quick and determined, and as the NAACP locally and nationally looked to slaying new dragons, the organization had to be vigilant about supposed "victories." In response to the varying sentiments about philosophy, rhetoric, and change processes to afford full black empowerment challenging the traditional approaches that some deemed outmoded and ineffective at mid-decade, supercharged efforts to build statewide membership ranks and coordinate voter education activities continued to fill the field director's calendar for the next several months.[22]

In what may be construed as a "premonition" of things to come in South Carolina, Roy Wilkins of the national office responded to the civil unrest and rioting raising the political consciousness, anger, and fears of people throughout the nation between 1965 (Watts, California) and 1967 (Detroit, Michigan). According to the National Advisory Commission on Civil Disorders (aka Kerner Commission) formed by President Lyndon B. Johnson in the midst of the Detroit upheaval, these uprisings and rebellions brought to the fore all the frustrations of marginalized and discriminated black citizens. The final statistics report seventy-five major riots in 1967 alone and eighty-three deaths.[23] Wilkins's directive to all NAACP units called for "riot prevention" plans to be drawn up. Newman called a statewide gathering of branch and youth council leaders at the Town and Tourist Hotel in Columbia on August 5, 1967. The long list of action plans that evolved from the gathering called for inclusion of citizens "from depressed communities." Working relationships with elected officials were proposed as a way to prevent racial outbreaks, with no specifics as to how such cooperation was to be attained. Primarily the initiative called for including poor people in the voter registration and NAACP membership drives. Weekly reports to national, via letters or telephone, were scheduled, especially as any tensions were deemed demanding of immediate action.[24]

While the efforts to "keep communities cool" seem incredibly naive in retrospect, most of the statewide leaders drawn together by Newman understood the necessity of taking advantage of the national hysteria over saturated black patience by pressing for official systemic changes that would signify changed policies on race: more blacks in the National Guard, State Highway Patrol, and South Carolina Enforcement Division, as well as on staffs of the attorney generals' and adjutant generals' offices were urged in suggestions to Governor Robert McNair and other state officials. Additionally the weight of prestige from such offices was to be brought to bear in support of federally sponsored housing programs and compliance with the new compulsory school attendance law.[25] A third set of suggestions was directed to county and municipal elected officials, urging the creation of antiriot task forces at their levels. Obvious to the NAACP leaders was the need to have policemen of color at all administrative levels in proportion to the racial demographics.[26] The August 7 meeting in the executive office of the State House with the governor, his legal aide Major Henry Lake, and press secretary Wayne Seal included NAACP representatives Reverend A. R. Holman, Reverend L. B. Burgess, the attorney Matthew J. Perry, Reverend David C. Francis, Dr. Charles H. Thomas, Reverend F. C. James, and Newman.

Newspapers such as the *Columbia Record* wrote encouragingly of the suggestions from the NAACP to build coalition forces in the "South Carolina way," which is to say "constructive, not destructive," to address the admitted inequities and injustices. Such problems were described as "not general, but usually are confined to specific sections or individual localities and the majority of (South Carolina) citizens are not aware of these vexations, and potential trouble spots."[27] Newman's choices for a voluntary citizen's task force included representatives from the Episcopal Diocese of Upper South Carolina, the *Methodist Christian Advocate*, the Columbia Urban League, the South Carolina Christian Action Council, the South Carolina Voter Education Project, and the longtime affiliate South Carolina Council on Human Relations. Additional members were added over the next few months as the ad hoc group met weekly to explore specific ways to keep the state from exploding from the combined forces of continued racial oppression and greatly increased militant rhetoric very much present, and especially promoted on high school and college campuses through a variety of youth-led organizations distancing themselves from the patient tactics of Newman and the NAACP. As much as it was hoped that the efforts to enlist dialogue between industrial, educational, and business power brokers would avert the possibility of street confrontations and possible violence, Newman had to address the continuing sets of racial insults and abuse reported across the state at a time when he most hoped to see state, county, and local officials take seriously the tinderbox conditions that could not be expected to bypass South Carolina.

In Ridgeville, South Carolina, 15 pupils and their parents were attacked and beaten at a football game by 150 white speculators angered by the desegregation of the Harleyville-Ridgeville High School. Allendale's city council refused to hire black officers. A white police officer shot a youth worker without cause in the town of St. Matthews, South Carolina. Much to Newman's dismay, local administrators of federally sponsored programs for assisting low-income blacks with rent supplements and other services chose to create havoc in an effort not to offer the services as designed. In order to keep peace, South Carolina officials were going to have to ensure more consistent transitions, which much of the white community was reluctant to embrace.[28]

The Explosion

The Monday, February 5, 1968, demonstration of South Carolina State and Claflin College students in Orangeburg before the segregated All-Star Lanes Bowling Alley evoked the outrage of the state. Within twenty-four hours, five hundred students staged a protest, insisting upon service as first-class customers. The protest resulted in extreme brutality at the hands of local police officers, spurring some of the protesters to throw bricks at police cars and into downtown business windows. Three Claflin students were wounded by gunfire on Wednesday night and required hospitalization. Because of Newman's longtime rapport with so many students at both campuses, state NAACP officials urged him to return to the state from Cincinnati, Ohio, where he was attending a meeting of the National Conference of Negro Methodists.

Meeting first with Claflin student body president Cynthia Ziegler and South Carolina State College student body president James Scott, Newman proceeded to confer with representatives of the branch, the youth council, the two college chapters, and their advisers. By the time the turmoil had finally subsided, a Wilkerson High School student and two South Carolina State students had been killed on the campus of South Carolina State College (now University); some forty others from the two campuses were wounded from weapons fired by the South Carolina Highway Patrol, who were called in by Governor Robert McNair to quell the disturbance.[29] Newman solicited a commitment from the national office and received "a pledge of full support of the authorities and students of both colleges if the quest for redress of grievances and civil rights objectives were perused [*sic*] within the framework of NAACP policy and that there be no vandalism, violence, rock throwing, etc."[30] Such wording speaks volumes to the state of national and local affairs. As the patience with process and gradualism that was always maintained by the NAACP found strong resistance from those demanding immediate attention to the age-old contempt for people of color, Newman's entire career and lifelong contribution to the struggle for first-class citizenship never vacillated, even in the midst of the most disturbing set of statewide events of his lifetime. His belief in nonviolent protest, in ordered change, and in agitation without malice had all been challenged in this era of militancy. In calling together seventy-five state conference officers and branch presidents to analyze the shootings and concurrent events, he would lead the effort to formulate an official response to the crisis. In addition to a "self-defense spending" campaign, in other words urging Orangeburg residents to refrain from purchasing products manufactured in the city of Orangeburg, particularly Azalea Brand meats, Paradise ice cream, and Sunbeam bread, the NAACP urged that "all other buying be restricted to the purchase of only what is necessary." Thus Newman supported an effort to make the entire community take notice of its culpability in the tragedy.[31]

The events of February 8,1968, were described by the South Carolina NAACP Conference as the result of a "problem of police brutality [that] has reach[ed] epidemic proportions in South Carolina." The conference "expressed the view that unless the ominous trend is halted and repressed it will lead to heartaches, pain, and miseries heretofore not experienced in the last fifty years." The NAACP called for statewide hearings to further investigate all charges of police brutality and with the support of over eighteen hundred college students developed a litany of demands ranging from the closing of the All-Star Bowling Alley if it remained segregated, the formation of a Fair Employment Commission, evaluation of the news media deemed responsible for spewing racist interpretations, rapid implementation of the Food Stamp Act, and the launching of an all-out attack on poverty throughout the county and state.[32]

By March 1968 Newman and the executive committee announced plans for two events: the Parents' March to the State House and the Conference of the Indigent Needy (COIN). The Parents' March called on all fraternal, civic, religious, and educational groups "cleared for participation" by the NAACP to join in.[33] Taking any opportunity to publicly honor the memory of the three youths slain in February, efforts to push for low-income housing, fighting "choice plans" that allowed whites to avoid integration of public schools, and generally reiterating the ongoing goals of the NAACP filled Newman's agenda. As evidence of the attempt to merge traditional civil rights issues of access and overt discrimination of the 1940s, 1950s, and early 1960s with the more clearly defined economic thrusts made clear by the social upheavals of the mid- to late 1960s, the state field director organized yet another statewide conference in August 1968.

COIN was originally planned for March 1968 but was postponed because of the Orangeburg crisis. It was held at W. Perry Junior High School with approximately three hundred low-income residents on August 24 for a series of seven workshops led by representatives of state, regional, and national agencies regarding services available to the poor.[34] In addressing the participants, Newman said that "information concerning programs to help the indigent achieve autonomy seldom filters down to the grass roots level." Further he attributed violence in America to little or no communication between blacks and whites but also to those needing help and those wanting to help. Efforts were promised through COIN to develop and implement similar workshops across the state in order that dialogue between those at the bottom of the economic ladder and tax-sponsored agencies could be increased and made more productive. Newman saw the voice of the indigent as necessary to any successful effort to relieve the despair that had been for so long described in racial terms but was now being articulated as that of poverty and class in addition to race. In order to continue the work, he appealed to the national office to give financial support, but no record shows evidence that funds to support his drive were received.

Summary and Conclusion

Newman's resolve for an ordered transition to a more open society remained throughout his years as a servant leader. Newman moved the focus of his agitation onto the next realms from which he expected change to evolve. He would never fully understand the motivations of those who took chances with their own and others' lives in seemingly ill-thought-through confrontation with forces known to be better equipped and more powerful. This was not only outside the agenda of the organization to which he gave so many years of his service but also just as much outside his character as a minister and follower of Christian tenets that he interpreted as always working from a position of love. Newman's discomfort and distancing from tactics and philosophies not built on love and patience would remain throughout his life, but especially throughout his term as field director, ending in 1970. When asked by his widow, Anne Newman, which of his alliances had been his most endeared calling, the NAACP or the ministry, her reply was interesting. According to Anne Newman, even after all the tremendous amount of energy expended and risk taken as a state leader and organizer for the years before and the ten years spent as field director of the NAACP, the call to the ministry had been DeQuincey's sustenance and motivation through it all.[35] There was no reason to believe that his next set of experiences in yet another aspect of civic engagement as a public service administrator and state senator would find him responding any differently.

Notes

1. Adeboyejo, "NAACP Archive."

2. Gloster B. Current to I. DeQuincey Newman, December 2, 1959, Papers of the National Association for the Advancement of Colored People (hereafter NAACP Papers), Part 25: Branch Department, Series D, Branch Department General Subject Files, 1956–63, Reel 30 (Bethesda, Md.: University Publications of America). Reproduced from the collections of the Manuscript Division of the Library of Congress, accessed from holdings of Joyner Library/East Carolina (N.C.) via Bluford Library/North Carolina A&T State University.

3. I. DeQuincey Newman to John Morsell, September 27, 1960, NAACP Papers, Part 25: Branch Department, Series D, Branch Department General Subject Files, 1956–63.

4. I. DeQuincey Newman to unidentified, December 19, 1960, NAACP Papers, Part 25: Branch Department, Series D, Branch Department General Subject Files, 1956–63.

5. I. D. Newman to unidentified, December 19, 1960, NAACP Papers, Part 25: Branch Department, Series D, Branch Department General Subject Files, 1956–63.

6. I. DeQuincey Newman to Roy Wilkins, May 16, 1960, and Gloster B. Current to I. D. Newman, June 7, 1960, NAACP Papers, Part 25: Branch Department, Series D, Branch Department General Subject Files, 1956–63.

7. Civil Rights Bill of 1964, Pub L. 88–352 78 Stat 241.

8. Emily Morris DeQuincey Newman, interview by Sadye Logan and Millicent Brown, Columbia, S.C., July 2007; I. DeQuincey Newman, "Columbia's Valley Park," unpub. report, circa July 1960. Newman Papers. S.C. Political Collections.

9. Anne Newman and Emily Newman, interviews by Brown, August 1987; J. Arthur, interview by Brown, Charleston, S.C., August 1987.

10. Brown, "Civil Rights Activism," 180.

11. Ibid., 175.

12. I. DeQuincey Newman, report, January–February 1963, NAACP Papers, Part 25: Branch Department, Series D, Branch Department General Subject Files, 1956–63.

13. Ibid.

14. *Charlotte Observer*, August 22, 1963.

15. I. D. Newman to Roy Wilkins, June 4, 1963, NAACP Papers, Part 25: Branch Department, Series D, Branch Department General Subject Files, 1956–63.

16. I. D. Newman to Roy Wilkins, September 23, 1963, NAACP Papers, Part 25: Branch Department, Series D, Branch Department General Subject Files, 1956–63.

17. Frankye Brown to Bobbie Branch, October 2, 1963, NAACP Papers, Part 25: Branch Department, Series D, Branch Department General Subject Files, 1956–63.

18. I. D. Newman to Roy Wilkins, February 13, 1964, NAACP Papers, Part 25: Branch Department, Series D, Branch Department General Subject Files, 1956–63.

19. Gloster B. Current to I. D. Newman, February 17, 1964, NAACP Papers.

20. Anne Newman, interview by Brown, January 1, 2008.

21. "Suit Filed to De-segregate the Medical College Hospital," (Charleston, S.C.) *News and Courier*, February 19, 1965; "Beginning of End to Tax Supported Segregated Facilities in SC." (Columbia, S.C.) *State*, February 22, 1965; *Methodist Newsletter* 7.7 (March 3, 1965).

22. I. DeQuincey Newman, field report, January–February 1965, NAACP Papers, Part 29: Branch Department, Series A, Field Staff Files, 1965–72.

23. *Civil Rights Chronicle*, 330.

24. I. DeQuincey Newman, report, August–September 1967, 1, NAACP Papers, Part 29: Branch Department, Series A, Field Staff Files, 1965–72.

25. Ibid., 2.

26. Ibid., 3.

27. *Columbia Record*, August 26, 1967.

28. I. D. Newman, "Build a Coalition South Carolina Way," August–September 1967, 7, Part 29: Branch Department, Series A, Field Staff Files, 1965–72.

29. Grose, *South Carolina at the Brink*, 199–240. See also Bass and Nelson, *The Orangeburg Massacre*.

30. I. DeQuincey Newman, "Day-to-Day" accounts, February 6–21, 1968, NAACP Papers, Part 29: Branch Department, Series A, Field Staff Files, 1965–72.

31. News release, I. DeQuincey Newman, records, February 16, 1968. NAACP papers Part 29: Branch Department, Series A: Field Staff Files, 1965-72

32. Ibid.
33. Ibid.; I. DeQuincey Newman, records, March 21, 1968.
34. "Workshops Scheduled," (Columbia, S.C.) *State*, August 24, 1968, A8.
35. Anne Newman, interview by Brown, January 1, 2008.

Leadership in Black and White

Newman's Struggles with Race and Politics

Wim Roefs

Everyone has a right to be wrong in his opinions. But no man has a right to be wrong in his facts.

Bernard M. Baruch, as quoted in Benjamin Garling, *Never Sleep Again! The Most Dangerous Facts about Bernard Baruch*

This essay contains an examination of the approach and success of 1940s civil rights activism in South Carolina, which helped to shape the fight over desegregation in the state during the 1960s, and the influence of this period's leadership, which conditioned and gave opportunities for the style of leadership utilized by white and black leaders including Isaiah DeQuincey Newman in the battle for civil rights two decades later.[1] At the heart of this exploration is the critical analysis of what was generally described as moderation and a relative absence of violent confrontation during South Carolina's 1960s desegregation battle. This explanation, I contend generally ignored the influence of African Americans civil rights activism during the 1940s and the 1960s. The standard narrative for the 1960s instead focused above all on the levelheadedness and moderation of the state's white leadership. Furthermore this interpretation often reduces the black dimension to proclamations of black conservatism and especially the so-called accommodationist attitude of arguably the period's foremost black leader, I. D. Newman.[2]

The influence of Newby's suggestion that pre-Brown black-activism in the state amounted to little and that 1940s black leadership was ineffectual is illustrated in Sproat's discussion of black and white leadership during the black activism of the 1940s—Sproat's perspective reflected the sustained influence of I. A. Newby's book. In acknowledging black activism's legal and political success in the 1940s, Sproat correctly attached to it a level of substance and achievement that Newby denied. Yet, despite this acknowledgment, Sproat endorsed Newby's judgment of the 1940s black leadership as passive and conservative. According to Sproat, African American leaders in the 1940s failed "to mobilize the masses" and were perhaps "overly cautious and concerned about jeopardizing their own relatively comfortable, yet still precarious, positions."[3] Sproat argued that Newby's research had affirmed this style of black leadership during the 1940s, but in reality, Newby's research had shown no such thing, despite his claims to that effect. Barbara Woods' later research demonstrated, black leaders, including often overlooked women in the 1940s utilized effective legal strategies that changed racially segregated politics and education. Further, Peter Lau's recent research confirms that black leaders during this period did mobilize the masses, not for street demonstrations but through successful NAACP membership and voter registration drives. In addition black leaders such as John McCray, Modjeska Simkins, James Hinton, Osceola McKaine, and others were not "overly cautious"; nor did they all live in comfort or fail to jeopardize their positions.

For the 1960s, the emphasis on the moderate stance taken by the state's white leaders is unsatisfactory in that the phenomenon is in need of an explanation, especially since this moderation is usually portrayed as an exceptional response to a grave racial problem. Notions about the political conservatism of the state's African Americans are based on little more than historian Newby's contentions on the matter which suffer from his poor use of sources and dubious historical points of reference. Simply defining Newman as an accommodationist without a thorough assessment of his reasons and motives denies him much deliberateness, which is problematic. Newman was no Uncle Tom; he wanted results in the fight to desegregate South Carolina, not just the appeasement of whites by "going slow," which was just one element of an approach that was likely informed by what Newman thought would lead to results.

The first section of this essay contains the argument that the behavior in the 1960s of moderate white leaders and of Newman should at least in part be explained by their experiences with the state's civil rights activism of the 1940s and early 1950s. Further argument shows that the strength of the 1940s South Carolina NAACP allowed the organization to dominate the state's civil rights field even in decades to come, facilitating a relatively restrained approach to the struggle for desegregation of all public facilities including public schools. An analysis in the second section shows why the link between the 1940s and 1960s civil rights scene in South Carolina generally has been absent from the historiography. Civil rights historiography has suffered from longtime neglect of pre-Brown activism, but the analysis here focuses on the influences on this issue of Newby's book..[4]

South Carolina's Moderate White Leadership

The notion of the relatively moderate nature and levelheadedness of South Carolina's white leadership in the 1960s is well established.[5]These leaders did not encourage violent resistance to desegregation and mostly insisted that the state and its residents adhere to the law. This created an atmosphere in which violent opposition was frowned upon and limited. White leadership included state and local politicians, school administrators, and the state's metropolitan business elite. Together these groups managed in 1963 a late but peaceful desegregation of Clemson University and the University of South Carolina. Other colleges as well as several public facilities and businesses across the state also desegregated without much violent opposition but often with substantial white resistance. Although the relative peacefulness should not be confused with an absence of violence altogether, as it often is, South Carolina certainly compared favorably to the likes of Mississippi and Alabama.[6]

None of this means that South Carolina's political leadership was not reactionary. It was. Its commitment was to white supremacy, not to desegregation. Desegregation was at best an acquired taste force-fed by black activism and federal law, forces largely beyond the control of South Carolina's political establishment. Even as the state leaders went about being moderate by some standards, they initially closed South Carolina's state parks rather than desegregate them. Governor Ernest "Fritz" Hollings was a lieutenant governor committed to segregation during the fiercely repressive 1950s regime of George Bell Timmerman; he maintained that attitude for several years after becoming governor in 1958. His successor, Donald Russell, even in 1963 claimed personally to be against desegregation. Robert McNair, Russell's successor in 1967, rose politically as part of the country elites who generally were less progressive on race than the new moderates.[7]

Men such as Ernest Hollings, Robert McNair, and George Timmerman came of age politically, or were already active, in the 1940s and 1950s, when the state of South Carolina opposed black equality and desegregation as vehemently as did other southern states. The opposition included at least the threat of violence by state leaders, as when Governor Olin Johnston in 1944 declared that the state would stop integrated Democratic primaries by all means necessary. South Carolina led the South in opposition to African Americans voting in the Democratic primary after the Supreme Court, in *Smith v. Allwright*, declared that the whites-only Texas Democratic primary was unconstitutional. The state also led the opposition to the desegregation of public education. It harassed the NAACP and intimidated teachers and state workers who joined that organization or contributed to it. It put one black leader, John McCray, editor of the newspaper the *Lighthouse and Informer*, on a chain gang on concocted charges.[8]

This opposition to racial equality intensified in the second half of the 1950s after the *Brown* decision, in the period immediately prior to the phase of moderation. Governor George Bell Timmerman, Jr., used all means possible to stop desegregation, including intimidation, persecuting the NAACP and its members, closing a state park rather than desegregating it, and having fired those college professors at South Carolina State College who favored desegregation.[9]

The state's intimidation of the NAACP and its members certainly did not create an atmosphere of law and order among whites. Since the 1940s African American leaders such as McCray had received threats against their lives. Gunmen shot at state NAACP president James Hinton's home and state treasurer Modjeska Simkins's motel. Economic boycotts by whites squeezed several local NAACP leaders out of business.[10]

Still, in the early 1960s several white leaders, including Hollings, advocated moderation in behavior and spoke out for law and order and against violent resistance to desegregation. They did so despite their segregationist convictions. Historians have typically noted rather than explained this turn toward moderation, except to mention two factors. First was the influence on politics of the state's business elites, who were looking after their economic interests. Still, if businessmen elsewhere in the South did not have such influence, the attitude of those in South Carolina would have to be explained. If businessmen had this impact in other southern states as well—and there are indications that they did—this factor does not set South Carolina apart, and the turn toward relative moderations by the state's political leaders would need further explanation.[11]

Second, historians have observed that South Carolina's politicians learned from disturbances elsewhere in the South, such as those surrounding the desegregation of Little Rock Central High in 1957 and the University of

Mississippi in 1962. They did not want such confrontations in South Carolina, which was different from George Wallace in Alabama or authorities in Birmingham and Selma.[12] The reactionary impulse of South Carolina's white political leaders was in fact modified by their particular collective and individual experience with civil rights activism. Because of that experience they were susceptible to and eventually acted with relative moderation. Their experience with civil rights activism had put them on the defensive since the early 1940s. It had conditioned them to take South Carolina's civil rights leaders and their demands seriously, as, for instance, Paul Lofton has pointed out for the desegregation of Columbia.[13] Members of the white establishment had, in any case, been confronted since the early 1940s with forceful, sustained, and militant civil rights agitations that favored court actions and political pressure, and they had been careful to stay within the law. Fighting civil rights battles through politics and the courts had become the norm throughout other parts of the South as well as in South Carolina. African American leaders had made it the norm.[14]

What had also become the norm was victory for South Carolina's civil rights activists and defeat for the white political establishment. Especially in a world in which the days of legal segregation were clearly numbered, it is possible that South Carolina's white leaders anticipated further defeat, which may in turn have undermined their segregationist resolve. When by the early 1960s the serious push for desegregation came to the state and could no longer be sidestepped, the white leaders' hearts may have been with segregation, but they only were willing to go so far opposing what they now likely saw as inevitable.[15]

During the 1940s and early 1950s black activists defeated the state of South Carolina and the state Democratic Party in the courts on the three major issues. First the state was forced to pay to African American teachers salaries equal to those of their white colleagues. Next, with the nation's post–*Smith v. Allwright* eyes on them, South Carolina's white leaders lost the fight over the whites-only Democratic primary after several embarrassing knee-jerk reactions that led to as many defeats in the courts. Then came *Brown v. Board of Education*, a combination of several cases aimed at dismantling South Carolina's segregated education system, for which South Carolina's African Americans had provided the earliest one, *Briggs v. Elliott*.

Much of the civil rights activists' court action was accompanied by political pressure. Throughout the 1940s the state's white establishment had to endure one of the strongest and fastest-growing NAACP organizations in the country. The state's white Democrats were the first to face a black-led alternative Democratic Party, the Progressive Democratic Party (PDP), established in 1944. They also were the first to be challenged by an all-black delegation for seating at the National Democratic Convention (in 1944, 1948, and 1956). In addition they were the first in the South since Reconstruction to face a challenge, albeit nominal, from an African American candidate for a major statewide office when the PDP's Osceola McKaine ran against Governor Olin Johnston for the United States Senate in 1944. African Americans through organizations such as CORE and the NAACP in South Carolina organized massive, successful voter registration campaigns in the 1940s well before such campaigns become common throughout the South (see "Isaiah DeQuincey Newman" and "The NAACP Years" for more detail).[16]

South Carolina's white elites, such as James Byrnes and Strom Thurmond, were not immune to African Americans pressure. Byrnes lost the nomination to become Franklin Roosevelt's vice president at the convention because of opposition from labor leaders and northern black Democrats, an event that ultimately cost Byrnes the presidency. Byrnes certainly had a bone to pick with McCray, the editor of the state's largest African American weekly, the militant *Lighthouse and Informer.* The suspicion of McCray and others was that Byrnes personally had ordered McCray's arrest and subsequent stint on a chain gang in 1952 after dubious charges and a conviction. Byrnes resented the editor's refusal to give up his support for the *Briggs v. Elliott* suit and his opposition to Byrnes's 1950s gubernatorial campaign. Byrnes, who led "Democrats for Eisenhower," also resented that McCray campaigned for Democratic presidential nominee Adlai Stevenson.[17]

Strom Thurmond in 1950 lost the race for the United States Senate to Olin Johnston, who received the African American votes after black leaders had decided he was the lesser of two evils. By the early 1950s, even before the *Brown* decision came down, given the size of South Carolina's black population made up a large number of voters, it became clear to South Carolina's whites that they would have to accommodate the state's African American leaders.[18]

Still, in the second half of the 1950s South Carolina's civil rights establishment lost the initiative to the white backlash against the *Brown* decision, led by the Timmerman administration. Given the enormous resentment among whites over the prospect of integrated schools, this may have been inevitable. This was not specifically a South Carolina development but was in fact a regional one. The lost initiative, in any case, was to be only temporary. It was significant that it took place not just because of the white political establishment's backlash but also because South Carolina civil rights activism had lost a step. It appeared that the state's three influential NAACP leaders, John McCray, Modjeska Simkins, and Reverend James Hinton, became less involved with or even left the movement. The second half of the 1950s was a period of generational change. Given the state's threat to close public schools, the NAACP did not push petitions to desegregate schools but decided on a wait-and-see attitude.[19] In doing so the NAACP relinquished the initiative, killing its momentum but avoiding an even fiercer white backlash. This relative inactivity created controversy among civil rights activists in the state and further weakened the movement as a whole.[20]

Despite this apparent inactivity on the part of the NAACP, South Carolina's government did not achieve much beyond pettiness and ugliness for its own sake. However, once Newman took charge of the state NAACP and put it back on course, the initiative returned to the levels of the 1940s and early 1950s.[21]

Newman's Leadership of the State NAACP

Newman had been active in South Carolina's civil rights struggle since the early 1940s and held various other positions in civil rights organizations before becoming state NAACP president, then secretary, and later field director (see The Servant Leader and NAACP Years). Newman had experienced the dominant civil rights tactics of the 1940s and their success. His first step after taking over the leadership of the state NAACP was therefore not surprising, but it certainly was significant. He immediately established the NAACP Legal Committee in South Carolina and asked attorney Matthew Perry to become its chair. At the end of the 1950s Perry and the Legal Committee filed lawsuits to desegregate a golf course in Charleston and the waiting rooms at Greenville's airport. Those cases were followed in the 1960s with, in John Sproat's words, "a battery of suits against every bastion of segregation in South Carolina, from the state parks to most remote school district. Perry assembled a team of lawyers that easily matched the Gressette Committee's legal staff. Understanding that the momentum of events nationally was in their favor, they pressed the offensive with a confidence that was unnerving to some of the white defenders."[22]

In initiating the Legal Committee, Newman picked up where the previous generation of state NAACP leaders had left off. The 1940s successes, Sproat has suggested, convinced Newman and other African American leaders that the most effective strategy in South Carolina involved politics and the courts, "the traditional strongholds of white conservatism."[23] Still, in the 1960s with frustrated African American youths initiating demonstrations, sit-ins, and other direct actions, Newman expanded the arsenal of the state NAACP (see essay in this volume, "The NAACP Years"). He led demonstrations and marches and engaged in civil disobedience, including a "wade-in" at a state park. In 1963 he criticized the slow pace of desegregation in Columbia. During desegregation battles in Charleston that year he kept up the pressure through continued demonstrations rather than agreeing to a cooling-off period of negotiations. Newman's activism led him to be arrested five times. But direct actions in his hands were means to aid political negotiations, which remained a main part of his approach. Newman also insisted that direct action be nonviolent.[24]

Newman did not represent the conservative wing of the state's civil rights activists in the 1960s. He clearly navigated the tactical waters between militant young activists and conservative older blacks in a movement that was more massive and less homogenous than that of the 1940s. "His emphasis on nonviolent, persuasive tactics," Sproat has written, "doubtless undercut the demands of more militant and younger activists in the movement for direct action. Some even saw him as an Uncle Tom [and] criticized him bitterly for 'turning white.'" (see Servant Leasre)[25] At the same time older, conservative African American leaders as well as some relatively liberal whites condemned sit-ins and other direct action. In Columbia when the desegregation movement began to pick up stream in the early 1960s, the 1940s militants McCray and James Hinton were among the hand-picked African American leaders to whom Columbia's mayor at the time, Lester Bates, was prepared to talk. Newman was not, nor was Simkins. Hinton had ceased to be active in the movement and was then considered a moderate, and McCray did not care for the sit-ins in Columbia. He thought they were improper and that merely negotiating with Columbia's white leadership would do the trick.[26]

Newman surely had the temperament for combining a wide range of tactics and applying restraint at all times. He was, by all accounts, mild-mannered and a born diplomat and persuader. He was also a leader who was persistent, determined, and tough in pushing for change.[27] These personal qualities enabled Newman to chart a course that was informed by what worked in South Carolina in the 1940s and 1950s and by what was necessary for success in the political climate of the 1960s.

Unlike McCray, for instance, Newman realized that the new era not only demanded additional tactics but also allowed for tactics that would have been unfit for the 1940s. Unlike younger militants, Newman did not conclude from the lack of progress on desegregation in the late 1950s that politics and the courts were no longer viable areas for civil rights agitations. His experience since the 1940s convinced him that they were crucial in South Carolina, despite the stagnation evident in the late 1950s. He was probably less frustrated than the younger activists because he had historical perspectives and knew the reasons for that stagnation—reasons that could be overcome. Newman's deliberations suggest that it misses the point to argue that his restraint and "accommodationism" were defined by basic conservatism. Although Newman's personality may have facilitated his course of action, that course was informed by his earlier experiences and by what he thought would get results.

The South Carolina NAACP

The tactics and successes of South Carolina's 1940s movement did not have an impact on the 1960s civil rights scene just because of their influences on key players in the later decade. The strength of the 1940s movement, especially that of the state NAACP, also facilitated the relative restraint with which 1960s developments played themselves out. That strength was evident not only in the S.C. NAACP's prominent position on a national level but also in the way the organization dominated its home turf, to the extent that other civil rights groups never established much of a presence in South Carolina. The Southern Conference of Human Welfare (SCHW), the Congress of Industrial Organization's Political Action Committee (CIO-PAC), and the American Communist Party did some organizing in the 1940s in South Carolina (see the introduction to this book). In the 1960s the Congress of Racial Equality (CORE) had some presence in South Carolina. But more so than in other southern states, the South Carolina NAACP and organizations associated with it dominated the field. Certainly on an organizational level, this was still true in the 1960s.[28]

NAACP dominance was an important reason why the state's white leadership had the opportunity to learn from the desegregation disasters in Mississippi and Alabama. Stagnation in the push for desegregation in the late 1950s bought white leaders time to learn from developments elsewhere, and that stagnation was in large part due to the activity, or rather inactivity, of the state NAACP. On the one hand, the organization took a wait-and-see attitude toward desegregation, waiting to see what the state of South Carolina would do. But on the other hand, because the NAACP's domination was so strong among state civil rights activists, no other organization was ready to fill the temporary civil rights leadership vacuum in South Carolina.

The S.C. NAACP's dominance in the 1960s did two things. First, as before, the strength of the state NAACP kept other organizations on the margins of organized civil rights activism in South Carolina. These other organizations would have been groups such as CORE and SNCC, which employed more militant tactics than the NAACP did. Second, because of a lack of proliferation of other strong civil rights organizations, there was not the kind of intragroup competition that by itself could have had a radicalizing effect on tactics. All of these factors facilitated the relatively restrained process in South Carolina in the 1960s and were the result of the foundations laid in the 1940s (see also essay: The NAACP Years).

Historians and the 1940s Movement

According to Newby, the 1940s black leadership had been conservative and lacked militancy and resolve. Newby's argument somehow rubbed off on the 1960s black leadership.[29] Newby was right about the link between the decades, but for the wrong reasons. In the process, by defining away the scope and importance of 1940s activism, he implied that this activism was not worth much attention.

Sproat, however, made the connection between the 1940s and the 1960s in more precise and analytically more meaningful terms when he argued that the legal and political successes of the 1940s movement may have been the impetus for the approach of 1960s black leaders, especially Newman. But Sproat too, in Newby-like fashion, defined both the 1940s and the 1960s movements largely in terms of conservatism and accommodationism. The 1940s leadership, he added, may have been too cautious. Moreover Sproat made the meaningful part of his link between the two decades in a 1987 conference paper that was not distributed widely. In the earlier, frequently cited, published chapter he had not done so.[30]

Not until recently has the state's 1940s movement been portrayed as politically mature, militant, well organized, successful, and even a national vanguard whose actions had implications beyond South Carolina. This relatively new view comes largely from two groups of historians. There are those, such as Patricia Sullivan and John Egerton in the 1990s, who have studied the South Carolina movement within a regional or national context and as such judged it to be of great importance. As indicated earlier, in 1978, Barbara Woods, Aba Mecha, as well as more recent researchers, have conducted important research on black activism during the 1930s and 1950s. Her book, published in 1990, on women in the civil rights movement extended the discussion on black activism from a feminist perspective in the south, including South Carolina.[31]

Newby's analysis, however, of 1940s black activism remained dominant until the late 1990s. Essentially, Newby showed a poor understanding of 1940s black political activism in the state. HHe ignored some earlier, admittedly brief and scattered treatments of the issue that placed 1940s activism within a national context. He did not ignore an unpublished study at the end of the state's whites-only Democratic primary, although he did ignore the study's portrayal of an active 1940s movement.[32]

In later years several studies dealt with aspects of 1940s black activism, often adding insights that contradicted Newby's analysis.[33] Some of these studies looked at the reactions of whites to civil rights developments.[34] Others studied civil rights developments without paying much attention to African Americans politics.[35] That neglect of civil rights activism was, before and after Newby, also noteworthy in many biographical and autobiographical books about or by relevant white leaders.[36] As suggested above, the most important exception was Woods's 1978 dissertation on Modjeska Simkins, which was a powerful reinterpretation of Newby's portrayal of 1940s black activism. Woods not only showed and discussed the initiatives and successes of the 1940s struggle; she also stated its importance in explicit terms. "During the early stages of the civil rights movement of the last decades," she began her dissertation, "South Carolina did not capture the attention of the national media as did other southern states which experienced a wave of bombing of churches and homes, sensational murders and other outbursts of lawlessness. Yet, if South Carolina can claim a period of moderation in race relations, fewer deaths during the civil rights movement, and less violence in integration of public facilities, the credit must be given to the well-organized strong and aggressive cadre of black leaders who controlled organizations that paved the way for the change in public life by disseminating information, by working for reform legislation and by undertaking mass registration campaigns long before the decade of [the] sixties."[37]

According to Woods, the African American leadership of South Carolina in the 1940s and 1950s "was in many ways in the vanguard of the civil rights movement in the South." Many of the leaders, she wrote, were "militant, outspoken, and charismatic." Although Woods's dissertation was not published in 1978 as a book, and consequently did not gain similar influence as Newby's book, which was published five years earlier in 1973, her research on this period of the civil rights movement and the NAACP continues to provide a significant perspective on African American leadership in South Carolina.[38]

Interestingly, Newby discussed the victory in the Clarendon County school desegregation case as well, but not as a political victory for African Americans. He discussed it as a factor in the improvement of the quality of segregated black schools as the state of South Carolina tried to hold off desegregation by making separate less unequal. It is within that context, the improvement of schools for African Americans, that Newby also mentions briefly the successful 1940s teacher salary campaign.[39]

It is also interesting to note that there is no mention in Newby's analysis that the South Carolina NAACP was one of the fastest-growing state NAACPs in the country.[40] Newby does not mention that the NAACP had to go to court twice to achieve salary equalization or that the national NAACP sent its chief lawyer, Thurgood Marshall, to do so. This hard-fought battle was reduced by Newby to a matter of simply applying some undetermined amount of undefined pressure.[41]

A similar treatment was applied in analyzing the decisive 1947 and 1948 court cases that gave black South Carolinians access to the state Democratic primaries. These were court cases that had national implications, as they made South Carolina the main battleground for the enforcement of the U.S. Supreme Court's *Smith v. Allwright* decision regarding the Texas primaries.[42]

The PDP was a major part of the successful primary fight, but the party was, in Newby's analysis, not much of a success. He judged its level of success exclusively on whether the party managed in 1944, at its first attempt, to force the national and state Democratic Party into allowing African Americans to participate in its primaries. By that narrow test the PDP did indeed fail, but the party conducted highly successful voter registration drives, ran a candidate for the U.S. Senate in 1944, and made the difference in the 1950s race for U.S. Senate between Olin Johnston and Strom Thurmond. Newby ignored all that and claimed that it was not until the 1960 presidential race that African Americans in South Carolina determined the outcome of a statewide contest.[43]

Likewise Newby ignored the national implications of the PDP's 1944 challenge of the state Democratic Party delegation's seating at the National Democratic Convention. It was the first such challenge by an all-black delegation and, in John Egerton's words, made the PDP "a vehicle to force open the political process in [the] state and in the nation." The PDP, Sullivan wrote, "threatened to explode the uneasy accommodation that the national Democratic Party had maintained between its northern black constituency and its white supremacist southern wing."[44]

Newby's problems of definition and interpretation are evident in how he uses concepts such as "success," "moderate," and "radical" or "active" and "passive." Newby also had a peculiar notion of what makes for an "active" or "passive" movement. It was not until the 1960s, he wrote, that "Black Carolinians were swapping a largely passive role in race relations for a far more active one."[45] He seemed to define "active" and "passive" not by what was done or even by the immediate and potential impact on what was done, but by the number of people involved.

The demonstrations and sit-ins of the late 1950s and 1960s are in such a scenario "active" activities. The court cases, political pressure, NAACP membership drives, and voter registration of the 1940s and early 1950s are "passive" activities. In this interpretation the movement's activities in the 1940s were just "a gentle breeze," which in 1950 "assumed the dimensions of a threatening storm" and in the 1960s "mounted to hurricane force."[46]

Newby's mind-set toward pre-1960s activism is revealed by how he cited and quoted the historian Erwin Hoffman about the 1930s. Hoffman wrote, according to Newby, that prominent black Carolinians of the 1930s recalled the decade for its lethargy and inaction among blacks. Newby failed to include what Hoffman added. "But upon reflection," Hoffman wrote, "the prominent black South Carolinians of the 1930s remembered enough incidents of organization and struggle in the pre-war decade to suggest that the seeds of revolt were germinating and sometimes sprouting in the earlier years." According to Hoffman, "One of the South's most dynamic and successful movements for Negro rights flourished in South Carolina during World War II and the postwar decade. Striking victories were won by a complex of aggressive organizations which were deeply rooted in both the cities and countryside of the Palmetto state."[47] In Newby's opinion these African American organizations were not aggressive at all. However, recent research describes black leaders of the 1940s as significant contributors to ending segregation and discrimination; that they knew the long term consequences of their demands. McCray's editorials in the *Lighthouse and Informer* certainly did not suggest that his militancy depended on him being too dumb to realize what the sum of the demands would be.[48]

For his "moderate" judgment, Newby used several points of reference, none of them very useful. First, he leaned heavily on conservative black sources. To show the moderate nature of African American attitudes he quoted an African American Republican not closely linked to the movement, as well as the *Palmetto Leader*, a conservative black weekly with only marginal involvement with civil rights activity. Second, he compared South Carolina's black leaders to the state's white politicians of the 1940s and 1950s and found Thurmond, Byrnes, Johnston, and Timmerman much more extreme and irresponsible than, say, Hinton and Simkins. That observation is correct, unlike Newby's subsequent implication that the 1940s black leaders lacked militancy and persistence.[49]

Newby's third and perhaps most important point of reference regarding his "moderate" judgment about black leaders was the 1960s. He believed that engaging in court actions and political pressure while obeying the law was moderate. Such a view suggests that the norm for radicalism is confrontational action with a willingness to break laws, as happened in the 1960s. Complaining about moderate means makes sense only if the implication is that more radical means were viable and needed, and that is not a case Newby made. A 1960s standard also applied when Newby called the early movement's goals moderate simply because not all of them involved demands for desegregation.[50]

The emphasis on the early movement's "moderate" nature may reveal a lack of historical perspective. Taking historical setting into consideration, a vanguard is by definition at least somewhat militant since it is ahead of the pack. When the early movement demanded equal pay for black teachers, it was a vanguard within a South Carolina context, as the lack of active support from the teachers themselves indicated. When black leaders of the 1940s rapidly built the South Carolina NAACP, they built an organization that many African Americans did not dare belong to and that even in the second half of the 1950s was the target of specifically designed suppressive state laws. When black leaders demanded access to the Democratic primaries, they were on the cutting edge nationally. In the process they demanded desegregation, one of Newby's standards for radicalism. Newby, however, applied a narrow, provincial perspective. Unlike Hoffman before him and other historians later, he made no attempt to study the 1940s struggle within a regional or national context. Newby even defined the importance of *Briggs v. Elliott* in strictly local terms.[51]

Newby was a victim of his sources. In addition to using dubious sources for his claims about black conservatism, he mostly used newspaper reports from white dailies to chart political developments within the African American community in South Carolina. But the mainstream dailies mostly ignored blacks and were, in any case, rather selective in what they reported.[52]

The 1968 Orangeburg Massacre showed that despite the relative lack of violent confrontation until then, South Carolina would not escape some of the excesses that had plagued other southern states. The episode showed that South Carolina's white political leadership was indeed capable of acting like its less-heralded equivalents in states such as Alabama and Mississippi. In Orangeburg, Sproat wrote, the state's authorities for weeks failed to take effective steps to defuse the crisis. Moreover "they fell into the mode of the Wallaces and Faubuses by seeing the crisis only as a plot by 'outside agitators' to disrupt the 'felicitous relations' of blacks and whites in South Carolina."[53]

The Orangeburg episode was part of what underscored Marcia Synnott's conclusion that for South Carolina, "the meaning and viability of 'moderation' in terms of black aspirations and white compromises" await "final assessment."[54] This is true to some extent even today. The meaning of black moderation in the state remains ill-defined in the historiography and badly applied to different periods. For the 1940s the term does not define black activism well. For the 1960s the term is useful more as a description of certain elements of black activism than as an explanation; black moderation was a tactical device at times but certainly not a straightforward indication of black conservatism. For the state's white political establishment of the 1960s, "moderation" describes part of its activities but explains only so much. It does not address how deeply felt or tenuous or even voluntary white attitudes were or what their origins were.

Summary and Conclusion

A better understanding of 1940s black activism in South Carolina and its long-term impact could provide a better understanding of both black and white moderation in the 1960s. Without considering the range, approach, and success of 1940s black activism, the 1960s movement led by I. DeQuincey Newman is stripped of much of its rationale and consequently its deliberate nature. Without an understanding of the successful modus operandi developed by 1940s black activists, the explanation for the historically surprising white moderation in the 1960s has to rely too much on unsatisfactory notions about the innately peaceful nature of South Carolina's white leadership.

Notes

1. A version of this chapter was published in Moore and Burton, *Toward the Meeting of the Waters*, and was edited for this collection with supplemental research by Sadye L. M. Logan.

2. For studies presenting, citing, or reflecting this narrative or parts thereof, see, for instance, McMillan, "Integration with Dignity," 381–91; Sproat, "Firm Flexibility"; John G. Sproat, "The Limits of Moderation in South Carolina," paper

presented at the annual meeting of the Organization of American Historians, spring 1987, Philadelphia, Penn., Wyndham Franklin Plaza; Sproat, "Newman, Isaiah DeQuincey," also available at http://www.scencyclopedia.org/newman.htm. Accessed June 5, 2012; Hine, "Civil Rights and Campus Wrongs"; Edgar, *South Carolina*, chap. 22; Cox, "1963."

3. Sproat, "Limits of Moderation."

4. Lau, *Democracy Rising;* Woods, *Modjeska Simkins*

5. Grose, *South Carolina at the Brink.*

6. Edgar, *South Carolina*, 523, 538, 543; Cox, "1963," 151–55, 178, chap. 3, 470; Sproat, "Firm Flexibility," 170; Renick, "Solomon Black"; Burton, "Black Squint," 175.

7. Edgar, *South Carolina*, 523, 538, 543; Cox, "1963," 151–55, 178, chap. 3, 470; Sproat, "Firm Flexibility," 170; Renick, "Solomon Black"; Burton, "Black Squint," 175; Richards, "Osceola E. McKaine," esp. chaps. 6–9; Sullivan, *Days of Hope*, esp. chaps. 4–6; Roefs, "Leading the Civil Rights Vanguard." For the current paragraph, see also Sproat, "Firm Flexibility," 165.

8. Roefs, "Leading the Civil Rights Vanguard."

9. Howard Quint documented much of Timmerman's abuse in his book about the post-Brown reaction of white South Carolina; see Quint, *Profile in Black and White*. See also Edgar, *South Carolina*, 528; Synnott, "Desegregation in South Carolina," 58; Hine, "Civil Rights and Campus Wrongs," 318–19.

10. Woods Aba-Mecha, "Black Woman Activist," chap. 4; Hine, "Civil Rights and Campus Wrongs," 310–20; Sproat, "Firm Flexibility," 170; Cox, "1963," 71–78, 238.

11. On the role of businessmen, see, for instance, Cox, "1963," chap. 4; Lofton, "Calm and Exemplary"; Edgar, *South Carolina*, chap. 22; Sproat, "Limits of Moderation"; Sproat, "Firm Flexibility," 177–82.

12. See, for instance, Cox, "1963," 11; Sproat, "Limits of Moderation"; Edgar, *South Carolina*, 537–40.

13. Lofton, "Calm and Exemplary," 79.

14. In addition to the sources in note 5 for the 1940s and early 1950s, see also Sproat, "Limits of Moderation."

15. On the inevitability of desegregation, see also Sproat, "Firm Flexibility," 1969–71.

16. Richards, "Osceola E. McKaine," esp. chaps. 6–9.

17. Roefs, "John McCray," 474–76; Robertson, *Sly and Able*, chap. 13, passim.

18. Cohodas, *Strom Thurmond*, 206–16; Sproat, "Limits of Moderation"; Roefs, "John McCray," 479–81.

19. Synnott, "Desegregation in South Carolina," 52–53, 57–79.

20. Ibid., 55, 58; Cox, "1963," 71–78, 238; Smyth, "Segregation in Charleston."

21. Sproat, "Firm Flexibility," 170; Hine, "Civil Rights and Campus Wrongs," 310–20; Cox, "1963," 346–47.

22. Sproat, "Limits of Moderation"; Sproat, "Newman, Isaiah DeQuincey"; Cox, "1963," chap. 3; Porter, "The Legal Committee of the South Carolina NAACP."

23. Sproat, "Limits of Moderation."

24. Ibid.; Cox, "1963," 348, 386, 411–12.

25. Sproat, "Limits of Moderation"; Sproat, "Firm Flexibility," 171–73; Newby, *Black Carolinians*, 328–29; Lofton, "Calm and Exemplary," 78; Woods Aba-Mecha, "Black Woman Activist," chap. 4; Cox, "1963," 354–55, 362, 376–77, 382–88, 411–12.

26. Sproat, "Limits of Moderation"; Sproat, "Newman, Isaiah DeQuincey."

27. Meier, "Epilogue"; Fairclough, *Race and Democracy*, xiv–xv; Sproat, "Firm Flexibility," 173, 180; Cox, "1963," 350, 456–57; Roefs, "John McCray," 477–79.

28. Newby, *Black Carolinians*, 279–80.

29. Sproat, "Limits of Moderation"; Sproat, "Firm Flexibility."

30. Egerton, *Speak Now*.

31. Heard, *A Two-Party South*; Robinson, "Democracy's Frontiers"; Walton, *Black Political Parties*; Farmer, "The End of the White Primary."

32. Kluger, *Simple Justice*; Lochbaum, "The Word Made Flesh"; Faggart, "Defending the Faith"; Cohodas, *Strom Thurmond*; Bass and Thompson, *Ol' Strom*; Lofton, "Calm and Exemplary," 73; Terry, "J. Waties Waring"; Yarbrough, *A Passion for Justice*. David Southern's 1981 article about Waring is in this respect less productive; see Southern, "Beyond Jim Crow Liberalism."

33. Secrest, "Black and White Press Opinion"; Dora Thomas Martin, "The Attitude of the Spartanburg"; John Bartlow Martin, *The Deep South Says "Never,"* 43–79; O'Neil, "To Endure, but Not Accept"; Johnston, "Communism vs. Segregation"; Frederickson, "The Slowest State."

34. Ellenburg, "The Congress"; Lamis, "The Disruption"; Blicck, "Beyond the Politics of Color."

35. Huss, *Senator for the South*; Leemhuis, "Olin D. Johnston Runs"; Lachicotte, *Rebel Senator*; Sherrill, *Gothic Politics*; Thomas I. Johnson, "James McBride Dabbs"; Robertson, *Sly and Able*; Byrnes, *All in One Lifetime*.

36. Huss, *Senator for the South*; Lachicotte, *Rebel Senator*.

37. Woods Aba-Mecha, "Black Woman Activist," 1.

38. Ibid., 1, 211; Woods, "South Carolina Conference of NAACP," 3; Woods, "Modjeska Simkins," 99–120.

39. Newby, *Black Carolinians*, chap. 7.

40. Ibid., 278–79.

41. Ibid., 303–4; Woods Aba-Mecha, "Black Woman Activist," 176–94; Richards, "Osceola E. McKaine," chaps. 6 and 7.

42. Woods Aba-Mecha, "Black Woman Activist," 195–208; Richards, "Osceola E. McKaine," chap. 7; Walton, *Black Political Parties*, 71; Sullivan, *Days of Hope*, 143.

43. Woods Aba-Mecha, "Black Woman Activist," 202, 210; Richards, "Osceola E. McKaine," 170–76, 193; Walton, *Black Political Parties*, 69–74; Sullivan, *Days of Hope*, 170, 190; Newby, *Black Carolinians*, 291; McCray, "The Way It Was"; Cohodas, *Strom Thurmond*, 206–16; Faggart, "Defending the Faith," chap. 5; Sproat, "Limits of Moderation"; Banks, "Strom Thurmond," 226.

44. Walton, *Black Political Parties*, 74–77; Egerton, *Speak Now*, 227; Sullivan, *Days of Hope*, 170; Richards, "Osceola E. McKaine," chap. 7.

45. Newby, *Black Carolinians*, 278.

46. Ibid., 274.

47. Ibid., 229; Hoffman, "The Genesis," 346.

48. See, for instance, McCray's editorials in the *Lighthouse and Informer* for October 19, 1941; January 10, 1943; and February 6, 1944.

49. Newby, *Black Carolinians*, 277–80, 288. For the level of moderation and militancy of the *Palmetto Leader* and the *Lighthouse and Informer*, see Wim Roefs, "Expanding the Media Landscape for African Americans: South Carolina's *The Lighthouse and Informer* in the 1940s," paper presented at the American Journalism Historians Association Annual Convention, Pittsburgh, Pa., October 2000.

50. Newby, *Black Carolinians*, 278–79.

51. Ibid., 305.

52. For the coverage in white South Carolina newspapers of black life and politics, see Roefs, "Expanding the Media Landscape."

53. Sproat, "Limits of Moderation." For the Orangeburg Massacre, see Bass and Nelson, *The Orangeburg Massacre.*

54. Synnott, "Desegregation in South Carolina," 61.

A Vision for Change

Community Planning and Development in Rural South Carolina

Wallace Brown, Sr., G. Robert Cook, Carrie Crawford Washington, and Karen Ross Grant

What makes community organizing especially attractive is the faith it places in the ability of the poor to make decisions for themselves.

Paul Wellstone

The war on poverty was not officially declared in the United States until 1964. However, in South Carolina poverty was not "discovered" until 1968.[1] One of South Carolina's first responses to poverty was the development in 1971 of the Rural Regional Coordination Demonstration Project (RRCDP). Three years later, in October 1974, Governor John West appointed the Reverend Isaiah DeQuincey Newman as director of the RRCDP. From July 1971 to September 1975, the RRCDP, funded by the Office of Economic Opportunity, was housed in the Governor's Office. Governor West's decision to appoint Newman to this directorship was based on a number of factors. First, Newman was a self-described "country preacher" who knew people in every rural community in the state of South Carolina, having grown up and worked in rural South Carolina. Second, he brought to the governor's staff a deserved reputation as a bridge builder and savvy politician who had established relationships at all levels of government. Newman's career in state government can be viewed as illustrative of the focus and title of this book, as he was one of our state's most important sons and, most of all, an activist. Therefore we present in this article some of the initiatives proposed and promoted by Isaiah DeQuincey Newman for improving the lives of all South Carolinians.

Newman was respected and loved by his staff. The stately country preacher with a bow tie, suspenders, and brown derby was serious about the business at hand, and yet he had a sense of humor. He set the tone and made the work environment one in which his staff wanted to participate. He was inclusive, appreciative of skilled and talented workers. He empowered staff to do their best—holding each one accountable in a gentle way. Staff members knew that important work was at hand, that great things were to be realized, and that their contributions would impact people's lives. Many viewed him more as a father figure and mentor than just a director or leader. They knew that with Newman they could be possibility thinkers with can-do attitudes and find-a-way or make-a-way approaches. Newman had the knack for recruiting and retaining capable people who could get the work done. He instilled in his staff the ability to face adversity with a spirit of optimism and to see challenges as opportunities to problem-solve. He was of the view that a cluttered desk was a sign of a cluttered mind. By example Newman kept his many projects and initiatives organized. He could always find any paper he needed when he needed it, and he encouraged his staff to do the same. Staff and other participants in his many initiatives knew they must be ready for the unexpected. Newman was a reassuring and dependable leader.

Under Newman's leadership from 1974 until 1981, community planning and development involved working with communities with populations of fifty thousand or less. The intent of these community development projects was to address the desperate needs of the "people left behind," as Newman called the rural poor and disadvantaged. He saw citizens needing a voice, people who wanted to be involved in bringing positive social and economic changes and justice to their lives and communities. At the most basic level, this work involved improving poor living conditions and lifting the human spirit. At other times it involved challenging the power structure to become involved with its constituents in both incorporated and unincorporated areas. One of Newman's strategies was to peacefully find a common ground on which both parties could agree. To accomplish this he would offer one or two alternatives on which both parties could agree. However, one of the alternatives would always be one that the two parties could not refuse, and the other would be an extreme.

Those who knew Newman saw leadership at its best. He did not covet his leadership. Instead he shared it and empowered others to grow and to reach back and help others left behind. Newman's leadership style was based on meeting people where they were and going from there. Empowerment, capacity building, and grassroots organizing were important keys to his effectiveness. In other words, he was not just politically savvy but also had the vision and courage to believe that a partnership with all levels of government was necessary to address the needs of the state's most needy. It was simply extraordinary that such accomplishments evolved out of the work from a small staff, headquartered as a special unit in the governor's office. In addition Newman was able to call on private corporations to partner across the state and to help fund and promote the regional meetings.

Expanding the RRCDP

There was a special persona about this "country preacher" who stepped into the governor's office to build upon the progressive work of his predecessors, Mr. Rodney Albert (deceased) and Dr. Hiram Spain, Jr. The project operated in two planning regions of South Carolina: the lower Savannah (covering Aiken, Bamberg, Barnwell, Calhoun, Clarendon, and Orangeburg Counties) and the lowcountry (covering Beaufort, Charleston, Hampton, and Jasper Counties). In August 1982 a helping guide was disseminated to all grassroots leaders. The guide included documented past grassroots efforts and RRCDP objectives.[2] The objectives of the demonstration project were to test whether

1. a state government, by exercising leadership potential, can strengthen institutional response to the needs of the rural poor by insuring that such needs become an identified concern of appropriate state, multicounty, and local agencies and organizations; the state leadership can increase the resources available to deal with rural poverty;
2. the state technical assistance and strategies can strengthen the planning capabilities of multicounty regional institutions, making them more effective planners and coordinators of resources relevant to problems of rural poverty;
3. the inputs into the planning process by the rural poor and racial or ethnic minorities can significantly improve the effectiveness of programs for human resource development.

Continuing to implement the RRCDP objectives and building upon past successes in the lower Savannah and lowcountry planning regions, Newman appealed to a new governor for a statewide office to be established as part of his administration, not just housed there. On October 1, 1975, his request was acted upon. Governor James B. Edwards established the Office of Rural Development (ORD) within the Governor's Division of Health and Social

Development. At that time Carroll Campbell, who later became governor, was executive assistant to Governor Edwards. The interaction between and among the hierarchy in the administration with Newman was respectful, with a live-and-let-live mode of operation, from the staff's perspective. When Newman needed support for initiatives, he usually got it. Newman had paid his dues during the civil rights struggle and had a support base that any politician with sense would not have taken on or squabbled over.

Eleven years after poverty received national attention in South Carolina, Governor Richard W. Riley elevated the ORD in August 1979 to division status. With successful efforts evident, on August 3, 1981, Governor Riley signed Executive Order 81-28 and expanded the Division of Rural Development's (DRD) function to include the Office of Small and Minority Business Assistance, headed by Mr. John W. Gadson, Sr. With the Executive Order passed, the new division was named the Division of Rural Development and Special Economic Assistance (DRD&SEA). Newman answered Governor Riley's call to lead the newly created DRD&SEA, as its first director, to address specifically both rural needs and small businesses.

Newman earned widespread respect across the state governmental agencies in South Carolina because he not only "talked the talk" but also "walked the walk." No matter how great or small the venture, his devoted staff members were always optimistic that under his leadership and tutelage only great things would happen.[3] Many lives were touched and many new leaders were shaped because Newman helped pave the way. Self-help initiatives for economic advancement were key areas of concentration during the Newman years in state government and served as prototypes for many of the initiatives currently seen in the state and in local universities. Newman knew that for advances to be made in rural areas across South Carolina its citizens had to become involved at the grassroots level and that strengthening one's economic base was essential to advancing the plight of people left behind. Under Newman's leadership state-sponsored self-help economics served to empower citizens in rural South Carolina.

Self-Help Initiatives

The Self-Help Initiatives projects for rural advancement included Roadside Markets, Good Hope Farmers Cooperative, Fairfield County Farmers' Market, Lowcountry Crab Trap Project, Dorcas Quilting Cooperative, Pee Dee Crafters, Crossroads Crafters, the Chair Making Training Project, Bluffton Oyster Cooperative, Sea Island Farmers' Cooperative, a wood pallet project in the Pee Dee, and an ethanol project in Williamsburg County.

The Good Hope Farmers Cooperative, which was established in July 1979, provided roadside marketing opportunities for low- and marginal-income farmers of Sumter, Kershaw, and Lee Counties. Farmers came to the roadside market, located west of Sumter on Highway 378, for direct marketing of fresh vegetables grown from their farms. Sweet potatoes were a prime and successful crop grown by farmers. The market received support from the Green Thumb Program, which helped seniors grow and sell plants across the state.

The Fairfield County Farmers' Market was established in June 1978 by a small group of citizens with assistance from the Clemson University Extension Service. The project grew out of grassroots citizens wanting a suitable market for their homegrown produce. Working with county, city, and local merchants, the group located a lot in downtown Winnsboro, which was leased to the Fairfield County Farmer's Market for a nominal fee.

The Lowcountry Crab Trap Project was established in December 1978, created out of a Title XX (Social Services) Life Skills Education Grant. The project involved thirteen citizens from Ruffin, South Carolina, with part-time gainful employment from making crab traps from their homes.

The Dorcas Quilting Cooperative was established in Sumter County in 1976 as an initiative to preserve the art of quilt making and to support the economic growth of the cooperative. As a result of technical assistance from the Governor's Office of Rural Development a start-up grant was received. Women from several rural churches came together to share their knowledge of the craft and to make beautiful quilts, which were sold to local vendors and residents. As a strong advocate for women's empowerment, Newman frequently noted that this was the only supported project that was organized and staffed by women.

The Pee Dee Crafters in Marion and Dillon Counties, the Dorcas Quilting Cooperative in Sumter County, and the Crossroads Crafters in Florence County were established in 1978 to provide economic outlets to market quilts and other craft items to the public.

The Chair Making Training Project was established in July 1978 with five eager trainees under the instruction of master craftsman Archie Hunter (now deceased). Trainees learned from Mr. Hunter the diminishing folk art of hand-making chairs from oak and then bottoming them with corn shucks. The project was initiated as a rural economic development training and employment opportunity to benefit the physically disabled, unemployed and displaced farm workers, and others who depended on public assistance programs for a livelihood. Reverend Granville Hicks, a longtime colleague of Newman, was a supporter of the self-help projects. Reverend Hicks fondly remembered the Chair Making Training Project as one of the more exceptional of the various projects sponsored by the ORD. He described it as family-run and producing chairs that were highly sought after.[4]

Long before it became popular, Newman was advocating the use of corn and other agricultural products for fuel—for example, a Williamsburg County ethanol project. He was also an advocate of drip-trickle irrigation, a process by which water is slowly introduced via perforated hoses at the base of growing crops to ensure needed moisture. This was another initiative that showed Newman to be ahead of his time. The demonstration projects are exemplars of what is possible in times of hopelessness and diminished economy. These projects were maintained from two to five years.

Grassroots Citizen Involvement

From the mid-1970s through the early 1980s, under Newman's leadership, citizens' participation in community planning was at its height—more than ever before or since in South Carolina state government. Grassroots committees grew out of citizen participation rallies that were held in rural communities across the state. The committees were structured and designed to involve local community people coming together to problem-solve their own issues and concerns. The goal was to establish a grassroots committee in every county of the state. The I. DeQuincey Newman approach was not complicated: ask the people what their needs were, assess them, organize, develop a structure to address those needs, get the people to commit on their local priority, strategize, provide guidance if needed, and let the work begin. As committees became organized and recognized for their voices and efforts to promote self-help programs in rural areas, more government support and technical assistance were made available to them. Empowerment and capacity building were always important to Newman so that citizens could tackle their own problems in their own communities.

A rural development conference and consultation on rural needs was held in each of the state's ten planning regions. Attendees to the rural conferences were recruited from local media, churches, businesses, public and private agencies, organizations, and local citizens known to Newman. After a general session on grassroots participation, county meetings were held prior to departing the conference to determine if there were rural needs to be addressed locally. Each county agreed to come together within a given period to host a grassroots committee organizational meeting. Each did and was assigned a community consultant from the governor's office to work with it. At an initial grassroots organizational meeting, citizens adopted basic by-laws, elected officers, and moved forward to identify, assess, prioritize, and strategize on needs. A representative sample follows.

Bamberg County Grassroots Citizens Advisory Committee (GCAC) was organized in the fall of 1980. Members determined that their focus was on establishing legal aid and a referral service for citizens.

Chesterfield County GCAC was organized in the fall of 1980. As health care was a priority, members were instrumental in recruiting a doctor to the county.

Darlington County Rural Development Advisory Committee was organized in April 1978 to provide a forum for discussing rural problems and assessing rural needs. Another goal was to provide a vehicle for action to address identified needs.

Fairfield County GCAC was organized in October 1978. Over two hundred citizens turned out and elected officers and agreed on standard by-laws. In addition they agreed to focus on health service education, home weatherization, a farmer's market, a community choir, a temporary shelter for battered children, water and sewer grants, consumer education workshops, and road improvements.

Greenwood County GCAC was organized in May 1980 and voiced as priorities the following: recreation; protesting budget cuts for Title XX day care; and applying for Farmers Home Administration grants and loans. A countywide wood project and day-care services and an after-school study and cultural enrichment center grew out of citizens' efforts. In addition a partnership was formed with retired teachers and students majoring in education to become tutors and teachers at the center.

Hampton County GCAC was organized in May 1980. Priorities selected were programs for the elderly, transportation, and recreation.

Horry County GCAC in 1977 organized and developed a healthy working relationship with the Horry County Council. Fire protection, water and sewer grants, and recreational centers were the priority needs on which citizens worked.

Marlboro County GCAC was organized in 1977. The committee sponsored a wood project to help the needy, the elderly, and unemployed citizens who did not have access to wood and depended on it as a main source of heating during the winter months.

Grassroots committees were also active in the Appalachian region in Spartanburg and Greenville Counties. The Concerned Citizens of Upper Spartanburg County worked with the county and Farmers Home Administration in extending water lines for their community. In York County the Concerned Citizens for Rural Recreation worked with the county in establishing a countywide recreation commission. In Charleston County the GCAC worked with state and federal agencies in securing funding for safe drinking water in the Petersfield community.

It became evident that in order to respond effectively and to improve living conditions of rural poor families, a community infrastructure was a basic necessity. This recognition led to the development of grants for rural water, sewer, and housing across the state. Community leaders surfaced and pledged their support of the identified needs. Newman helped secure rural and sewer grants that supported communities such as Petersfield in Charleston County, Cassatt in Kershaw County, Hemingway in Williamsburg County, and Jenkinsville in Fairfield County. With assistance from the South Carolina Department of Health and Environmental Control and local government participation, these communities were able to see the fruits of their involvement in community planning. In Bamberg County housing conditions of the most needy were addressed by working with local officials and Habitat for Humanity.

After organizing forty-six GCACs, Newman viewed it as important to continue to keep local leaders apprised of resources to improve communities and sharpen existing skills and for them to network and learn from each other. Rural Leaders Schools were established in the late 1970s and early 1980s. Staff members continued with these schools in 1982, 1986, and 1987 for the same purposes. They were mostly held at White Oak Conference Center in rural Fairfield County. A faculty for this purpose was established, headed by Dr. Eddie Wynn of Clemson University. This opportunity was also used to recognize unsung male and female heroes in rural areas who were making positive things happen in their communities. An award program for outstanding services rendered was always a component of Rural Leaders Schools.

In 1982, during the Riley administration, the first Governor's Council on Rural Development was established to develop policy recommendations on rural issues after having heard from local leaders. Elected officials and agency leaders assembled for the purpose of drafting the state's first rural development policy for Governor Riley's consideration. Policy recommendations related to health care, economic development, water and sewer services, housing, public transportation, education, and other rural improvements were identified and put forward for the governor's consideration.

Grant development was viewed as significant in the formation of effective community infrastructure. In this regard, under Newman's leadership, the Rockefeller Foundation Grants, the first Volunteers in Service to America (VISTA) project (operating from the state level), operated out of the governor's office and DRD&SEA with a coordinator who was nationally recruited and twelve locally recruited volunteers. In addition the South Carolina Department of Social Services in 1978 awarded the DRD&SEA a Life Skills Education Grant to help people on public assistance develop better coping skills.

After Newman

Newman retired from state government in 1981, and Wallace Brown, Sr., succeeded him, continuing many of the previously discussed initiatives. Newman's retirement occurred at a time when the political climate had drastically changed. Different priorities and agendas were embraced, which impacted rural development initiatives and lessened support for the state's overall rural development programs. In 1982 the newly elected Senator Newman continued to have an impact on community planning, supporting bills and laws improving the quality of life for South Carolinians and continuing to support the Governor's Council on Rural Development. In cooperation with the staff from the governor's office, the council produced a report outlining a number of steps for the state to take in addressing the needs of rural South Carolina. The report was favorably received and supported the continuation of work in the areas of water and sewer services, housing, public transportation, and economic development. These initiatives continued to be supported with state, federal, and local funds. However, as a consequence of numerous social and political changes since Newman's death, many of the initiatives proposed and implemented under Newman's leadership have not been actively supported by any governors or legislative leaders since the mid-1980s.

This examination of Newman's role in community planning and development in South Carolina has included many of the rural areas of the state. Even though all of the initiatives illustrating his activism do not exist today in their original forms, these projects continue to influence and contribute to community planning and development in rural South Carolina. In 1990 state Rural Development Councils were created by a national Rural Economic Development Initiative. The councils, not unlike the work that Newman instituted under the ORD, were formed to coordinate rural developments efforts among federal, state, local, and private sectors. The South Carolina

Rural Development Council (SCRDC) was formed in 1991 and is housed at Clemson University Institute for Economic and Community Development. Unfortunately these current initiatives appear to be reinventing the wheel, as if nothing had gone before. The most striking thing about the current initiatives is what appears to be a lack of direct community involvement. The stakeholders are primarily state, federal, and regional agencies with university-based administrations.[5] An additional observation is the SCRDC 2008 discussion on the critical need for water and sewer infrastructure in rural South Carolina. The SCRDC report, unlike Newman's vision of the 1970s, warns that unless state policy makers start seriously addressing the important issues of water and sewer in rural South Carolina, the state's ability to sustain its rural economic and public health environment is in serious jeopardy.[6]

Hundreds or perhaps thousands of South Carolinians had the opportunity to interact with Newman during his struggles to create a viable sewer and water infrastructure while serving in the governor's office. Everyone held him in the highest regard.[7] His staff considered themselves fortunate on many levels for the opportunity to serve with him. Countless state and local government employees owed their jobs to his tireless efforts. An important component of his legacy can be seen in all the lives he touched around the state, the nation, and the world. We are better for knowing him, and our state is a better place because he was here.

Summary and Conclusion

Many of the projects and initiatives discussed herein involved a large cast of characters whose state government careers were launched and/or continued by Newman's presence in the governor's office. He recruited (or convinced to be retained) the following during his tenure in the governor's office, 1974–81: Wallace Brown, Sr. (as his successor), Valentine Burroughs (deceased), G. Robert Cook, Frazella Delaney, John W. Gadson, Sr., Dr. Jimmy Gilbert, Georgia Goode, Karen Ross Grant, Pam Grant, Alvin Hinkle, Mark Hoffacker, E. Fern Howell, Leila Jamison, Jill Jeter, Strom Thurmond Johnston, Barbara Kelly, Danny Koon, Lou Prather, Gail Samuels, Jean Samuels, Carrie Crawford Washington, and Wendy Wright. In addition to state employees directly under his supervision, Newman also helped recruit and supervise the activities of a large core of Volunteers in Service to America (VISTA). This program was the domestic equivalent of the Peace Corps and recruited people from across the country to help in community development and assistance projects in varied settings. Newman initiated the first (and only) statewide VISTA project in South Carolina supported by state government from the governor's office. Appropriately many of these volunteers were recruited from their communities to address problems specific to rural citizens in South Carolina. Many of the volunteers were retired educators and public servants who knew Newman from his years of service as a pastor and civil rights leader. As was the case in grassroots organizing for citizens' involvement in community planning and development, Newman's name and participation were sufficient to bring dozens of local citizens into service for their community. Notable among these volunteers were Corean Anderson, David Belton, Naomi Cannady, Sandora Cathcart, Bernice Graham, Frances Hill, John Hutto, Eudora Jolley, Nora McCaskill, Ethel Miller, Virginia Pringle, and James and Syble Scott.

Notes

1. Hollings, *The Case Against Hunger.*
2. M. Hoffacker, "Rural South Carolina Grassroots Committees: The Past and Ideas for the Future" (unpublished ms., Columbia, S.C., 1982).
3. Wendy Wright, interview by Karen Ross Grant, February and May 2007.
4. Reverend G. Hicks, interview by Sadye Logan, fall 2006.
5. srdc.mis/state.edu/sp/sc_final.doc; srdc.misstate.edu/entrepreneurship/Clemson.edu. Accessed June 9, 2012.
6. Walter Harris, "Rural Developments," 1, 3.
7. Jerome Noble, interview by Sadye Logan, summer 2006.

Impacting the State's Economy

Challenging Discriminatory Practices in Employment

Tanya S. Brice and Sadye L. M. Logan

> As the agitation which culminated in the abolition of African slavery in this country covered a period of 50 years, so may we expect that before the rights conferred upon us by the [Civil] war amendments are fully conceded, a full century will have passed away.
>
> T. Thomas Fortune, *New York Age* (January 25, 1890)

Isaiah DeQuincey Newman lived during a time of great economic transition in the state and the nation. He was born during an era when sharecropping was the major economic and employment activity for African Americans in South Carolina. This and related menial jobs kept African Americans dependent and impoverished emotionally, physically, and spiritually. According to I. A. Newby, 79 percent of all farmers were working someone else's land in 1920.[1] Newby goes on to say that for the majority of black Carolinians, living in poverty was an inescapable lifestyle.[2] By the 1960s, however, sharecropping was largely replaced by textile factories, bringing leveling prosperity to the state's African Americans. This prosperity transitioned to a rise in unemployment among African Americans by the mid-1980s and beyond. Newman became field director of the NAACP during the 1960s (see "Isaiah DeQuincey

Newman" and "The NAACP Years") and was concerned with the economic and employment plight of African Americans in South Carolina during this era. This essay contains an examination of the characteristics of South Carolina's economy and employment during the three periods 1910–60, 1960–70, and 1970–present and concludes with future economic and employment implications for the state.

Traditional Employment: 1910–60

After the formal end of the institution of slavery, African Americans in South Carolina and throughout the rest of the South were subjected to social and economic policies that moved them from being slaves to becoming sharecroppers.[3] There was little difference between their status as slaves and their status as sharecroppers except for the semblance of the opportunity to earn fair wages in the sharecropping system. In addition to sharecropping and tenant farming, African Americans were involved in other unskilled labor and domestic services. According to Newby, blacks who were engaged in agricultural and domestic services were viewed as failures and persons of low social and economic status.[4] Social and economic policies, such as the criminal and Black Codes, throughout many of the southern states supported a system of economic repression among blacks. These laws were intended to keep black laborers and tenants in their place and resulted in a system of peonage (see "Isaiah DeQuincey Newman"). Although African Americans were mostly rural people, they were an integral part of southern urban life. They performed most of the menial tasks that involved heavy, dirty work in the mills and turpentine and naval stores. It is important to note that black people were also artisans and craftsmen in significant numbers. While Reconstruction-era policies empowered blacks to pursue the American dream of equality, liberty, and happiness, the criminal and Black Codes quickly reversed any gains acquired during Reconstruction. In addition Black Codes created an environment of unchecked racial oppression of blacks through domestic terroristic acts by organizations such as the Ku Klux Klan, or the "white caps." These policies directly influenced employment practices and the economy in South Carolina during the early twentieth century.

The advent of the Black Codes initiated a time of migration of blacks from the South to other regions of the United States. This migration caused great concern for the U.S. government, as is evidenced by the formation of the following U.S. Senate resolution passed in December 1879:

> Whereas large numbers of negroes from the Southern States are emigrating to the Northern States; and,
> Whereas it is currently alleged that they are induced to do so by the unjust and cruel conduct of their white fellow-citizens towards them in the South, and by the denial or abridgment of their personal and political rights and privileges: Therefore,
> *Be it resolved,* That a committee of five members of this body be appointed by its presiding officer, whose duty it shall be to investigate the causes which have led to the aforesaid emigration, and to report the same to the Senate; and said committee shall have power to send for persons and papers, and to sit at any time. ["Report and Testimony of the Select Committee of the United States Senate to Investigate the Cause of the Removal of the Negroes from the Southern States to the Northern States," 1880]

After the 1910 census, approximately nine million southerners left the region for other areas in the first half of the century.[5] The principal path of migration was from the rural South to urban areas within the South and in other regions.[6] As is depicted in the table below, a large number of those migrants were black. These migration patterns are significant because the rural South provided more migrants to other regions than it received. In addition a large number of its labor force left the South.

Net Migration from the South: 1910–60

	1910s	1920s	1930s	1940s	1950s
Whites	-559,900	-764,400	-689,500	-1,126,900	-1,453,000
Blacks	-482,300	-824,700	-458,000	-1,345,400	-1,362,900

Sources: *Historical Statistics of the United States . . . to 1957; Historical Statistics of the United States . . . to 1962;* from Kirby, "The Southern Exodus, 1910–1960," 594.

This mass migration of black labor created racial tensions in the South. White landowners were concerned about the loss of black laborers.[7] Consequently the incidences of terrorism against blacks increased. Between 1880 and 1920 more than three thousand blacks were burned, shot, and mutilated by lynch mobs, with less than 1 percent of the murderers prosecuted by the states.[8] Additionally with respect to black employment in the cotton mills in 1915, racial discrimination was written into the law. Some historians have viewed this abomination as the most important fact of economic life for urban African Americans. Essentially the legislature made it unlawful for cotton mills to permit black and white employees to work together in the same room, to use the same doors of entrance and exit at the same time, and to use at any time the same lavatories, toilets, drinking water, cups, bowls, or buckets. Particularly from 1910 to 1930 this may have contributed to increased migration by blacks.[9] However, Charles Johnson, the National Urban League's first national director of the Office of Research and Investigation in New York City, in his survey of migration patterns from 1865 to 1920 observed the following regarding motivations for black migration from the rural South: "Reasons are one thing; motives another. . . . Persecution plays its part—a considerable one. But when the whole of the migration of southern Negroes is considered, this part seems to be limited. It is indeed more likely that Negroes, like all others with a spark of ambition and self-interest, have been deserting soil which cannot yield returns in proportion to their population increase."[10] Johnson's observations suggest that black migration was primarily driven by economic conditions.

In the early 1920s there was a boll weevil infestation primarily among cotton crops in the South. In 1921 the South Carolina cotton crop had 100 percent infestation, resulting in the loss of those economically important cash crops.[11] Agricultural wages also plummeted as a result of the infestation. In South Carolina the average pay for picking one hundred pounds of cotton decreased from ninety-five cents in 1904 to seventy-eight cents in 1927 to fifty-three cents in 1930. This infestation also resulted in mass migration of blacks in South Carolina to primarily the southern and northeastern industrialized centers. In fact there were more blacks than whites migrating from the South during this decade.

The 1930s ushered in one of the most devastating economic times of that century, best known as the Great Depression. As a result of the depressed economy, economic policies, as part of Roosevelt's New Deal, were enacted to relieve the daily suffering of citizens. However, these policies often had a negative impact on the African American laborer. The Social Security Act of 1935 largely excluded agricultural and domestic laborers,[12] in turn excluding African Americans, and essentially did nothing to change the relative economic status of African Americans in South Carolina. Furthermore the New Deal programs were often discriminatory toward African Americans. As Thelma P. Kube, an African American woman reared in Edgefield, South Carolina, during this era, recalled, "One of the first New Deal agencies was the Public Works Administration (PWA). My dad, Milton Percival, worked on PWA for $1 a day repairing roads. When he used his mule, Sam, he received $2 more per day. When he was promoted to foreman, he was on equal pay with Sam: $2 a day!"[13]

The U.S. government, in an attempt to assist agricultural landowners, enacted the Agricultural Adjustment Act of 1933. This act was intended to raise the prices of agricultural goods and dairy products by decreasing supply and increasing demand for the products. Farmers were paid stipends to produce a fraction of their potential yield of produce and dairy products. This rationing of production would create increased price demands in the market. The Agricultural Adjustment Act had unintended consequences. While it was meant to benefit farming landowners, African American laborers on those farms often received less pay, less sustenance, and less work.[14] The following quote highlights the plight of black sharecroppers: "It was 1933, and we were poor black sharecroppers—eight children, Mom and Dad . . . no longer did we have the freedom to grow and raise things and live off the land. Everything went to the Brown family [the landowners]. We learned what it meant to be hungry. Mostly, we ate what we called 'chunk up' (cornbread/buttermilk) and mush made from cornmeal, leaves from cabbages (we couldn't wait for the heads to form), creasy greens (which grew wild) and, at times, some pole beans, corn or even a chicken, pilfered by my sisters from the Browns."[15] This unintended consequence led to increased migration by blacks to industrialized centers in the South and other regions.

The Civilian Conservation Corps (CCC), a significant employment program of the New Deal, served as a transition to an upward economic trend for some African Americans in the 1940s. The CCC was created in 1933 by the Roosevelt administration as a public works program responsible for the building of roads and trails in parks, conservation dams, and campgrounds, as well as the planting of trees, draining of swamps, replanting of grazing land, and renovating of historic buildings. In addition the CCC was responsible for the stringing of telephone lines. This program provided an opportunity for young men ages eighteen to twenty-five to work for wages, approximately thirty dollars per month, of which all but five dollars was sent back to their families for support.[16] The government ensured that about 10 percent of the CCC workforce was African American. Laws establishing the CCC forbade discrimination on the basis of race, color, or creed. Initially blacks and whites were in the same companies in some places, but this practice was immediately disbanded. According to Robert Fechner, the national director of the CCC, occasional placement of a few blacks in camps that were for white enrollees was permissible and workable "because of the natural adaptability of Negroes to serve as cooks."[17] Blacks were generally assigned to policing the kitchen or similar camp duties. Given the camps' practices of segregation, discrimination against blacks occurred throughout the nine years of the CCC's existence.[18] While the program's first name was "Civilian," it was managed by the U.S. Army. Corps members were subjected to military-style boot camps and discipline. While they were obligated to serve in this corps for six months, many reenrolled for up to two years. Many corps members enlisted in the U.S. military when the nation became involved in World War II. In spite of ongoing practices of discrimination, the need for work pushed African Americans toward enlisting. Their service in the U.S. military marked a period of significant economic progress for the African American community.

The 1940s also marked the beginning of what some scholars term the "Second Great Migration."[19] During this period approximately 1.5 million African Americans moved from the rural South to urban areas in the northern, midwestern, and western regions of the United States. This migration was the beginning of African Americans becoming more urban than their white counterparts. It also marked the primary employment shifts from agricultural labor to industrial labor in urban centers. While migration patterns reduced the agricultural labor force of African Americans in the South, this was a time when they experienced a relative increase in economic prosperity.[20]

As African Americans migrated to urban centers, farming became more mechanized. This technology shifted African American labor in South Carolina to textile manufacturing.[21] In fact the employment rate of African Americans was a stable fraction of total employment between 1940 and 1965.[22] As manufacturing jobs increased, African American jobs grew proportionately.[23]

In the era between the mid-1930s to the 1950s, the educational gap between black and white schools dramatically narrowed.[24] These gains in educational quality resulted in an increase in wage earnings for African Americans.[25] African Americans knew the importance of quality education, having taken advantage of opportunities to better themselves from the early 1870s,[26] and they took extraordinary efforts to pursue quality education. In 1948 South Carolina's first case challenging discrimination regarding inequities in educational quality and access was filed in Clarendon County. As was the case throughout the South, there were parallel social institutions, including schools; there were schools for white children and schools for African American children. These schools also had parallel, and inequitable, funding structures. The state's per-pupil expenditure for white students during this era was $111, while it was $50 for African American students. Teacher salaries were just as disparate. The average teacher salary was $2,057 for whites and $1,414 for African American teachers.[27] These issues were at the forefront of the NAACP protests and legal confrontations (see "Isaiah DeQuincey Newman," "The NAACP Years," and "A Vision for Change").

While this information was well known by African Americans, their initial request of the state was to provide some support for the transportation needs of their children, as many traveled up to ten miles to school.[28] The state provided transportation for white children but not for African American children. African American families collectively purchased two school buses and requested some support in the purchase of gas and maintenance for these buses (also known as *Pearson v. Clarendon County*), but to no avail. As a result the state NAACP convinced Henry and Eliza Briggs to file a federal lawsuit (known as *Briggs v. Elliott*) not only challenging the transportation needs of African American children but also requesting the desegregation of publicly funded schools. This case morphed into the more well-known 1954 *Brown v. Board of Education* of Topeka, Kansas.[29]

Equitable access to education also affected employment opportunities for African Americans in South Carolina. High schools in the state offered courses that prepared students to enter the workforce upon graduation. However, these course offerings were impacted by the parallel educational system described earlier. The curricula have been described in the following way:

> When the Rosenwald Fund sought to provide financial support for black high schools in the South during the 1920s and 1930s, the fund sponsored a series of surveys of "Negro jobs" in various cities, so as to adapt the curricula to the jobs actually available. In place after place the response indicated that there were no black jobs for which a high-school education would be useful. Thus, black schools typically did not offer training in such subjects as stenography, accounting, bookkeeping, printing, or typing. The fund's curriculum expert acknowledged: "If commercial courses were offered in the negro school there would no doubt be tremendous pressure to get into them and the only result would be keen disappointment for everyone."[30]

The black high school in the textile center of Greenville, South Carolina, excluded education on textiles entirely. So while there were efforts to provide education to African American children, it was clearly not equitable access to necessary training for economic advancement. Given that South Carolina's employment practices were heavily influenced by the social mores of the times, Newman saw this as a major area of concern. Additionally the public schools in some ways continue to maintain a strict social structure of apartheid. The fight for equal access to educational opportunities was and is an effort to access economic opportunities.

Another issue related to economic access through a quality education was that 10.5 percent of African American South Carolinians ages twenty-five and older had no formal education, as compared to 2.6 percent of whites. In addition 12 percent of African Americans had some high school education and 5 percent had some college education, compared to white South Carolinians at 49 percent and 25 percent respectively.[31] With the inequitable curricula in South Carolina high schools, a relatively small number of African Americans attained levels of educational access equal to those of whites, ensuring that African Americans would remain at the lowest levels of the socioeconomic ladder (see the conclusion).

A Time of Transition: 1960–1970

The 1960s and 1970s made up a time of transition and change for the United States. The country was in turmoil exacerbated by increasing race relations. It was in this context that Reverend Newman became the field director of the NAACP (see "Isaiah DeQuincey Newman" and "Leadership in Black and White"). In 1954 the U.S. Supreme Court decided that public schools were to be desegregated with the accompanying funding necessary to implement this ruling. This ruling influenced the subsequent banning of discriminatory employment practices, voting rights, and access to housing, public accommodations, and other social structures characteristic of the Jim Crow South.

The NAACP was instrumental in these progressive efforts. Since the organization's inception in 1910, the NAACP has fought three forms of racial oppression: 1) the disenfranchisement of black voters; 2) the inferior education of blacks; and 3) the denial of civil liberties. This organization indefatigably fought for more than half a century to keep these issues at the forefront of American policy makers' decisions. This was done through the use of skillful attorneys, such as Nathan Margold, a white who challenged the constitutionality of "separate but equal" policies, and Charles Houston, a Harvard-educated attorney who established the legal department of the NAACP in 1935. Working cooperatively with those attorneys were social scientists such as W. E. B. Du Bois. In a keynote address at the fifty-first annual convention of the NAACP in St. Paul, Minnesota, in June 1960, Robert Weaver, then chair of the board of directors, described how this early planning was instrumental in the implementation of desegregation efforts post-1954: "There were always three ingredients: an organization led brilliantly in my day by James Weldon Johnson, Walter White, and Roy Wilkins; a public relations program which effectively articulated the issues and presented them within the framework of the American ideal; and a great source of legal, research, and writing talent which has kept the cause of equality in the minds and in the hearts of most of our citizens. Backing up and supporting these three resources are some three hundred thousand members who function through over 1,800 local units in 45 states and the District of Columbia."[32]

Weaver went on to describe how this force of organizational history and robust membership served as the foundation for socially progressive efforts of the time. Beginning in the 1950s the labor participation rates in South Carolina took an interesting shift. During this time the African American labor participation rate became lower than that of whites. The state unemployment rate for African American males was 4 percent compared to 2.7 percent for white males. The unemployment rate for African American females was 5 percent compared to 3.2 percent for white females (see the conclusion).[33] The unemployment rates were higher among African Americans in urban areas than for those in rural areas,[34] partially due to the increase of the minimum wage from seventy-five cents to one dollar. Employers were unwilling to pay the increased wage to African Americans in urban areas.[35] At the same time the unemployment rate of urban African American males may be due to the increased institutionalization of this population in the county jails and state prisons.[36] Jobs held by African Americans continued to be concentrated in the least desirable sectors of employment, such as agricultural and domestic labor. Jim Crow laws restricted small business ownership among African Americans.

During the 1960s, the period of Newman's activism, African Americans saw a relative increase in economic status.[37] There was movement from the "traditional sectors into operative and craftsman jobs concentrated in manufacturing."[38] African Americans moved from rural, farming occupations to urban centers.[39] As a result African Americans accounted for a quarter of the wage growth in the South, although it is important to note that African American income was significantly less than comparable white income. Scholars have suggested several possible explanations for this relative growth: antidiscriminatory policies, equal access to education, and economic demands. It is important to note, however, that the quality of life was dismal for black Carolinians living in rural South Carolina (see "A Vision for Change"). This sector of the population was a major concern for Newman, not only as director of the RRCDP but also as NAACP field director.

The passage of antidiscriminatory policies facilitated the improved economic status of African Americans in South Carolina. Title VII of the Civil Rights Act of 1964 prohibits employment discrimination based on race, color, religion, gender, or national origin. This act established the Equal Employment Opportunity Commission (EEOC) and also generated protest in South Carolina from the NAACP. Executive Order 11246, commonly referred to as Affirmative Action, requires that employers of federal contractors and subcontractors take affirmative action to ensure equal access to employment opportunities for qualified applicants. In general this package of employment policy directly impacted the economic status of African Americans. Although African Americans were increasingly employed in government and other nontraditional sectors, this was not the case in South Carolina. This was reflected in the list of demands concerning more equitable employment opportunities in governmental organizations and in white-collar jobs made by the South Carolina NAACP under Newman's leadership. With the dismantling of segregation, the dual wage structure characteristic of Jim Crow policies was abolished, so the wage gap between African Americans and whites for similar occupations was reduced, although never equal.[40]

Another explanation for the relative economic growth of African Americans may be the limited social policies and practices regarding the provision of greater access to quality education.[41] Despite the growing realization of the importance of human capital and its impact on overall economic prosperity in the state, this recognition was not being translated in an appreciative way for its African American citizenry. Newman believed as well that the more educated the workforce, the more skilled labor available, resulting in high-quality production of goods and services. In addition Newman was convinced that as African Americans began to realize their political influence through the power of the vote, they would have greater access to employment. Further he believed that this political influence would result in increased demands for access to employment opportunities, such as the increased hiring of African American teachers.[42]

Newman's and the NAACP's influence on the employment sector can also be seen in the textile industry. In this regard the state realized the rising cost of discrimination in tight labor markets, particularly those associated with increased industrialization.[43] Textiles were South Carolina's major industry. With the advent of the EEOC, textile manufacturers were closely monitored for discriminatory employment practices.[44] More than 140 charges of wage and employment discrimination were filed against textile firms in the Carolinas in 1965. Subsequently government contracts with these companies were withdrawn for a brief period in 1968 due to noncompliance with Executive Order 11246.[45] These sanctions helped the state to weigh the costs of discrimination against the benefit of market competition and demand.[46]

Contemporary Economic Policies and Employment Practices

After this era of increased economic gains among African Americans in South Carolina, a downward trend began. As a result of increased parental expectations that African American children would complete their formal education, entry into and continued participation in the labor force among African American teens, particularly males, declined significantly.[47] This was most apparent in urban areas of the state. African Americans were more likely than their white counterparts to work in unsafe, low-paying, and low-prestige occupations requiring the lowest amount of education and specialized training. These occupations were often difficult, dangerous, and unpleasant.[48]

Quality of education resurfaced as a demarcated factor in economic gains. Students in high-poverty rural communities were more likely to have inequitable access to educational opportunities. For example high-poverty, rural school districts were usually predominantly African American. These school districts spent significantly less on resources and had fewer resources than wealthier school districts (see Bud Ferillo, *Corridor of Shame: The Neglect of South Carolina Rural Schools*). Furthermore these school districts had more difficulty in recruiting and retaining highly qualified teachers.[49] This has had a significant impact on the available occupations for African Americans from rural, high-poverty communities. They are more likely to have low-skill, low-wage employment. Given this forecast of the quality of life for many African American families and children, it is understandable why Newman was concerned about educational progress in South Carolina. When he campaigned for the senate in 1983, he based his campaign on educational improvement and environmental protection. When he reflected on the impact of the movement on South Carolina's educational system during his tenure, he said, "I consider the schools of South Carolina now as being desegregated. Of course, there are pockets of segregation remaining which could be wiped out if administrators and local boards can summon enough temerity to do the job. But those are exceptions rather than the rule."[50] Newman went on to commend Richland School District One for its attempts at desegregating the district. However, he noted that though the job had not been done perfectly in School District One or anywhere else in South Carolina, he thought that District One had essentially done a good job.

Summary and Conclusion

It seems clear from the foregoing and current developments in South Carolina that in order to realize the goals of the civil rights movement and Newman's vision for a strong educational system, the state must focus on increasing the quality of public education for all of its students. This would entail equitable funding, especially in high-poverty school districts, for improvements such as facilities and technology. Additionally the state must engage in purposeful economic development strategies that promote access to employment opportunities, including the promotion of small business ownership by African Americans. It would be imperative that the legislature hold firm to affirmative action policies that ensure that qualified applicants are given equal access to employment opportunities. Additionally the minimum wage should be raised to reflect a living wage, so as to support the upward mobility of all citizens, including African Americans.

Notes

1. Newby, *Black Carolinians.*
2. Ibid.
3. Ruef and Fletcher, "Legacies of American Slavery"; Blackman, *Slavery by Another Name.*
4. Newby, *Black Carolinians.*
5. Kirby, "The Southern Exodus."
6. Meier, *Negro Thought.*
7. Beck and Tolnay, "The Killing Fields of the Deep South."
8. Hutchinson, *Betrayed*; Sitkoff, *A New Deal for Blacks.*
9. Smith and Welch, "Black Economic Progress."
10. Charles S. Johnson, "How Much."
11. "Billon Dollar Bug War," *New York Times,* April 2, 1922.
12. Davie and Derthick, "Race and Social Welfare Policy."
13. Bigger, *The Great Depression,* 165.
14. Ruef and Fletcher, "Legacies of American Slavery."
15. Bigger, *The Great Depression,* 13.
16. Salmand, *The Civilian Conservation Corps.*
17. Gower, "The Struggle of Blacks."
18. Ibid.
19. Bontemps and Conroy, *They Seek a City*; Hamilton, "The Negro Leaves the South"; Shin, "Effects of Migration."
20. Lemann, *The Promised Land.*
21. Wright, "The Economic Revolution."

22. Freeman, "Political Power"; Smith and Welch, "Black Economic Progress"; Welch, "Catching Up."

23. Wright, "The Economic Revolution."

24. Boozer, Krueger, and Wolkon, "Race and School Quality"; Smith and Welch, "Black Economic Progress."

25. Liu, Mulvey, and Hsieh, "Effects of Educational Expenditures."

26. William Edward Burghardt Du Bois, "Some Efforts of Negro Americans for Their Own Social Betterment," paper presented at the third annual conference for the study of the Negro problems, Atlanta, Ga., 1898; Du Bois, "The Talented Tenth"; William Edward Burghardt Du Bois, "Some Efforts of Negroes for Social Betterment," paper presented at the fourteenth annual conference for the study of the Negro problems, Atlanta, Ga., 1909.

27. Quint, *Profile in Black and White.*

28. DeLaine, *Briggs v. Elliott.*

29. Thompson, "Equal Education Opportunity."

30. Anderson, *The Education of Blacks*; Wright, "The Civil Rights Revolution."

31. Swinton, "The Economic Impact."

32. Weaver, "The NAACP Today."

33. U.S. Census Bureau, *U.S. Census of Population: 1950.*

34. Swinton, "The Economic Impact."

35. Margo and Finegan, "The Decline"; Quint, *Profile in Black and White*; Welch, "Catching Up"; Wright, "The Economic Revolution."

36. Swinton, "The Economic Impact."

37. Wright, "The Civil Rights Revolution."

38. Heckman and Payner, "Determining the Impact."

39. Donohue and Heckman, "Continuous versus Episodic Change"; Heckman and Payner, "Determining the Impact," 139.

40. Ibid.; Swinton, "The Economic Impact."

41. Smith and Welch, "Black Economic Progress"; Margo and Finegan, "The Decline."

42. Welch, "Catching Up."

43. Wright, "The Economic Revolution"; Donohue and Heckman, "Continuous versus Episodic Change."

44. Freeman, "Political Power."

45. Wright, "The Economic Revolution"; Wright, "The Civil Rights Revolution."

46. Margo and Finegan, "The Decline."

47. Swinton, "The Economic Impact."

48. Welch, "Catching Up"; Thompson, "Equal Education Opportunity."

49. Swinton, "The Economic Impact."

50. Page, "New Role for Newman."

Narratives

DeQuincey Newman Remembered

As you live, believe in life! Always human beings will live and progress to greater, broader and fuller life. The only possible death is to lose belief in this truth simply because the great end comes slowly, because time is long.

W. E. B. Du Bois, farewell message to his wife, dated June 26, 1957

This collection of thirteen personal narratives about Isaiah DeQuincey Newman provides a diverse mixture of voices that paints an informative, moving, and sometimes passionate collage of the challenges, triumphs, and small and large everyday acts of courage in living. It has been said that when memory speaks, as it does through these narratives, it tells a powerful truth that comes to have more influence than historical truth. The power of narratives is that they situate the people who are their focal points in their cultural contexts and allow the narrators to bring into play the intricacies of time, place, and event from a very personal perspective.

It is possible that the reader of these narratives may experience some redundancy across these thirteen powerful recollections. This was also the experience of the editor as she interviewed, taped, transcribed, or edited the narratives. However, it is important to note that this is the power and beauty in narratives. It is an important indicator of truth telling when the story lines converge into recognizable patterns across narratives.

These narratives reflect the vitality and moral energies that directed Newman's vision and action as an advocate for change. In many ways these narratives reflect the sum total of what these contributors believe in general about life, being, existence, and relationships, but more specifically about Newman in the context of these remembrances.

Gloria Blackwell (Rackley)

My work and involvement in the civil rights movement might have been formed and born from the same force as Reverend Newman's because I too was a South Carolinian, a native of South Carolina, and a Methodist. Also my mother was the daughter of a Methodist minister—just as DeQuincey Newman was the son of a Methodist minister.

Newman was an interesting figure and had a most distinguished and arresting voice. He spoke slowly and clearly. We used to say it would take him maybe thirty minutes to say "Good morning." To my mother he would say, "How do you do, Mrs. Blackwell?" It was as though nothing else in the world mattered. His entire focus was on greeting the person. Although he was a very very handsome man, there was nothing about him that seemed pampered. You wouldn't think of him as someone who stood in the mirror and did anything to himself. He seemed comfortable and casual with himself and his surroundings. It was not until his funeral that I realized the impact he had on so many people's lives. I noticed all of those people who kept coming in throngs and all of them saying how important he was in their lives, the tremendous impact he had on them and the direction they chose, and the strengths that they had because of him. I had thought almost up until that moment that our friendship was unique, but I realized that the way I experienced him was exactly the way he was with everyone. It was amazing, almost deflating, but at the same time so marvelous to know that this was really the miracle of his character and personality that he could make everyone feel special.

In retrospect, I remember meeting DeQuincey Newman the fall when my mother decided to prepare me for college. I was admitted to Claflin at the age sixteen and was under the tutelage of Trinity Methodist Church, where Reverend Newman was the pastor and Mrs. Newman was the first lady of the church. I didn't stay at Claflin long; I married and went away with my husband. My husband went into the navy; however, I later returned to Claflin and graduated. Reverend Newman and Mrs. Newman were still there. DeQuincey's being selected as the pastor at Trinity was viewed as an accomplishment. Although there was not a great deal of money in the appointment, the appointment itself carried prestige and importance.

Some people question Newman's movement from the church to the NAACP. However, as he explained it, he wasn't leaving the church—the church was in the street already. In his way of thinking he was simply following the dictates of the church to the streets where the people were, where the activity was. He thought that this was where Christian leadership needed to be. He was ideally suited for this role. Sometimes you can see the hand of God working in earthly ways. I believe that it was the hand of God directing Newman in his role as NAACP field director. DeQuincey knew every nook and cranny in South Carolina, and he knew people in all of those places. He had the quality of knowing people very well. Wherever he went, he could easily persuade people to become involved. All he needed to say was, "Could I depend on your support?" He knew how to organize the entire state for the kind of help that we needed so that the civil rights movement, a movement that was totally professional in the 1960s, could achieve its goals.

I would guess that a major challenge for Newman was being equipped to meet the difficulties that came with his role as NAACP field director. However, it's important to remember the significant role that Mrs. Newman played in assuring that her husband successfully accomplished his goals. Mrs. Newman was well equipped to serve as the secretary to the field director. DeQuincey had to have a well-run office and be able on a regular and ongoing basis to communicate effectively with the NAACP national office. This was no small task for his wife, who also had a child by that time to care for. Mrs. Newman is to be commended for being able to do all those things effectively and efficiently.

I can recall DeQuincey's love for Scrabble playing. Scrabble playing was a centerpiece at the meeting of the steering committee of the Orangeburg freedom movement. This committee worked closely with Newman and the NAACP and was very effective in bringing change to the racist practices in Orangeburg. Members of the steering committee included James Sulton, Reverend Matthew W. McCollum, John Brunson, Grace Palmer, and many others.

It is also important to acknowledge Newman's role as a state senator. I believe that he was most deserving of the recognition as the first black senator since Reconstruction. He didn't accept that office for any self-glory; he did it because he knew that it was important to take advantage of the opportunity that had been presented to us. There was nobody who had been there before who could step into that job the way he did. There was never anything small about DeQuincey. He was a visionary, and he was something rare. He was a

Christian. He lived the Christian life principles. The person who gave the eulogy at his funeral kept saying that he was the kind of person who walked humbly, who loved mercy and believed in justice. And he really did believe in a just and peaceful world. He was never a braggadocio, although one might say that he dressed in a somewhat flamboyant manner. For example, he wore those interesting bow ties and a special kind of hat. And yet his appearance was always modest. He was well read but was able to speak with everyone. He never spoke above anyone's head. Anyone could converse with him about anything.

DeQuincey was truly a son of South Carolina, a wonderful composite of what South Carolina could be. He lived up to his opportunities and was a wonderful role model. Using his life and accomplishments as a prism, we are able to see black people more clearly, the church more broadly, and human strength and character at their best. I'm very glad that he lived, and that I had the great good fortune to know and work with him.

Donald L. Fowler

Few people younger than fifty would recognize the name I. DeQuincey Newman, aka Deek, Dr. Newman, Senator Newman, Reverend Newman—and this is unfortunate, for not to know him or know about this wonderful man is not to fully know one of the most challenging, mean, exciting, rewarding, and progressive periods of our state's history. No single individual did more to guide South Carolina through its most critical, tension ridden, and transformative period in the twentieth century than I. D. Newman.

Many remember I. D. Newman because he was the first African American elected to the South Carolina Senate in the modern era. He was also one of the first African Americans to head a significant division within South Carolina's economic development agency. He was a highly respected minister and leader in the South Carolina Conference of the United Methodist Church. He was also secretary of the South Carolina Conference of Branches of the National Association for the Advancement of Colored People. All of these things describe what he did, and they are important but not as important as who he was.

Reverend Newman, as I always addressed him, was first and foremost the quintessential Christian gentleman. I use the term "Christian" intentionally because his behavior was always motivated and permeated by a commitment to put the interests of others ahead of his own. He truly believed that we should love our neighbors (and our enemies) as we love ourselves. He was always polite, even humble, and considerate of others. Even when people treated him with a lack of respect, he never retaliated in kind.

Reverend Newman was very smart. Not only did he know a lot about a lot of things (his mind comprehended expansive volumes of information and facts), but he also had an exceptional understanding of people and what motivated them. He was a near genius in being able to get people to do the right thing, even when they were not fully aware of why they were doing what they were doing.

People trusted Reverend Newman—even those who sometimes opposed his aims and goals. Everyone knew that his word was his bond. In light of the many delicate matters he treated in his time, these qualities of trust and creditability were indispensable.

All of these attributes are noteworthy and important—for anyone. Because of the role that Reverend Newman played as a leader of the NAACP in the 1950s and 1960s, they were absolutely necessary. These two decades were difficult for South Carolina. During these twenty years our state was transformed from a segregated to an integrated society—at least in legal terms. These years were marked by tension between blacks and whites. This transition was wrenching for many people—stiff, determined resistance marked the attitudes of many whites; absolute heroic determination was characteristic of many blacks. There were demonstrations, sit-ins, court cases, and tense moments over days and weeks. Hostile confrontations threatened violence in many areas of South Carolina.

Reverend Newman was always at the forefront of these events. He was a crusader for justice, equal rights, and opportunities. He exposed himself to danger and was threatened personally with severe physical harm. Yet he never wavered, nor did he ever do anything to precipitate violence on either side; just the opposite: he always urged people to be calm. This was his genius.

He was explicitly trusted by the struggling black community and, in an intriguing way, by white leaders—governors, mayors, sheriffs, and church leaders among others. This trust—this creditability—that he enjoyed on the part of leaders and rank-and-file people on both sides probably saved South Carolina from many violent, even deadly events. Reverend Newman, with his wisdom, goodwill, judgment, and sensitivity, was able to pour oil on many troubled waters during these troubled years.

In many instances Reverend Newman was the indispensable link between the black community and the white community. This unique role led to great progress for African American citizens without the violence that attended this struggle in other southern states.

It is not an exaggeration to assert that his wisdom and leadership—his ability to talk with credibility to both sides in these very difficult times—saved the state and its people many violent occurrences and led to a more equitable society for everyone.

Reverend Newman's judgment and his understanding of people enabled him to push and push hard for reform, but not to push so hard as to create diminishing returns, hurt people, or set back the cause of human rights.

Reverend Newman combined great courage with unfailing judgment. More than any other person, public or private, his work saved South Carolina much violence, and yet it hastened the day when African Americans achieved full legal rights.

All South Carolinians owe Reverend, Senator, Dr. Newman great thanks, tribute, and gratitude. As a great poet once wrote, "That which he did, he did out of a good conscience and a common concern for all."

Robert E. McNair

The Reverend I. DeQuincey Newman is one of South Carolina's greatest heroes, and his legacy has been a better South Carolina for all her citizens. It is so important that we preserve and perpetuate his heritage and his legacy for all South Carolinians, present and future.

He always thought of the struggle for racial equality as a matter of the spirit—as well as a social and political concern. Vernon Jordan, one of his protégés, who became a major political figure in our country, always said that he "listened carefully when Reverend Newman prayed because he felt that when he prayed, God listened."

In many ways I. DeQuincey Newman never left the ministry. He was a deeply devout man who considered the state of South Carolina to be his ministry—and the public forum to be his pulpit. His political agenda of fairness and equal opportunity mirrored his Christian message of love and human compassion. He helped to establish the Orangeburg branch of the NAACP and served with that organization in many roles, including as field director from 1960 to 1969—one of the most difficult and turbulent periods of our history, and one with which I am most familiar.

He was a gentle, patient man who believed in negotiation rather than confrontation. He was a man with great skills of diplomacy and political ingenuity. He was not one to make demands of people, but rather negotiated and compromised and squeezed every ounce of progress out of every pound of opportunity. If that meant setting up a meeting at Owens Field or some other quiet location at midnight—and that was sometimes how we'd meet—then that's how we did things. He was always willing to talk and became a trusted confidant of mine, of Senator Hollings, and of Governor John West, among many others.

Yet for all his politeness, he was willing to actively challenge the status quo. He was a tenacious advocate for simple justice in race relations, and he was a man of raw human courage and determination. He was a man in his fifties leading younger people less than half his age into demonstrations and protests. He was a father figure to many—one who led by example and who led by the sheer force of his own personal commitment.

Those of us who worked with Reverend Newman knew he valued above all things the power of communication. He believed nothing could be solved if people weren't talking to each other. He and I agreed that communication was more than just conversation—it was keeping people apprised of different angles and forces at play. We worked together not only to find solutions, but also to let each other know where potential trouble spots were. His involvement in the civil rights movement paved the way for much of South Carolina's progress during turbulent times. He was elected to the South Carolina Senate in a special election in 1983, becoming the first African American since Reconstruction to serve in that body. He loved that one of his oldest and most powerful foes—Senator Marian Gressette, earlier known as "Mr. Segregation"—asked to have his picture taken with him and welcomed him to the senate as a colleague. How times have changed since he shined Senator Brown's shoes!

In remembering and honoring Reverend Newman, I believe he would want us to recall that his cause was not simply working on behalf of minorities and all their rights through opportunity and social justice, but working for all South Carolinians. He believed that by making South Carolina a better place for minorities, it would be a better place for everyone. I believe he would want us to remember that if we're not moving forward, then we are in danger of slipping backward. I believe his message today would be the same as it was through all his life: Have hope, keep the faith, and bring energy and courage to the good fight.

Reverend Newman left behind a legacy of ministering to all those who were hurting—hurting because of segregation and lack of opportunity, hurting because of poverty and disadvantage, hurting because of illness and age. His dedication and determination never hid behind his kind and gentle spirit.

By passing on and bringing to life his dreams, his values, and his ideals, we can make those dreams possible for generations to come—just as Reverend Newman would want.

Jerome Noble

My acquaintance with Reverend Newman began during my tenure in South Carolina state government during the late 1970s and early 1980s. At that time he was the director of rural development in Governor Richard Riley's administration.

Six years prior to meeting Reverend Newman, I enrolled in Massachusetts Institute of Technology (MIT) in September 1974 to complete my graduate studies in transportation. Dr. Tom Jones, a former president of South Carolina State University, was a vice chancellor at MIT. Dr. Jones had a way of discovering students enrolled at MIT who were from South Carolina. Once we met, my charge was to meet with him at least once a month to monitor my progress over a two-year period. When I graduated, not knowing exactly what I was going to do, it was Dr. Jones who helped me to focus and find my grounding. He reminded me that there were a lot of exciting things going on in the field of transportation back home in South Carolina. At the time, I was married and we were new parents of our first child.

Returning to Columbia, I took a position with the city in its new Economic Development Office as an economic development analyst. After nearly two years in this position, I received a call from a local businessman saying that there was an opportunity for me to join the South Carolina Department of Highways and Public Transportation. This was an opportunity to get back into my field. As the director overseeing various pilot programs in mostly rural transportation, I one year later was appointed executive assistant, replacing the previous executive assistant who had moved over to the new administration of Governor Richard Riley. This was an exciting, intensive time of change in this new Interagency Council, which was established in 1976 by the legislative to be adviser to the Department of Highways and Public Transportation in the undertaking of various pilot programs and research demonstration projects.

As the Department of Highways and Public Transportation continued to evolve, Reverend Newman was no longer the director of rural development. In 1983 he was elected state senator. There were advocates for as well as opponents against the proposed legislation to create a separate Department of Transportation. Senator Isadore Lourie chaired the Senate Transportation

Committee, which included Reverend Newman and Senator Tom Smith, who was based in Florence, South Carolina, and was very familiar with transportation issues. The other two members were located in Sumter and Beaufort/Jasper Counties. The Department of Highways and Public Transportation's board of commissioners was uncertain about the proposed change.

Reverend Newman, of course, supported this legislation. One day I got a message to come over to the senate chamber. While I had been accustomed to making testimonies about rural transportation and urban transportation to various legislative committees, I don't recall ever before having been on the senate floor. Reverend Newman, who referred to me as Brother Noble, told me that he wanted me to join him on the senate floor around noon. We sat in this legislative session from noon of that day when I joined him until the wee hours in the morning, when that legislation was finally passed. He advocated, Senator Lourie advocated, Governor Riley sent messages to the senate—it was so awesome. And the bill did pass.

As I worked with Senator Newman on more expanded transit pilot programs around the state, he would always ask, "Brother Noble, is there any legislation you need us to include in the Appropriation Bill?" Once we advised him what needed to occur, it was taken care of. When I left state government in 1995, I felt a real sense of accomplishment in that we had expanded mass transit services to the general public from twelve counties to twenty-four.

Perhaps the last major initiative that I witnessed in the department occurred in 1987 over the need for more revenue. At the time Governor Riley and others were no longer in office. Governor Carroll Campbell, who succeeded Governor Riley, was the incumbent. The Department of Highways and Public Transportation lobbied for an increase in the gas tax, and they coached me about supporting their effort. Of course, that was very difficult for me, but as an employee of that department, heading up one of its three or four divisions, I consulted with the leadership at the local level about what transit could get out of this deal. Ultimately we came to an understanding that we would support a gas tax increase, and so did many of our supporters in the General Assembly. The senate and the house provided that a portion of the increase would be earmarked to improve and extend mass transit throughout the state of South Carolina. The legislation passed. For the first time mass transit was provided with gas tax money for the purpose of helping local areas operate, manage, and provide transportation.

It is important to remember that the focus on mass transportation, especially in the rural areas, started under Reverend Newman's leadership with the Office of Rural Development. After he left Rural Development and became senator, I began working closely with his protégés Wallace Brown, Karen Grant, and others in expanding the transportation needs of the state and learning more about the rural transportation program. The work that I had done in South Carolina took me to the national level as part of a White House initiative. In that capacity I was on an advisory panel looking at rural transportation needs across the state. I had initially been invited to the White House when Jimmy Carter was president to provide technical assistance at the national level on the rural transportation initiative. It was during that time that I learned that Senator Newman's health was failing.

One cannot forget people like Reverend Newman, who played a vitally important part in helping to shape and improve impoverished conditions in South Carolina. There was only one overriding source that caused the naysayers to come around. When you saw Senator Newman take the mike and say, in so many words, that this is vitally needed in South Carolina, his colleagues in that senate chamber responded. There were others who played equally important parts, but it was on the strength of his words, on his request, that I think the difference was made in transit legislation becoming law or at least being enacted by that body, such as on that night that I described earlier. It was an interesting and powerful eye-opener to me as a young man growing up in South Carolina.

Some of the things that I sensed Reverend Newman wanted and advocated for were not newsworthy to those who were listening to what he had to say. They may have thought, now is not the time, but it *was* the time. He was right on task when he chose to be the spokesman for rural South Carolina. What he brought to the table through his quietly spoken words unquestionably was needed and necessary. He was convinced that it was the right time for the transportation question. He was a visionary. He was always willing to listen, and he made you feel as though your concern was important and worthy of his full attention. He was not a detail person. He left the details up to you. He wanted me to stay away from technical jargon. He was a person who gave me strength. In that environment I needed all of the strength that I could have.

You had to understand the minds and attitudes at that time and probably today within the Department of Transportation. There had been some reservations about whether or not mass transportation should have been housed in the Department of Highways and Public Transportation. Some felt that it would be there and sit in a corner and not do anything that should be done, or that it would be controlled by Highways and Public Transportation and would not provide the services that were envisioned. My role was to keep things moving forward because I had to think about those who helped make this a reality, and I would rather lose by doing than allow failure to set in by doing nothing. It was the right time. With Senator Newman's support and through my job, I had an opportunity to work throughout the state of South Carolina, particularly in the rural areas. Driving on weekends in the state car into the Beaufort and Jasper County areas, I witnessed some of the most deplorable conditions imaginable. These sights would bring tears to my eyes and made me want to work even harder when I returned to the office on Monday. In many ways I felt and experienced what, perhaps, Senator Newman already knew.

Those of us who had an opportunity to interact with Reverend Newman learned through him. He was a deep thinker, calculating and determined in his actions. In my early thirties I wanted things to happen now. He had a grasp, certainly a better grasp of the political and the business environments in South Carolina than most people in the state. When it came to the unfolding of major developments, he demonstrated patience. He gave deep thought and care in his words to his colleagues. He was a man, a statesman of principles. When he said he would lend support, I can say that there was never a moment in those years in South Carolina state government in working, even as briefly as I did, with Senator I. DeQuincey Newman when I was ever disappointed or not supported.

Matthew J. Perry, Jr.

This statement serves to capture my reflection on the life and contributions of the Reverend I. DeQuincey Newman, whom I had the pleasure to know and work with for over two decades.

I. DeQuincey Newman was born at a time when conditions in our state, certainly from the sociological perspective, were not good. Let's think back for a few moments. The Constitutional Convention of 1895 had passed approximately fifteen years prior to his birth. It's important to note that during the course of that convention many of the rights that the citizens of South Carolina had come to enjoy following the Emancipation Proclamation of 1865 were effectively eradicated. You may also recall that the Congress of the United States of America approved several amendments to our Constitution: the Thirteenth (abolish slavery, 1865), Fourteenth (provide citizenship, equal protection, and due process of the law, 1868), and Fifteenth (right to vote, 1870) Amendments. It was intended that these amendments protect and establish black freedoms. During this period some of the former slaves began to enjoy their freedom. They especially enjoyed the right of franchise and managed to get elected in various positions in government and to enjoy the fruits of citizenship. However, that was not to last long. The beginning of the end to this freedom occurred in 1877. There was a compromise between the presidential candidates and the electors of three states: South Carolina, Louisiana, and Florida. The leadership of both parties in these states came together and decided to give the bulk of the electoral votes to the nominees of the Republican Party. It's important to note that Republicans and Democrats of that period were not comparable to members of those two parties today.

The compromise referred to above was that if the electorate gave their votes to the Republican nominee, he would, upon his election, withdraw the federal troops from the South. This action would in turn result in an immediate change in the freedom enjoyed by blacks in the South. White citizens who took a dim view of blacks in certain elected positions proceeded to do all they could to oust black people from these positions, and in many instances violence was used as a form of persuasion to keep black citizens from voting. During this time the Ku Klux Klan (KKK) came into prominence and lynching became rampant. Along with these violent acts, Black Codes and vagrancy laws helped in moving the black community toward complete disenfranchisement. It is also important to note that during this turbulent period, the practice of racial segregation was solidified in every aspect of life in South Carolina. Similar moves were taken in other states.

Following the 1895 Constitutional Convention, the United States Supreme Court decided the important case of *Plessey v. Ferguson*. This case signaled the beginning of the period of "separate but equal" policies. This case served to affirm the separation of the races throughout the United States, especially in the South. The southern United States relied on this decision to maximize the effect of disenfranchisement and the advent of other racial practices, such as lynching and other violent acts.

Consequently at the beginning of the twentieth century all of the black political office holders were driven out of office. A way of life had come into being, a way of life that still exists in some form even today. It was in that climate that I. DeQuincey Newman was born and raised. As a young man he had to exist in the presence of repressive acts against black citizens nationwide. Young I. DeQuincey Newman was among the fortunate and received a good education. He matriculated at Claflin College in Orangeburg and at Clark College and Gammon Theological Seminary in Atlanta. Also he became a builder of churches. He became widely known for the excellent renovation of Trinity Methodist Church in Orangeburg. He viewed his calling as a minister as the means by which he would contribute to the well-being of all people: those who would attend his churches as well as the people of the broader community.

I. DeQuincey Newman was widely revered and respected as a Methodist minister. He was very proud of his calling as a minister. He was also well known because of his dedication to the improvement of the quality of life for all people. It was also in Orangeburg, South Carolina, that he became active and practically singlehandedly built the Orangeburg branch of the NAACP.

My acquaintance with I. DeQuincey Newman began upon my return from serving in World War II. I had commenced my studies at South Carolina State College before I was drafted. When I was discharged in January 1946, I returned to Orangeburg and took up the matter of completing my undergraduate studies. It was during this time that I also learned about a meeting of the Orangeburg branch of the NAACP at one of the local churches. I attended this meeting with some of my friends. There I met and heard a talk by this very important and impressive minister with a deep voice and excellent enunciation. I was immediately impressed with his commitment, intelligence, and zeal, and with the articulate style with which he displayed his leadership abilities.

I eventually enrolled in the South Carolina Law School, which had come into existence as a result of a lawsuit against the University of South Carolina, where black people were not allowed to matriculate. I graduated in 1951. During that time a lawsuit was taking place in Sumter, South Carolina, where a local citizen sued all the members of the NAACP. We were called upon to offer the NAACP a defense. This was my first contact with I. DeQuincey as a client. In 1957 I. DeQuincey was elected as the state NAACP field director, and the first thing he did was to invite me to a meeting. We became colleagues as well as good friends. I observed him challenge the Constitution of the United States in his various leadership roles. He also provided inspiring leadership in the NAACP. This included his protest against the segregated parks of South Carolina as well as other inequities practiced within the state. In his role as NAACP field director, he also encouraged his constituencies to challenge racially segregated schools, theaters, and other programs controlled and operated by state authorities. He believed in human dignity and pressed his views with everyone with whom he came in contact. He challenged people to be good citizens. He urged citizens to register to vote and to participate in elections. He urged them to send their children to schools and obtain an education; he sought to improve the quality of life of all citizens, especially citizens of color.

The 1954 *Brown v. Board of Education* case gave a new legal underpinning to what DeQuincey Newman and other civil rights leaders were advocating for. The decision gave new meaning to the Fourteenth Amendment. Interestingly, following this decision the United States Congress passed the Voting Rights Act. On the basis of these new enactments, the civil rights movement became quite active. Nationally several great movements were going on. This was the beginning of the civil rights movement giving prominence to people such as Martin Luther King, Jr., and Rosa Parks, who refused to give up her seat on a bus in Montgomery, Alabama. (It is important to acknowledge that a year or two prior to the incident with Ms. Parks, a young woman named Sarah Mae Flemming, of South Carolina, had refused to give up her seat on a public bus. Of course, we fought her case and obtained victory on her behalf.) During this time Newman began to press the issue in every corner of the state. The NAACP began to organize student protests against practices that enforced racial segregation in the services they rendered.

DeQuincey Newman found himself advising and giving leadership to students protesting. I can recall the first major student protest that occurred in Orangeburg, South Carolina, where some 360 people were arrested for simply walking down the street peacefully and asking that discrimination conducted against black citizens cease. Newman had this penchant for moving on without the cover of legal advice. He would inquire, "Where are you going to be about 12:00 noon or 1:00?" What I didn't know was that the possibility existed that more than 360 people could be behind bars at that time. In such cases I had to call upon a group of lawyers. After dealing with such an incident in Orangeburg, the next year a similar thing happened in Columbia. An outcome of this stance was the case known as *Edwards v. South Carolina*, recognized as a seminal case and decided by the United States Supreme Court. The Supreme Court overturned the students' conviction for staging a peaceful march in protest of the discrimination of blacks, saying, "The Fourteenth Amendment does not permit a State to make criminal the peaceful expression of unpopular views." Years later I visited DeQuincey Newman on his deathbed. He acknowledged that this case was most meaningful. His fight for peace and justice in South Carolina, including efforts to eliminate the public school system of South Carolina by awarding tuition grants for white parents to send their children to nonsectarian schools, took us into every corner of South Carolina. We indeed persuaded the court to rule that the statute was unconstitutional and at the same time saved the public education system in South Carolina. This was his mark.

It was through Newman's urgings and teachings that we successfully challenged the exclusion of black citizens all across South Carolina. These activities of course originated in the mind and imagination of I. DeQuincey Newman. He deplored the status to which black citizens were relegated. He spoke loudly, clearly, and constantly not only to South Carolina but to the United States as well. His message to those discriminated against was to stand erect and proclaim themselves free citizens with all due rights and privileges.

Newman was seemingly inexhaustible, always with new rivers to cross, new tasks to tackle, new challenges to meet. He lived in the exciting world of anticipation. He lived in the creative world of hope. He went about the business of advocating his views for those without a voice. Eventually, in the early 1980s, his work led to a seat in the South Carolina Senate. That was the time and event that gave us all pride. He devoted his entire life to bettering the lives of all people.

However, by the time he was elected state senator, I. DeQuincey was beginning to show signs of fatigue and battle weariness. Not long after he became state senator, the ravages of age and illness confined him to a wheelchair. However, he never lost his vitality. He was a dignified man. If you came in touch with him, he was always dressed impeccably. In the final analysis, let it be known that he served like no other and did with courage all that he was called upon to do.

Harrison Rearden

I am a life resident of South Carolina, and one of the few who have remained in South Carolina all of my adult life. I view myself as a surrogate son of Reverend Newman.

I built a career in the life insurance business before assuming the role of a public servant. I can recall that fateful day in the spring of 1974, while doing very well in the life insurance business; I was visited unexpectedly by Reverend Newman. During this visit, he spoke of having a vision in which he was directed to speak to me about replacing him in his current position as assistant to the commissioner for the S.C. Department of Social Services (DSS).

It is important to note that during this time the department at the executive level was totally white. The commissioner was Reverend Archie Ellis (who was generally referred to as Dr. Archie Ellis), the pastor of First Baptist Church in downtown Columbia. Dr. Ellis was appointed by Governor Robert E. McNair to head DSS. Archie Ellis viewed DSS as a ministry because its mission was to serve the poor among us. Although it was never acknowledged, according to my observations Newman was appointed as assistant to Archie Ellis to keep the lid on the mounting racial tensions in the state. Given that Newman had broad contact with and the respect of people all across the state, he was viewed by the white establishment as the perfect person for the position. However, by 1974 Newman had decided to move on to the political arena for which I believed he was perfectly suited. I don't think there could have been a better linkage than him between religion, politics, and civil rights. Of course many people may not agree, but I am convinced that religion, politics, and civil rights must come together if people are going to be treated humanely and equally.

I replaced Newman in 1975 as deputy state director of the Department of Social Services. This appointment really changed the face of DSS in state government. This change was not because of me, Harrison Rearden, but because of circumstances, timeliness, and quite frankly appropriateness. There were a lot of eyes on me—or shall I say, a black man in a true executive position in the South Carolina Department of Social Services. Newman also did good work in his role as special assistant to the commissioner. His function was basically public relations and networking. He must also be credited with having paved the way for people like me. I don't know what would have happened to me as a person of color in a predominately white institution had it not been for the prior work of Reverend Isaiah DeQuincey Newman.

In my judgment, one of Newman's greatest accomplishments was his ability to instill confidence in others. As we know, in Newman's days there was an unspoken place where black people were supposed to fit into and stay. Newman raised our vision to levels above that and said "no" to the powers that be. How did he do it? He confronted the enemy face-to-face. He did not put his personal circumstances in front of him. He even had to leave family, friends, and personal aspirations behind at times as he confronted the system and spoke truth to power. I view this as being one of the real highlights of his accomplishments.

In working with Newman in Greenville, South Carolina, in the 1960s, I recall a situation at a restaurant involving a waitress who became unraveled—this establishment didn't know what to do, but they didn't want to serve us either. We waited and waited until finally one of the waiters walked over and said in a low tone, "You know we can't serve you." As I was leading the group, I asked to speak with the manager, who was also the owner. He came out from the back with a meat cleaver in his hand and said, "Don't you guys know we don't serve niggers and dogs in here?" Of course we retorted, "We don't eat them either." The next day this story was front-page news in the local paper.

Newman not only traveled to places such as Greenville to attend NAACP meetings on weekends or whenever they were scheduled; he also traveled all over the state. In my opinion he was a giant of a man. I know in some small sense all that was involved in his role as South Carolina's NAACP field director. However, it is also important to acknowledge what I consider an important or unique strength that Newman possessed, and that is keeping a right relationship with God. Mankind, on the whole, I think, gets sidetracked on this issue. There is a tendency among some of our so-called community leaders to be more interested in pointing out personal accomplishments than truly helping those in need. For example, there were politicians who would come into impoverished communities, particularly when they were running for office, and would promise many things to help the poor, but once the election was won, that was the end of the promises made. There is also a segment of the community whom I don't appreciate, especially when they use racist behavior in the name of God. However, my experience with Reverend Newman affirmed that he dealt equally across the board with all people. I saw him with white people, I saw him with black people, I saw him with poor people, I saw him with powerful people, but I always saw God working in and through him without prejudice.

In my opinion, under Newman's leadership an extraordinary contribution to improving the quality of life of poor people in rural areas was made through the Office of Rural Development. This was a prime example of his sensitivity to the poor. He was instrumental in bringing running water where there was none, and also transportation. Because people in the rural areas didn't have access to transportation, the welfare department was not serving the people. It is sad, however, to admit that not much has changed in some rural communities since the days of Reverend Newman. Today when I am asked about the needs of poor people, my response is that all we need to do is take an inventory of our own homes. Do we have food? Do we have clothes? Do we have a floor in our house? Do we have running water? Do we have electricity? The interesting thing is that this inventory is primarily addressing basic human needs. It was at this level of awareness that Newman anchored his focus and concerns. Overall, Newman's sensitivity for all people was very real. I can also attest to the fact that for a lot of us who have come through the ranks and have been fortunate enough to hold leadership or upwardly mobile positions in society, we are the evidence of Newman's work. He was a giant in the social, spiritual, health, and political arenas.

Richard W. Riley

Reverend Isaiah DeQuincey Newman was a special person and a special friend of mine. We had many experiences together during the challenges of the civil rights movement. I never saw him on the wrong side of a critical issue. Yes, he was my friend and also my mentor—and a great South Carolinian.

Reverend Newman's first mark of leadership was in Orangeburg, where he helped organize that branch of the NAACP. Appreciated by everyone for his calm but effective manner, he quickly moved to the top of South Carolina's NAACP leadership. It was from this platform that he became recognized as a man with a mission—a good man with a good mission.

Reverend Newman later served as the first African American member of the South Carolina Senate. He also was an important adviser to me while I was governor, as well as to Governors Bob McNair and John West and to Senator Fritz Hollings. However, it is probable that I. D. made his greatest contributions to South Carolina while serving as the state field director of the NAACP.

It is hard for many people, especially younger folks, to understand and appreciate how difficult the 1950s and 1960s were for a person in I. D.'s position. He lived in constant physical danger and faced daily death threats. The manner in which he conducted himself as field director of the NAACP—which to I. D. was just an extension of his Christian ministry—caused many conservative white South Carolinians to rethink their positions regarding racial equality. He helped them realize that the time for change had come.

All political leaders of the last half of the twentieth century, including me, owe a debt of deep gratitude to I. D. for his stellar leadership during that time. The citizens of South Carolina should be aware of the enormous contributions he made to the progress of our great state.

Like most of the very small number of African Americans who were politically active in the mid-twentieth century, I. D. was involved in the "Party of Abraham Lincoln." In fact, he was a South Carolina delegate to the national GOP convention in 1956. By the 1960s, though, he perceived that the Democratic Party was more committed to civil rights, and Reverend Newman then became a staunch Democrat. However, he never let politics soften the fervor of his mission. He used his influence *within* the Democratic Party to become one of the clear leaders of our civil rights movement.

A wonderful speaker and a great student of the Bible, Reverend Newman was a beloved and effective preacher. Regardless of other positions he may have held—NAACP field director, adviser to governors and senators, and even his own service as a state senator—he was always a preacher. I heard him speak and preach many times. His audience was always quiet and attentive—obviously moved by his message and his personal commitment. His command and use of the English language were such that the most hardened listener was always affected in some positive way.

When I think of the great leaders of South Carolina during the turbulent 1960s, I always include the Reverend I. DeQuincey Newman high on the list. Those were difficult times, and leaders were tested. The negative forces of segregation were always present. But I. D. never became negative in response. His South Carolina was going to be a state of one people, concerned and interested in each other. Reverend Newman had the courage of his convictions. Ernest Hemingway defined courage as "grace under pressure." That describes I. D. so well. He had that kind of courage—always courteous and kind, but always strong and powerful.

When a vacancy occurred in the Richland County senate delegation as a result of Alex Sanders's election to the South Carolina Court of Appeals in 1983, I. D. decided to run for that senate seat. This surprised many people. He was thought to have very little chance of being elected in an overwhelmingly white district, especially in a special election, which traditionally had low voter turnout. He met with Joe Sapp, his longtime friend and colleague in politics. Assuring I. D. of his support if he decided to run, Joe also advised that he did not believe Reverend Newman could win. He said, "I. D., I just don't believe the time has come yet. I just don't believe the people are ready for a black state senator." Showing his courage—and his sense of humor—I. D. responded, "Joe, I love you like a brother, but I sure am glad you weren't around to advise President Lincoln on the Emancipation Proclamation—you would have told him the people weren't ready yet."

Reverend Newman proved Joe Sapp and all the pundits wrong. He won the election and forever changed South Carolina politics and the South Carolina Senate. But he didn't just change history; he also changed hearts. I witnessed older members of the senate—who previously had been Reverend Newman's avowed enemies—change their views on a number of social issues because of the gentlemanly conduct and diplomacy of Senator I. D. Newman. He was able to effect these changes because he was so well respected by all forty-five of his senate colleagues.

I. D. Newman's tenure in the senate was all too short. He became ill, and life itself became his daily struggle. Being pushed in his wheelchair, Senator Newman came to me in the governor's office and informed me that he was going to retire. I urged him to continue, even though he would miss some legislative sessions. He said to me, "Governor, I have tried to stand for something to the young African Americans of our State. I don't want them to watch from the Senate balcony and see me in my frail and weakened condition." I understood—"grace under pressure." I. D. continued to serve with dignity and remained effective until his last day of service. By the end of his tenure, he was the most beloved member of the senate. I. D.'s senate colleagues recognized his "grace" by voting to hang his portrait in their hallowed chamber—an honor reserved for only a very few in the entire history of the South Carolina Senate, and one richly deserved by the Reverend Senator Isaiah DeQuincey Newman.

Alex Sanders

I. DeQuincey Newman's election to the South Carolina Senate marked the end of an almost century-long period during which African Americans were largely excluded from participation in the democratic process in South Carolina. When he was elected in 1983, no African American had served in the senate since 1887. With the end of the Civil War in 1865 and the enactment of the Thirteenth, Fourteenth, and Fifteenth Amendments to the Constitution, the newly freed slaves as well as African Americans who were previously free were accorded full citizenship. Federal forces stationed in South Carolina after the war, joined by the largely black state militia, rigorously enforced the newly enacted constitutional rights.

With citizenship and the right to vote came the right to hold public office. At that time a majority of South Carolina citizens were African American. They went to the polls and elected African Americans to public offices throughout South Carolina. According to Professor Thomas Holt, who studied under C. Van Woodward at Yale, 487 men were elected to various offices in South Carolina between 1867 and 1876, and more than half were African American. Included among these offices was membership in the South Carolina Senate and House of Representatives. Then came the presidential election of 1876 between Republican Rutherford B. Hayes and Democrat Samuel J. Tilden. The election was the most fiercely contested in the history of the country.

Although Hayes had strong support—and even Mark Twain stumped for him—most people, including Hayes himself, expected the Democrats to win. When the first returns seemed to confirm this, Hayes went to bed, believing he had lost. The popular vote was 4,300,000 for Tilden to 4,036,000 for

Hayes. But the all-important vote in the Electoral College depended upon contested votes in South Carolina, Louisiana, and Florida. If all the disputed electoral votes went to Hayes, he would win, whereas a single vote would elect Tilden.

Months of uncertainty followed. Congress established a commission to decide the dispute. White politicians in South Carolina, Louisiana, and Virginia gave their support to Hayes, based on his pledge to withdraw federal troops from the South. The final electoral vote was Tilden 184, Hayes 185. As the bell on top of Columbia City Hall tolled twelve, signaling the removal of federal troops from the State House, the *Charleston News and Courier* proclaimed that Republican rule was dead, never to be reborn. (Quite obviously, the proclamation later proved somewhat overstated.)

Without the federal troops to enforce the rights of African Americans, white politicians proceeded to reclaim the government of the state. The constitution of 1895 locked out African Americans from participation in the political process. Impediments to voting—including literacy tests, poll taxes, rigorous voter registration requirements, and the requirement of property ownership—eventually disenfranchised thousands of African Americans. By 1902 no African Americans remained in the South Carolina legislature. The legislature—the senate and the house of representatives alike—remained all-white for sixty-eight years.

Fast forward to 1965. Congress enacted the monumental Voting Rights Act of 1965. The act removed the impediments to voting by African Americans. Literacy tests, the poll tax, and the requirement to own property were outlawed. Voter registration was simplified and made more broadly available. Federal poll watchers were brought in to monitor elections. The states were prohibited from changing election laws to discriminate against African Americans. Any changes in the election laws had to be approved in advance by the Justice Department in Washington, D.C. African Americans began to register and vote in significant numbers.

Unsurprisingly, they elected African Americans to public offices throughout South Carolina. Integration of the legislature came about when three African Americans were elected to the house of representatives in the general election of 1970. In the decade that followed, more African Americans were elected to the house. The senate, however, remained all-white through the 1970s and into the 1980s.

Practical considerations made the election of an African American senator difficult. The power of incumbency in the senate was hard to overcome. As election year 1984 approached, no incumbent senator showed any inclination either to retire or to die. There was no "vacancy," so to speak. That's where I came in.

I had been elected to the legislature in 1966 in the first election following the enactment of the Voting Rights Act. My election was wholly unexpected, especially by me. I was young, unknown, and a card-carrying member of both the ACLU and the NAACP. The newly registered African American vote put me over the top by fewer than fifty votes. By 1983 I had served a total of eight years in the S.C. House of Representatives and seven years in the S.C. Senate. I was ready to go on to something else.

I gave notice of my intention to vacate my seat in the senate. Remembering how I had first been elected to the legislature, I made a speech urging that an African American be elected in my place. I. DeQuincey Newman was the natural choice to succeed me. He became the first African American to serve in the S.C. Senate in almost a century. History will surely record that the best thing I ever did in the legislature was to leave.

At the time I. DeQuincey Newman was elected to the state senate, many people—even people of goodwill—did not see any point in having an African American as a member of that body. They were mistaken about that. To be sure, there were at the time a number of enlightened white senators who did their best to represent the needs of their black constituents. But no amount of good intentions on the part of those senators could ever take the place of having I. DeQuincey Newman actually sitting among them. He led the senate from within and in a way no white senator could ever duplicate. He became their conscience, a moral force in their midst, never letting them forget their responsibility to all the people of South Carolina and reminding them of that, sometimes simply by his presence, whenever they forgot.

When I. DeQuincey Newman was elected, Jim Fields was the clerk of the senate. Jim told me about going to see Senator Newman immediately after he was elected to make him aware of the more mundane aspects of his position. Jim told him about the office assigned to him, his secretarial assistance, office supplies, and telephone services—everything he would need to represent his district, consisting of Richland, Fairfield, and Chester Counties.

Jim says he will never forget what Reverend Newman said to him. "You must understand, Mr. Clerk," Newman said, "I will be representing much more than the district from which I was elected." That was very true. Reverend Newman undertook to represent the broadest possible constituency: all the people of South Carolina who needed him—black and white alike—from every nook and cranny of the state and even from beyond her borders. His areas of interest brought forward from his ministry and his work with the civil rights movement were education, housing, medical care, the environment, the aging, and social services in general, particularly in rural areas. The senate committees to which he was assigned fairly reflected his interests. But he did not confine his senate work to these areas. On any given issue he spoke for the last, the least, the lost, and the left out. He provided a voice for those who could not speak for themselves.

Frank Caggiano succeeded Jim Fields as clerk of the senate and held that post throughout DeQuincey Newman's term of service. I asked him to describe how Reverend Newman was received by his fellow senators, coming, as he did, as a stranger to most of them. Without hesitation Frank replied, "Reverend Newman commanded respect." Frank then proceeded to tell me about the first speech Senator Newman made on the floor of the senate. His subject was the compelling needs of children in South Carolina. Children are not always well represented in the legislative process. After all, they can't vote.

DeQuincey Newman told his fellow senators that the needs of children must be their very first priority. He eloquently explained why. The senate is normally a hurly-burly place, with much more talking than listening going on. Frank said he remembers vividly the senate becoming eerily quiet as Newman began to speak. A solemn atmosphere—entirely unusual for the senate—immediately came about, as the senators stopped what they were doing and paid rapt attention to his words.

I. DeQuincey Newman was a great orator, but he did not deal in aphorisms. We judge our leaders the way the Greeks judged their orators—not so much by what they say but by who they are, and we judge who they are by what they have done. On this basis Reverend Newman will always be judged as one of South Carolina's great leaders.

Senator John Land of Calhoun County is one of the senior members of the South Carolina Senate. He served with Senator Newman the whole time Newman was in the senate. I asked Senator Land how he would describe Senator Newman. He said that Senator Newman was a "consummate gentleman." He described an occasion on which Senator Newman brought a whole new dimension to the legislative process. The issue was whether or not to censure a senator for having made an improper use of a state airplane. The senator was clearly in the wrong. A great public clamor had been stirred up by the press. People were outraged. Censure was unanimously demanded. By that time I. DeQuincey Newman was thought of as the conscience of the senate. To everybody's amazement, he defied all expectations and voted against censure. He explained his vote this way: "The Senator has admitted his wrongdoing; he has said he is sorry; he has made amends to the State for wrongfully using the airplane; he has asked forgiveness." Newman concluded, "We can require no more of him than he has given; we are powerless to withhold our forgiveness." Newman was expressing the philosophy, whether intentionally or coincidentally, of another great black leader who was in prison at the time but would someday assume a high political office. His name is Nelson Mandela.

Newman always said that everything he did in his life, including during his service in the senate, was merely an extension of his Christian ministry. He was a godly man, but he was never pious or judgmental toward any individual. He was a gentleman of enormous dignity. By his very presence he radiated integrity and goodwill toward all, even toward those who would do him harm.

Indeed, DeQuincey Newman was as Senator Land described him, a consummate gentleman in every sense of the word. But he was without vanity or pretense. By the time he was elected to the senate, he had become something of a celebrity in South Carolina. He was always a powerful presence everywhere he went, but he was never the least bit enamored of himself. He was self-effacing to a fault. I once asked him what it was like to be so widely recognized in public. "I am most often mistaken for a headwaiter," he said. "Except when I am in Washington," he added. "There, I am mistaken for a diplomat from a third-world country."

Senator Newman did not serve a long tenure in the senate. He never achieved great seniority. He was reelected to a second term, but his health failed and he was forced to resign before his term was over. He died soon thereafter. Immediately after he died, the senate did something without precedent. Although he had served less than two years in the state senate, his fellow senators moved to commission a full-length portrait of Senator Newman. They directed that the portrait be hung in perpetuity in the senate chamber.

Today the portrait of I. DeQuincey Newman joins the portraits of John C. Calhoun, Strom Thurmond, and other famous South Carolinians of another day. He looks down for all time on the senate he once inspired by his presence. I would like to think that when the senate is embroiled in debates of difficult issues in years to come, at least a senator or two or maybe three may glance up and see him looking down and once more be inspired to do the right thing by the Reverend I. DeQuincey Newman.

William "Bill" Saunders

I am a life resident of Johns Island, South Carolina. After being discharged from the army in 1954, I started working with Esau Jenkins and the Voter Education Project. I met I. DeQuincey Newman through a statewide voter education association. Reverend Newman had a presence. If he entered a room, there could be twenty-five or thirty people walking in with him, but his was the presence that made a difference.

Reverend Newman and people such as Esau Jenkins were so consistent that they stood out among the many. A lot of people were going this way and that way, and they reminded me so much of ants, continuing to do the same things over and over. One of the most amazing things about Reverend Newman was that he was a Methodist minister but was able to bring together people from many faiths. It was as if he saw no distinction between the denominations. Unfortunately today the different denominations appear not to be able to come together and work as a team.

It is interesting that the challenges we face today are the same challenges that we faced when Reverend Newman served as the NAACP field director. People are still on a tightrope. Newman spent most of his life on this tightrope or in the eye of the storm. Interestingly he was not uncomfortable in that danger zone. I can recall having Newman on one of my radio talk shows, and when he was on, everyone would be glued to the radio listening to him. He had a voice that was just unbelievable. It seemed as if he ordered it and God said, "You can have it." But more important, he was a man of character and substance, as is illustrated by an event that occurred when he was on one of our radio programs involving Dr. Mary McLeod Bethune. He spoke of Dr. Bethune as a beautiful woman. Having worked with her, he praised her accomplishments. Following his praise, a listener called in and said that although he agreed with Reverend Newman about her accomplishments, he thought that Dr. Bethune was an ugly woman. Reverend Newman ignored the caller and continued to talk about Dr. Bethune. When the caller called in one final time, he stated that he continued to agree with Newman's assessment about Dr. Bethune's accomplishments but still considered her physically unattractive. At this point Reverend Newman responded that beauty is as beauty does. That was the end of that conversation.

I am also reminded of the time when I ran for the state senate against Newman in 1980. The state NAACP, however, opposed me. They thought that Newman should be the first black senator. After I lost the election in

Charleston, there was a special election held in Columbia in which Newman was elected. Following that election Newman expressed an interest in the radio business. He contacted me and asked for my assistance in the development of radio station WDPN. We put together a radio station in Columbia, South Carolina. This situation helped me to see the kind of person Newman was up close and personal.

Those are the kinds of things that don't get acknowledged. Newman was a mediator, a negotiator, and a leader. Many of our leaders are really managers. There is a big difference between a leader and a manager. A leader, I believe, is someone who can motivate. I. DeQuincey Newman was such a motivator; he could line up people to go to jail for a cause. People believed in him and trusted him. It was amazing to observe how he was able to sit in meetings and not say anything; but when he did speak, everyone gravitated toward him. He was an amazing person who dedicated his life to helping others.

Newman had no personal agenda. There were a lot of people around him who tried to emulate him, but they didn't have the ability, they didn't have the stamina. History will have no choice other than to view him as someone who really made a difference. I sincerely believe that the white leadership of this state owes him. If he considered you a friend, it was an unconditional friendship. If he thought your approach was not correct, he would help find the right approach. To me, that's a true friend. He was consistent and committed. Unfortunately we do not have leaders like I. D. and Esau Jenkins today, and little or nothing has been done to preserve their legacies.

Hiram Spain, Jr.

My first encounter with Reverend I. DeQuincey Newman was in Orangeburg, South Carolina, in the early 1960s. A number of students at South Carolina State College (now University) had become frustrated with prejudicial conditions existing in the city, in addition to the fact that there were several business establishments in Orangeburg where blacks were not admitted.

On this particular day a number of us decided to march to downtown Orangeburg to protest what we thought was dire injustice. Included in that group were James E. Clyburn (now a congressman) and Emily England (now the wife of Congressman Clyburn). Both were students at South Carolina State and were classmates of mine. We left the campus and marched for several blocks before we were stopped by police officers with water hoses. They ordered us to turn around, but we refused, and they began to spray water on us from the fire hoses. We marched as far as we could under the ferocious pressure from those hoses. We were finally arrested and herded into a fenced-in yard surrounding an Orangeburg County government building that we named the "Pink Castle." We remained there, wet and cold, until someone contacted Reverend I. DeQuincey Newman, who was in Columbia at the time. Meanwhile there were folks from the community who came by and brought us boxes of sandwiches and blankets. Reverend Newman came to court to secure our freedom. I very vividly remember him, adorned in his famous derby, as he entered the courtroom along with a young lawyer named Matthew Perry, Jr. Funds were collected for our bonds from the community, and we were released after the intervention of Reverend Newman and Attorney Perry.

Reverend Newman made several other trips to Orangeburg on behalf of demonstrating students, but I never had a chance to meet him personally. I did not see him again until after graduating from the university, completing a seven-year stint teaching at Carver High School in Spartanburg, becoming a student at Howard University law school in Washington, D.C., and then returning to Spartanburg, South Carolina. I recall his coming to Spartanburg to speak with several groups regarding justice and fair treatment in America and in our state.

In 1972 I relocated to Columbia as a result of efforts on the part of (now Congressman) James E. Clyburn, who at that time was an assistant to Governor John C. West, who offered me a position with the governor's office. Shortly after 1972 Reverend Newman was appointed special assistant to the commissioner of the South Carolina Department of Social Services. Due to the nature of my job as head of the Rural Regional Coordination Demonstration Project (RRCDP) (now the South Carolina Office of Rural Development), I had the opportunity to work with Reverend Newman on several projects. I vividly remember once traveling with him to Beaufort County, where we boarded a small boat and traveled to Daufuskie Island, which was separated from the mainland and did not have many basic conveniences, such as indoor toilets. We were both struck by the conditions of folks living on this island. Their quality of life made it seem that they were out of step with the rest of the world. I will never forget Reverend Newman's statement as we left Daufuskie: "Hiram," he said, "there must be something done on behalf of these people to improve their living conditions and enhance the quality of life for them and their children."

Late in 1974 I was called to the Columbia Urban League as executive director. Ironically my replacement at the Rural Regional Coordination Demonstration Project was Reverend Newman. Our relationship was strengthened after this move, as I had to work with him very closely on several of the projects that we undertook at the Columbia Urban League. At that time we had several offices for South Carolina, one of which operated out of Augusta, Georgia. We also had a number of activities based in the lowcountry, which was one of Reverend Newman's areas of concentration. Because of his abilities, his political astuteness, his savvy, his understanding of people, and his determination, I was drawn to Reverend Newman and became one of his mentees. We traveled together on a number of occasions. One trip in particular was to Sumter, where we participated in the opening of a building project and posed for photographs together. I shall always cherish those moments that I was able to spend with him. Another moment that I shall never forget is a luncheon that was sponsored by the Columbia Urban League supporting our Labor, Education Advancement Program. This program trained students for jobs in construction and small business operations. At the end of the luncheon, I posed for photographs with two giants, Dr. Benjamin E. Mays and Reverend I. DeQuincey Newman. Very few young men my age experienced such privilege.

After his tenure with the RRCDP he was elected to the South Carolina Senate. I found myself visiting with him whenever he was available to spend time with me. One of the things I learned from him and will always treasure is the ability to deal with others in the world of politics and business. He stated to me on one occasion, "Hiram, if you want to make an impact in this world you must be kind, you must smile, and in situations of conflict you must operate with a steel fist enclosed in a velvet glove." I have never forgotten this statement, and it has taken me through many situations.

I was approached in late 1978 by DSS commissioner Virgil Conrad, who shared with me that he was looking for a bureau chief at the Bureau of Human Services at the State Department of Social Services. He told me that my name had been given to him by Reverend Newman. At first I was not interested in the position; however, after several meetings with Commissioner Conrad, I learned that forty-plus applicants had applied for the job and that I would be the first black to hold the position at the Department of Social Services. Needless to say, I accepted the position. I was especially encouraged in my decision to accept it after Mr. Conrad shared that Reverend Newman thought that of all the applicants, I was the most qualified for the job. After leaving the Urban League and accepting the position at DSS, I sought the advice of Reverend Newman on numerous occasions. Each time I went to him I left a better person than I was when I approached him. His memory and candid advice will always be part of my life.

James S. Thomas

I met Reverend I. DeQuincey Newman many years ago. We were members of the same annual conference of the then Methodist Church and became very good friends. In fact, he was the best man at my wedding, and my wife and I have been married for sixty-three years now. So Newman and I had a long history of friendship, intellectual inquiry, and mutual respect.

When I was chaplain at South Carolina State College in the mid-1940s, it was Newman who took me down to Orangeburg to register to vote. In those days that was a difficult undertaking; I have that voter registration certificate to this day. It was in part this determined and focused nature that made him such an effective NAACP leader. He had, among other attributes, two gifts that are not generally thought of as directly connected to good leadership, but I believe that they went a long way toward helping him do his job well: he had a good sense of humor, and he did not take himself too seriously.

In addition Newman knew where he was going and how he wanted to get there. He was an excellent preacher and even-tempered enough to share tough talk with his congregation and others while maintaining great composure and sense of purpose. It is no coincidence that some of the very important civil rights cases handled by the NAACP came from Clarendon County, South Carolina. In fact in large part because of Newman, South Carolina enjoyed regular visits from Thurgood Marshall, Ruby Hurly, Vernon Jordan, and other members of the NAACP national office. He was one of those highly effective leaders who worked behind the scenes, forgoing the notoriety that some others crave. He wasn't interested in headlines so much as he was in getting things done.

It was interesting to observe how Newman reconciled his leadership within the NAACP with his ministry. I happen to be very much a supporter of his point of view—which was, essentially, that the treatment of human beings is fundamental to the teachings of the gospel. Regardless of one's station in life, every individual has a right to basic human rights and dignity. He believed that human beings are equal in the sight of God and that no one has the right to take others' dignity from them. So then, following a proud tradition in African American culture, these vocations—civil rights activist and minister—were complementary and mutually supportive pursuits for

Newman. He saw it as a part of his ministry to get people from his congregation to the polls, even if he had to take them himself. There was a certain calm assurance within him that social action was a natural and necessary part of his ministry; that was the way he approached life. Frankly, that's the way it should be. I wish we had more of this in these times.

At the same time, Newman never allowed a battle to consume him, nor would he allow the group with which he was working to lose focus. If arguments erupted and threatened to deflect the purpose of a specific agenda, he did not get emotionally involved; instead he had a way of defusing the situation with calm and single-minded redirection to the task at hand. He was, consequently, able to work effectively with various groups of people. While some white people might have feared him because of the intensity of his focus and his words, he was universally respected. Having supervised pastors for a quarter of a century, I know that it is a rare and unusual ability for individuals to maintain focus and to allow, at the same time, others to express themselves. I'm sure that Newman was criticized—every pastor is—but that never deterred him from his mission. I never heard him say, "We've got to do this" with an edge in his voice. He just did it through powers of persuasion, strong relationships he had built with others, and determination. He never compromised his integrity in the process.

Newman had the ability to rise above traditional ways of doing things in the interest of the NAACP and moving on with a different strategy. For example, he shared with me his assiduous work in getting Harvey Gantt admitted to Clemson University. It was difficult, but with solid strategy it got done. And then of course, many of us who were enmeshed in the early days of the civil rights movement are still stuck back there. Sometimes even now groups of people want to march simply for the sake of marching. Marching is fine, but simply marching doesn't solve anything anymore; it's not an end to a means in and of itself; some important goal has to be on the agenda. Newman didn't get caught up in self-limiting techniques. If a march would do something that led somewhere, he'd go with it; but you've got to have more than one arrow in your bag, and he did. This approach kept him from constantly fighting little wars, as we were often forced to do in the 1950s and 1960s. While some might call it courageous to dare to deviate from the norm, for Newman it boiled down to just good old common sense. You have to understand the time you're living in, and while you're fighting battles that are important to fight, you must also be careful to fight them with the most effective weapons.

All of us detested the cruel system of segregation, right down to the pervasive "colored only" signs. Those days are gone and will stay gone. But that doesn't mean that the pathology of racism has passed; this makes the need for today's advocacy to be different from the advocacy Newman lived and practiced. This country's history and its experience with centuries of slavery, segregation and Jim Crow, and denial of access for black people and other disenfranchised groups gave Newman's advocacy a kind of "in-your-face" edge. It is questionable whether we could have ever achieved a "level playing field," as it is called these days, without Newman's style of advocacy. But today racism is generally more subtle, and black people are often accused of "playing the race card." What is important to recognize is that black people didn't invent the racial divide in the first place; we didn't bring it from Africa. White people invented it long before this country was born. After working in the church's structure for my entire career, I am very sensitive, as was Newman, to the fact that discrimination can and does occur in myriad ways. Even at my age, in this new millennium, I continue to hear of instances when people are continually being denied access based on race, usually through creative and historically indefensible arguments: policies against Affirmative Action, for example. We must recognize that America is that kind of country —wanting to see itself as rooted in equality but still far from that goal and often in denial of that fact—and act accordingly. The spin that this country puts on race relations is debilitating for people of color. Newman recognized the subtleties of the issue and the burden that we bear if we are to be effective activists.

On the whole, I believe that several things accounted for Newman's successes. He had a great sense of timing. He was a powerful leader, a focused and effective strategist. He often addressed situations with a sense of humor and had the self-assurance that also allowed him to laugh at himself. He knew who he was. That is the kind of man he was.

Isaac "Ike" W. Williams

I serve as district liaison to Congressman Jim Clyburn. I also served as a former field director of the South Carolina NAACP (1969–83).

My first encounter with Reverend Isaiah DeQuincey Newman was in 1958 through my sister, Mildred Williams, who attended the Highland Folk School in Tennessee. That school conducted informal adult education programs focused on the southern labor movement, citizenship, and civil rights.

At that time Reverend Newman was pastoring at Wesley United Methodist Church in Charleston, South Carolina. I was impressed with his deep voice, commanding personality, and distinctiveness. My involvement with the NAACP began when Reverend Newman asked my mother if he could "borrow" me for a few weeks. He and I would travel across the state doing voter registration work. Through his encouragement we organized a local youth council of the NAACP in Charleston. I subsequently became the local youth president of the NAACP and expanded our membership to five hundred youths in the North Charleston area.

I will never forget my first real speech in the summer of 1963 before a public audience. That summer I received a call from Reverend Newman. I can recall him saying in that distinct voice, "Brother Williams, I wonder if you could help me solve a problem. I have this dilemma of needing to be in two places at the same time. I am supposed to be in Spartanburg and in Orangeburg this afternoon and there is no way I can do that. I wonder if you could help me." Without waiting for a reply, he continued, "I have arranged for you to take a flight from Charleston Municipal Airport to Columbia where my Volkswagen will be waiting for you. You can take my car and drive to Orangeburg. All you need to do is to speak to the people of Orangeburg about the need for them to organize and get active." I thought, here I am, a recent high school graduate, speaking to a group of people at Trinity United Methodist Church across the street from the campus of South Carolina State College! Just the thought of this task was mind-blowing. When I arrived, on the front row in the meeting room were college professors from South Carolina State and other dignitaries from Orangeburg, including Dr. Hubert Manning, the president of Claflin College. To say the least, I was somewhat intimidated. I had written some notes about what I was going to say. However, I realized quickly that I was going nowhere with this speech, so I pushed my notes aside and spoke from my heart. So, you can see that Reverend Newman was very much my anchor, which allowed me to increase my involvement with the NAACP. Subsequently, through Reverend Newman's genius, I was eventually elected president of the National Youth Committee of the NAACP.

Another experience I had with Reverend Newman in the summer of 1963 really and truly speaks to his essence concerning the protection and care of his family. That summer Medgar Evers, a contemporary of Reverend Newman, who visited the Newmans' home on numerous occasions, was assassinated. His assassination touched Reverend Newman deeply. It was the only time that I had witnessed his vulnerability and concern for his family's safety. The Newman house was situated almost exactly like Medgar Evers's house, across from a wooded area. One night when we returned from our travels all over South Carolina, he pulled up to his garage and blew the horn of his car. Mrs. Newman, as usual, came downstairs and raised the garage door for him to drive in. During the pause between when he blew the horn and when Mrs. Newman came to raise the garage door, he looked at me, a mere teenager of seventeen years, and said, "If anything ever happens to me, I want you to take care of Anne and Emily." It was an awesome request, but it helped me to focus. It made me more serious about how I thought about and viewed the work that he was involved in.

Over time it became very clear to me that Reverend Newman was an astute and impressive figure. He had an aura about him. He was a profound speaker and a very committed person. People responded naturally to his proposals for change. He could preach a sermon and convince and convert you. He had a passion about what he did, and that was his essence. I really respected his mind, his intellect. He had a way of putting things together. He was unlike anybody I have ever known, and I must say without hesitation that as a person and male role model, he has left an indelible mark on me. My father, Reverend Willie Williams, died when I was eight, and Reverend Newman became the next important male figure in my life. I learned many lessons from Reverend Newman. Perhaps the most important one he taught me is how to work effectively with people. He helped me to be more confident.

Reflecting back on Reverend Newman's involvement in the NAACP, as I recall it, he was the local president of the South Carolina Chapter of the NAACP, a former president of the South Carolina State Conference, and later the South Carolina field director. He worked directly for the national organization. His job as South Carolina field director was to organize the NAACP chapters around the state. He did a very good job. The issues at the time were very hot. I tell people it's easy to organize behind a common theme. However, it is another story when the common theme is civil and human rights and at a time when it is opposed by the establishment.

When Reverend Newman became field director, he created a lot of support for the organization because he was committed to justice. The racial problems that dominated the state were evident. Everybody felt those issues. He rallied people around the unfairness of the practices. As field director for the NAACP, he spearheaded a tremendous organizational effort statewide. He initiated the NAACP Freedom Fund dinners, originally known as Honor Guard dinners, and he also initiated a strong life membership drive. Overall he was a great organizer, a tremendous speaker, and a very convincing leader. In my opinion, one of his greatest moments was when he began to focus on poverty in South Carolina. The poverty tour brought to light the deplorable health and sanitation conditions among the poor. Even though he was one heck of a civil rights leader, I really think his heartfelt care was for the poor and oppressed. When he did the poverty tour, I saw in his spirit and essence a commitment to the underprivileged. Finally, when he was elected to the senate, he did an impressive job in the General Assembly as the first black senator after Reconstruction. His greatest contribution was that he was not interested in being top dog. He took pride in making top dogs. He left an indelible mark on the state's social, political, and economic life.

I believe that Reverend Newman's biggest challenge was that he was a race person. Race persons, unlike racists, always consider their work in light of its relationships to the progress of their groups—for example, Jewish people, white people, or any ethnic group looking toward a movement to support their own. It's not a bad thing to be a race person because as you raise the lowest of your group, you raise the entire group. W. E. B. Du Bois spoke about group consciousness. Newman was very much like that. He wanted to move not by himself but with and on behalf of the people. He was an able minister and a great builder of a congregation. He was believable and convincing. He took entrepreneurial risks, not only in building the NAACP but also in terms of community development. He initiated a statewide effort to provide homes to the disadvantaged. He always pushed the envelope and saw opportunities for people of color to expand their horizons. He also saw opportunities in the business sector. For example, he created a radio station. Among other things, in the church he had concerns about control and equity. Although he was not a separatist, he fought hard to make sure the playing field was leveled.

His final challenge, in my opinion, was to make certain that African Americans had their proper place in the political arena. DeQuincey Newman was probably the best politician I knew. He was as shrewd, cunning, and sharp as they come. You had to get up very early to fool Reverend Newman. Sometimes those he interacted with would think that they had the edge, but the fact is, he had it from the very beginning.

Above all, I believe without question that Reverend Newman was an honorable person. He was an honest person, but there were times when, to some, he didn't appear to be straight up. That's the part of him I refer to as cunning. He never exposed his full hand, and that worked to his advantage. However, I know that Reverend Newman played a full court when it came to community, business, religion, and politics. He was one of a kind, the likes of whom we have not experienced since his passing in 1985.

Esther Nell Knuckles Glymph Witherspoon

I lived in Gaffney, South Carolina, until I was a junior in high school. I left to complete my education in North Carolina and later in Cleveland, Ohio. I earned a bachelor of arts degree in elementary education from Johnson C. Smith University in North Carolina and a master of science degree in library science from Western Reserve University (now Case Western Reserve). I returned to Gaffney when I married my first husband, Clarence L. Glymph, Jr. Mr. Glymph died after eighteen years of marriage. I left Gaffney in 1975 when I married my second husband, Dr. James W. Witherspoon of Columbia, South Carolina.

I had seen Reverend and Mrs. Newman once in the 1930s at a meeting at the local church in Gaffney, South Carolina, where I was a member. I didn't meet them in person until much later. However, I knew about Reverend Newman because of his ministerial and community work. He was known throughout the South Carolina Conference of the Methodist churches. I again met the Newmans in the mid-1970s when I came to Columbia to live. At the time I was still attending church in Gaffney, approximately one hundred miles away. This was quite a distance to travel and was becoming a bit of a challenge. At that time my second husband, Reverend Dr. Witherspoon, was a partially retired minister, but I was not affiliated with his church or any church in particular. Over time I heard Reverend Newman deliver several sermons. I was also aware that the congregation at his church was smaller than the congregation of the church I attended in Gaffney. Eventually I came to feel that Reverend Newman's church was the place where I wanted to be. Further, I was quite impressed with his work with the NAACP.

Reverend Newman had so many outstanding qualities about him. But if I were to attempt to sum them up, I would say that the way he battled against the odds was extraordinary. He was a man of great integrity. I was especially impressed with the way he stood up for what he believed. Being a man of principle and courage was one of his most outstanding characteristics.

I think it is also important to consider the danger involved in his work as a civil and human rights advocate in a state where lynching of black people was a common practice, especially of blacks who were considered "uppity" or didn't know "their place." There were many who were out to get him. Despite the enmity and danger, he continued his work. I recall an incident that occurred in the lower part of the state when the Ku Klux Klan was threatening his life. When he related this incident to his congregation, he said that he was so afraid when he got to his destination and to safety that he was unable to speak. Despite the apparent dangers, he was willing to continue to take risks of that kind—risks that would lead to the creation of a more just and equal world for all South Carolina citizens.

I think his most significant contribution is his legacy as a fair and godly person. He helped and inspired so many people. The young people he encountered, such as Ike Williams, have spoken admirably of how he inspired them. He was the root of so many things that will live on. He has changed the face of race relations in this state. One of the most important outcomes of Reverend Newman's work was raising the consciousness of both black and white people in realizing that black people were not satisfied with the status quo. It was amazing to see that so many white people, including those at the highest levels of state government, thought that black people were satisfied with living in enslavement or in impoverished conditions. Reverend Newman's work woke people up. Not only did black people want freedom, but they also had the potential to become leaders of their destiny. Given our history, one cannot help but be amazed when looking at some of the accomplishments that blacks have made; for example, a black man is president of the United States, a black woman served as secretary of state, there are black judges at all levels of the judiciary system, and there are black high-ranking administrators, physicians, scientists, educators, and legislators. I contend that blacks must learn to take advantage of all the opportunities around them; they must learn to appreciate and build on the hard work of people such as Reverend Newman and not let the difficult work that he did be in vain. White people, on the other hand, need to get out of the era of slavery. South Carolina must come into the twenty-first century. Together we must recognize that although we live in the South, we are still a part of the world.

Conclusion

Newman's Vision of a "Just" South Carolina

Sadye L. M. Logan

Every great dream begins with a dreamer. Always remember, you have within you the strength, the patience, and the passion to reach for the stars to change the world.

> Harriet Tubman, as quoted in Sarah H. Bradford,
> *Harriet Tubman: The Moses of Her People*

At the turn of the century and at the time of I. DeQuincey Newman's birth in 1911, the United States was on the brink of major transformation. This was a time of great hope. The progressive spirit of reform was spreading rapidly across our nation. One might surmise that this was the perfect time for the birth of a future activist, a visionary. Many have referred to I. DeQuincey Newman as a visionary. It is generally believed that visionaries do not see or experience the world in the same manner as everyone else does. This simple presumption suggests that visionaries are different or special in some unique ways. It has been established throughout this book that I. DeQuincey Newman was unique, that he was a man with a special mission of peace and justice. In reviewing the time line (see the chronology, p. xvii) that captures the events of his seventy-four years of life, it seems impossible that the events of the world as well as the events of his life could have been crammed into so few years. This time line suggests that I. DeQuincey Newman was at the forefront of many historical events in South Carolina and witnessed many others as an activist citizen of the world. His life encompassed the experience of thirteen different United States presidents: Wilson (1913–21), Harding (1921–23),

Coolidge (1923–29), Hoover (1929–33), Franklin Roosevelt (1933–45), Truman (1945–53), Eisenhower (1953–61), Kennedy (1961–63), Johnson (1963–69), Nixon (1969–74), Ford (1974–77), Carter (1977–81), and Reagan (1981–85, when Newman died). He experienced four wars, including World War I (1914–18), World War II (1939–45), the Korean War (1950–53), and the Vietnam War (1964–75). He also witnessed the Great Depression, abject poverty, gross racial inequities and disparities in all spheres of life (income, health, education, welfare, employment), and major civil and human rights events such as *Brown v. Board of Education* and the civil and voting rights acts.

Newman's focus was as a change agent. He addressed South Carolina's legally sanctioned system of racial segregation, such as all-white political parties and all-white schools, as well as employment opportunities and the environment in terms of inadequate or nonexistent water and sewer services and poor health care, especially in impoverished rural areas of the state (see "Leadership in Black and White"). In the years following his departure from the role of NAACP field director, Newman summed up the results of over a decade and a half of work aimed at changing South Carolina's racially oppressive systems as having had limited success. He said, "We've achieved a modicum of political integration and to a lesser extent economic integration, but there is not much evidence of social integration."[1]

In 1948, when Newman was elected vice president of the NAACP's South Carolina Conference of Branches, the conference resolved that the acid test for democracy in South Carolina and the rest of America was the inclusion and the realization of equality for all people of color. In 1958, a decade later, but before Newman's appointment as state field director, the South Carolina Conference of Branches declared, "It is our belief that timing, and not time, is a dimension of social change, and that it is the quality of the experience which matters in our common associations, and not the length of time we are exposed to one another. As a mode of human association, segregation prevents the realization of even the most elementary demands of equality, making democracy impossible. Consequently, we believe that the elimination of segregation from all aspects of life is the first step toward the realization of true democracy."[2]

It was within the context of this vision that Newman took up the helm of the NAACP leadership. He was guided by the concept of full inclusion of black Carolinians in the political, economic, educational, and social lives of the state and the nation. In this phase of NAACP leadership, however, he was faced with the overt rage of white Carolinians toward black Carolinians and the all-out resistance to the Brown *decision* regarding segregated schools

Newman greeting President Jimmy Carter. Courtesy of the Newman family.

Anne P. and I. DeQuincey Newman at a social event with Michael D. Jarrett, commissioner for the Department of Health and Environment Control. Courtesy of the Newman family.

in South Carolina and the nation.[3] Newman's assessment of his work on the front line for human and civil rights begs the question, How far had the state progressed in nearly three decades? A useful baseline and more expanded perspective are reflected in an important event that occurred close to the time frame of Newman's assessment. In 1976 Vernon E. Jordan, director of the National Urban League, delivered a powerful speech in a special address to the South Carolina joint assembly. This address was in celebration of the United States Bicentennial. It provides a concrete image of the state of South Carolina in terms of race relations and social and economic disparities. At the time of Jordan's address, Hiram Spain, Jr., was serving as executive director of the Columbia Urban League and DeQuincey Newman had been serving for approximately one year in a new position as director of the Governor's Office of Rural Development (see "Isaiah DeQuincey Newman" and "A Vision for Change").

Jordan began his message to the South Carolina joint assembly with a focus on the state of the nation. He said,

> This year we celebrate America's Bicentennial, the 200th anniversary of our nation's independence. It is also an election year. It is then, a time, uniquely situated for self-examination, for redefining what America is all about and for dealing with the unfinished business of the American dream, the still-to-be-completed promise embodied in our Declaration of Independence that "all men are created equal, that they are endowed by their Creator with certain inalienable rights, that among these are life, liberty and the pursuit of happiness." Those words shine like beacons through the ages. They have inspired men in far-off countries, as they have inspired our own people. They stand today as reminders that the barriers of race, of poverty, and of joblessness should not be tolerated in the birthplace of liberty and the fount of equality.[4]

Then Jordan moved his focus to the South and the state of South Carolina. He said,

> Here in the South, the situation is even worse; the poverty rate, involuntary part-time work, and sub-employment are all higher. And both nationally and regionally, Black people fare worse than do Whites. Southern Black unemployment is over double the White rate; a third of all Black families are poor and half of them do not receive a single cent from welfare; earnings of Black workers average only about two-thirds that of Whites, and in almost every measure of socio-economic status,

> Blacks lag behind Whites and in many instances, the gap is growing, not closing. Just as a disproportionate number of southern Whites are poor and sub-employed, so too, do we find a disproportionate number of southern Blacks lagging behind their White neighbors.[5]

Almost four decades have passed since the above observation was made about the United States of America and South Carolina. Observing South Carolina today, it would be impossible to say that change did not occur in that time. However, available data suggest that though South Carolina may look different, unemployment and poverty continue to plague a disproportionate number of the state's black population. These systemic problems are further exacerbated by a lack of available health care, chronic health conditions, and a poor quality of education.[6]

Newman and other advocates of human and civil rights recognized that many more whites than blacks were jobless, poor, and receiving welfare; blacks were and continue to be disproportionately affected by social, economic, and health disparities.[7] It seems evident that South Carolina must sooner rather than later recognize the need for a paradigm shift in addressing the needs of its poor whites and its impoverished people of color. The issues must not continue to be framed in racial terms or to be seen solely as "minority" issues. Instead all South Carolinians must work to "eracism" and create an equal and just South Carolina.

There are no arguments with those activists who believe that it is not possible to legislate the attitudes and hearts of humans, but there is no denying that it was the civil rights laws of the 1960s and 1970s that provided the impetus for a new and expanded South Carolina and the new South. In 1976 the optimists in this new South, while acknowledging that discrimination and remnants of the old order still existed, boasted of a new dawn in the relation between the races. Thirteen years earlier (1963) Newman, in a move to intensify his attack on racially motivated discrimination, had announced in several local newspapers a set of nine "goals" that would move South Carolina toward a more just and equal treatment of all its citizens. These goals were

- desegregation of public facilities and institutions
- desegregation of all publicly sponsored restaurants and accommodations
- desegregation of public drinking fountains, restaurants, lounges, and reception rooms
- equal employment opportunities in various departments and agencies

appointment of Negroes to the county registration boards
appointment of Negroes to several standing committees, commissions, and boards of state government
inclusion of Negroes in white-collar jobs
opening of all technical and training centers on a nonracial basis
appointment of a racial committee with a view to resolve the problems of racial segregation and discrimination.[8]

These goals were a direct outgrowth of the earlier *Briggs v. Elliott* in 1950 and the laws passed after the 1954 Supreme Court *Brown v. Board of Education* decision by the South Carolina General Assembly. At the writing of these goals, South Carolina was a racially segregated state (see the table on right).

The Transition of African Americans in South Carolina: 1600 to Present

By law black Carolinians were second-class citizens whose existence was based on the principle of benign neglect. During this time blacks existed on the fringes of the employment sector. The state agencies dependent on federal funds employed blacks primarily in service positions such as laborers, mail clerks, or messengers. This pattern of employment went as high as the governor's office. Limited exceptions existed in health and mental health, welfare agencies, the Employment Security Commission, the Department of Education, the Department of Correction, and the federal government.[9]

The educational system was segregated and grossly unequal. The state's political system with a multicounty, multisystem plan was designed to effectively deny the election of a black senator. South Carolina was the last state legislative body in the South to adopt a single-member district system (in 1984).[10] At the time, of the forty-six state senators, nine or 19.6 percent were African Americans and twenty-eight or 22.5 percent of the 124 representatives in the S.C. House of Representatives were African Americans.[11] In 1992 James Enos Clyburn became the state's first African American to serve in the U.S. House of Representative since 1897. In 2007 Clyburn was the first South Carolinian to become majority whip, the third-ranking Democrat in the U.S. House of Representative. Clyburn represents South Carolina's Sixth District, serving fifteen counties that include the state's six most impoverished counties with the lowest per capita income. "Many of these counties are found along the I-95 corridor, which bisects the Sixth District. This two hundred mile stretch of interstate has been dubbed the 'Corridor of Shame' because it is home to inadequate public schools, high unemployment rates, widespread poverty and alarming rates of strokes, diabetes, and

Capture, Transition, and Enslavement	Slavery Abolished	Black Reconstruction	White Reconstruction	New Reconstruction	Emergent Democratic Transformation
(1600–1864)	(1855–72)	(1873–77)	(1878–1962)	(1963–99)	(2000–)
Sold as property	Emancipation Proclamation—passage of Thirteenth, Fourteenth, Fifteenth Amendments	Supported the right of all citizens to vote	The Tillman movement and white supremacy	*Briggs v. Elliott*	Spiritual/religious integration
Slave codes	Passage of Black Codes	Blacks elected to political office and became members of a national political party	Constitution of 1895 was designed to disenfranchise blacks	*Brown v. Board of Education* of Topeka	Political integration
Plantation and backcountry lifestyles	Blacks could not vote, own guns, or serve on juries; employed only as servants or farm laborers	Provision of free education for all people regardless of race and gender	Intimidation, violence, fraud, and lynching	Sit-ins and other racial demonstrations	Economic integration
No common language	Designed to prevent political participation or economic power	Supported economic and social equality	Distrust widespread between whites and blacks	Voting Rights Act passed	Educational integration
Creation of a common language	Widespread illiteracy, poverty, and poor health	Unity between the races	Unjust legal system	Low-income occupations; Corridor of Shame (poor quality education)	Social integration

Capture, Transition, and Enslavement	Slavery Abolished	Black Reconstruction	White Reconstruction	New Reconstruction	Emergent Democratic Transformation
(1600–1864)	(1865–72)	(1873–77)	(1878–1962)	(1963–99)	(2000–)
Re-creation of a spiritual life	Continuing spiritual life	Encouraged hopefulness	Rigidly segregated systemic structures; black oppression	Continuing health disparity	Housing integration
				Rural poverty	Progressive law enforcement system
			Repression, health, poverty, and poor poor quality of education	Substandard housing	Progressive health, mental health, and welfare systems
				Civil Rights Act passed	
			Use of church to oppress and control		

prostate cancer. Textile plants have closed throughout the district due to outsourcing, and tobacco farmers in the eastern portion of the district have seen their livelihood evaporate."[12]

As indicated earlier, Newman described his fight to resolve the problems of racial segregation and discrimination as moderately successful, in that the obvious signs of racial discrimination and segregation no longer existed. Others have described the once racially desegregated South Carolina as progressive: the economy is growing; there is an infusion of industrial capitals; and new job-producing industries are established by national and international corporations.[13]

As indicated in the table above, the time is long overdue for the full transition and inclusion of black Americans in American life. Despite the obvious advances of black Carolinians in city government across the state, they continue to be severely underrepresented in law enforcement, the federal government, and the judicial system. As we entered a new century, African Americans, other people of color, and some poor white families in South Carolina remained seriously disadvantaged. The 2000 census and other available data highlight a telling profile of African Americans as South Carolina's most disadvantaged group. This profile includes total number of African Americans in the state's population, where they lived, and their levels of education, employment, income, and poverty status.

According to the U.S. Census Bureau in 2000, 54 percent of the black or African American population lived in the South. South Carolina ranked third to the rest of the nation on the percentage of African Americans (29.5 percent) of the total population. South Carolina was still considered to be more "rural" than the United States as a whole, although the majority of its "rural" populations no longer lived on farms. Due to affordability of housing, the state had one of the highest rates of home ownership in the nation. African American home ownership rates were between 60 to 65 percent. There was a 20 percent gap between white Carolinian home ownership and that of black Carolinians.

The level of educational attainment for African Americans in South Carolina and the nation varied greatly. South Carolina ranked forty-eighth in the nation for African Americans having less than a high school diploma, with 35.1 percent. Nationwide 27.7 percent of African Americans had less than a high school diploma. It is important to note that having less than a ninth grade education has often been used as a measure of illiteracy. The state ranked fiftieth in the nation in the percentage of African Americans with a graduate or professional degree. In 2000, 3.1 percent of African Americans in

South Carolina held a graduate or professional degree. The state continued to bicker over adding adequate funding to change its policy of minimally adequate education for its impoverished rural districts.[14]

Given the recent economic downturn, the employment rate for black Carolinians has continued to fluctuate as the state's overall employment rate dropped. However, using the 2000 census data as a baseline, in South Carolina 10.9 percent of African Americans in the civilian labor force were unemployed. This percentage was lower than the national average of 11.6 percent, giving South Carolina a ranking of twenty-second in the nation in 2000.

With respect to income and poverty, 11.8 percent of households in South Carolina reported incomes of less than ten thousand dollars in 1999, compared to 9.5 percent nationwide, placing South Carolina forty-first in the nation in this category. Interestingly, 8.1 percent of households in South Carolina reported incomes greater than one hundred thousand dollars in 1999, compared to 12.3 percent nationwide, giving South Carolina a ranking of thirty-fourth in the nation. Overall the percentage of African Americans living below the poverty line was higher for South Carolina than the United States for all age groups.[15]

Several theories exist for why the conditions described above have continued to persist over time in South Carolina. One compelling theory is that within the context of South Carolina racial history, many white South Carolinians have continued to believe that political and public equality means social equality and that social equality is synonymous with racial intermarriage. But more important, they believe that such equality may place African Americans in positions of leadership and authority.[16] The sentiments about positions of authority and leadership are reflected in the old 1868 document titled *The Respectful Remonstrance of White People of South Carolina:* "We do not mean to threaten resistance by arms. But the white people of our state will never submit to Negro rule. We may have to pass under the yoke, you have authorized, but by moral agencies, by political organizations, by every peaceful means left us; we will keep up this contest until we have regained *the heritage of political control handed down to us by our honored ancestry* [emphasis added]."[17] This theory is fueled unintentionally by an ongoing belief held by many black South Carolinians, especially those in positions of leadership or owners of small businesses. The belief is that in order for a black person to be successful, it was or is imperative that he or she have the support or friendship of a white person with name and/or position recognition. Such stances, though outdated, are dangerous and potentially destructive if not examined and applied by individuals possessed of critical thinking and a solid sense of self.

More important, it is imperative that South Carolina not allow another century to pass without fully embracing and moving through the long period of transition into a more ordered, open, and just South Carolina that was envisioned by Reverend Newman and champions of civil and human rights before him—some of whom gave their lives in the quest to expand the boundaries of a free and just society. Newman and others believed that South Carolina was in a unique position to teach the region, the state, the nation, and the world about antiracist practices and behavior.[18] Our state can, with its natural resources, new technology, and the creative minds of its citizenry, forge a social order that could serve as a prototype to address the confusion and destruction that plagues not only South Carolina but also the rest of the world. Newman's leadership of the NAACP during the 1960s brought South Carolina to the forefront of the civil rights movement and the black struggle for equality and inclusion. This phase of the struggle served as a prototype of a social order that would include the true acceptance of all humans as equal beings, denounce the destructiveness of poor and inadequate quality of education and economic exploitation, and embrace people of color as full economic equals living the values of racial reconciliation and partnership based on dignity and respect.

We must begin to view our state as well as the world as one big extended family, not unlike a vision espoused by DeQuincey Newman. In this regard, scholars of family life have learned over time that to help families, including extended families, move forward, it is necessary to challenge not only the symptoms that derail families from their normative path and bring them into treatment but also the family system and the family system's view of the presenting concerns that have caused the families to get off track. In other words, we must learn to respectfully stay in dialogue with all members of the family and ask very hard questions of ourselves and everyone else in the family. We must, according to one expert on family life and dynamics,

> ask questions about the symptoms until all can see that our problems go beyond the symptoms to include the entire society;
> help all parties see how their interaction is perpetuating the problem and accompanying symptoms;
> help everyone see how this view of the symptom came to be the accepted view of the symptom and its continuation; and finally

develop a team/collaborative/group response to solving the problem[s] or concerns of the group.[19]

This seemingly simple approach is powerful and can lead to a new social order—a world that is free from distinction of country, language, sect, and race and that is based on love and respect for self, others, and the planet. Living this vision would afford every person with an equal opportunity to reach his or her highest potential. We have the resources; we simply need to do it!

Twenty-eight years have passed since Reverend Newman's death. Although externally South Carolina looks very different than it did at that time, a scratch of the surface reveals a distressing and disturbing image for a significant portion of its citizenry. This disturbing image suggests that there is much work to be done. In this regard, South Carolina is being challenged to move forward into the twenty-first century with a new attitude and commitment to make democracy work in the state and in all of the United States of America—in other words, to live Isaiah DeQuincey Newman's vision of a just South Carolina and a just world.

It seems fitting to conclude this piece with the epigraph of John Stuart Mill from John Henry McCray's keynote address, delivered at the annual NAACP meeting of the South Carolina Conference, October 10, 1941, Orangeburg South Carolina:

> "The worth of a state, in the long run, is the worth of the individuals composing it."

Notes

1. Brinson, "The Reverend Mr. Newman."

2. Statement of the eighteenth annual meeting of the South Carolina State Conferences, file 958-1957, II-c-143, NAACP Papers. Microfilm. University of South Carolina, Thomas Cooper Library.

3. Cox, "1963"; Brown, "Civil Rights Activism"; Lau, *Democracy Rising*.

4. Mr. Vernon E. Jordan, address to the joint Assembly, journal of the South Carolina General Assembly, House of Representatives, March 10, 1976, 1279–89.

5. Ibid.

6. Sheheen, ". . . And Miles to Go."

7. U.S. Department of Health and Human Services, *Healthy People 2010: Understanding and Improving Health*, 2nd ed., 2 vols. With understanding and improving health objectives for improving health. 2 vols. (Washington, D.C.: U.S. Government Printing Office, November 2000).

8. I. D. Newman to Roy Wilkins, June 4, 1963, NAACP Papers, Part 25: Branch Department, Series D, Branch Department General Subject Files, 1956–63.

9. Newby, *Black Carolinians.*

10. Page, "New Role for Newman."

11. I. D. Newman to Roy Wilkins, June 4, 1963, NAACP Papers, Part 25: Branch Department, Series D, Branch Department General Subject Files, 1956–63.

12. Newby, *Black Carolinians.*

13. Brinson, "The Reverend Mr. Newman."

14. See http://www.scschoolcase.com. Accesed June 9, 2012.

15. "South Carolina: Who Are We Now?," http://www.sccommunityprofile.org/pdf files/who are we now pdf. Accessed June 9, 2012.

16. Logan, "Social Justice"; Cox, "1963," chap. 2.

17. Edgar, *South Carolina*, 377.

18. Mr. Vernon E. Jordan, address to the joint Assembly, journal of the South Carolina General Assembly, House of Representatives, March 10, 1976, 1279–89.

19. Minuchin, Nicholas, and Lee, *Assessing Couples and Families.*

Appendix

Time Line of the Central Jurisdiction and Events Leading Up to Its Creation

1784 The Methodist Episcopal Church was organized. This is recognized as the founding date of the United Methodist Church.

1787 Richard Allen and others in the congregation of St. George's Methodist Episcopal Church withdrew in protest of segregation.

1796 James Varick led the founding of the African Methodist Episcopal Zion Church and became first black bishop.

1816 Black Methodist Episcopal churches united to form the African Methodist Episcopal Church. Richard Allen, founder, became its first bishop.

1864 Separate African American annual conferences were formed.

1870 The Colored Methodist Episcopal Church, later renamed the Christian Methodist Episcopal Church, was formed.

1939 The Methodist Episcopal Church, the Methodist Episcopal Church, South, and the Methodist Protestant Church merged to form the Methodist Church. The segregated Central Jurisdiction was formed as a racial compromise.

1948 The Central Jurisdiction Conference formed a committee to study ways of eliminating the jurisdiction.

1952 The General Conference established the Board of Social and Economic Relations.

1956 The General Conference conducted a study of the jurisdictional system. The General Conference adopted legislation, which later became Amendment IX, allowing churches in the Central Jurisdiction to transfer to geographical jurisdictions.

1958 Amendment IX of the Methodist Church's Constitution, adopted by the 1956 General Conference, became effective.

1960 General Conference set up the Commission on Interjurisdictional Relations to continue a program to abolish the Central Jurisdiction.

1964 Conferences within the Central Jurisdiction began merging into geographical annual conferences.

1967 Bishop L. Scott Allen became the fourteenth and last bishop elected by the Central Jurisdiction.

1968 The Central Jurisdiction was abolished with the merger of the Methodist and Evangelical United Brethren Churches into the United Methodist Church.

Bibliography

Primary Sources

Davis, Jake. Letter to Reverend Newman appealing for help. November 11, 1969. Isaiah DeQuincey Newman Papers, Modern Political Collection, University of South Carolina, Columbia.

Dawes, Kwame. *Grace: Poems Honoring Columbia and Richland County's African American Leaders*. August 21, 2008. Historic Columbia Foundation, Columbia, S.C.

Jenkins, Esau. Collection. Avery Research Center, College of Charleston, Charleston, S.C.

Logan, Sadye L. M. "In Their Own Voices." Isaiah DeQuincey Newman Institute for Peace and Social Justice, Columbia, S.C.

Manning, Hubert V. Introduction of I. D. Newman to new congregation. 1940. Wesley Methodist Church, Charleston, S.C.

National Association for the Advancement of Colored People (NAACP). Papers on microfilm.

Newman, Isaiah DeQuincey. Papers, 1929–2003. South Carolina Political Collection, University of South Carolina, Columbia.

Newman, Isaiah DeQuincey. Papers, October 21, 1956. Modern Political Collection, University of South Carolina, Columbia.

Peck, J. Richard. "Many White Methodists Joined Fight against Segregated Church." 2005. http://archives.umc.org/interior.asp?ptid=2&mid=6696. Accessed April 9, 2009.

"Report and Testimony of the Select Committee of the United States Senate to Investigate the Cause of the Removal of the Negroes from the Southern States to the Northern States." U.S. Senate, Forty-sixth Congress, Second Session. p.x., 1880.

Resolutions Adopted by the South Carolina Conferences of the NAACP, October 1948, South Carolina State Conference of Branches file, II-6-181, NAACP Papers. file, II C-181. Microfilm, University of South Carolina, Thomas Cooper Library.

Snider, Jan. "Remembering Central Jurisdiction: The Story Needs to Be Told." http://archives.umc.org/interior.asp?ptid=2&mid=6723. Accessed March 5, 2009.

Published Sources

Bailey, N. Louise, Mary L. Morgan, and Carolyn R. Taylor, eds. *Biographical Directory of South Carolina Senate, 1776–1985*. 3 vols. Columbia: University of South Carolina Press, 1985.

Charron, Katherine Mellen. *Freedom's Teacher: The Life of Septima Clark*. Chapel Hill: University of North Carolina Press, 2009.

Huss, John E. *Senator for the South: A Biography of Olin D. Johnson*. Garden City, N.Y.: Doubleday, 1961.

Jordan, Vernon E., Jr., with Annette Gordon-Reed. *Vernon Can Read! A Memoir*. New York: Public Affairs, 2001.

"The Journal of South Carolina Conference: 1954." In W. M. Jenkins, *Steps Along the Way: The Origin and Development of the South Carolina Conference of the Central Jurisdiction of the Methodist Church*, 39. Columbia, S.C.: Socamead Press, 1967.

Lau, Peter F. *Democracy Rising: South Carolina and the Fight for Black Equality since 1865*. Lexington: University Press of Kentucky, 2006.

Logan, Sadye L. M. "How Anne Newman Changed Our Lives." Editorial. (Columbia, S.C.) *State*, November 2, 2011.

McCray, John. "Lighthouse and Informer, 1939–1954." In Charles Payne and Adam Green, eds., *Time Longer than Rope: A Century of African-American Activism*, 462–91. New York: New York University Press, 2003.

Meetze, George, Chaplain, S.C. Senate. Invocation for Memorial Service in S.C. Senate Chambers, 1985, Memorial Service for Newman. South Carolina Political Collection.

Renick, Timothy D. "Solomon Black: A Segregationist in Moderation." *Proceedings of the South Carolina Historical Association* (1991): 61–68.

Robertson, David W. *Sly and Able: A Political Biography of James F. Byrnes*. New York: Norton, 1994.

S.C. Conference of Branches 26th Anniversary Convention Program. Richland County, University of South Carolina Political Collections, November 16–19, 1967.

Sellers, Cleveland, with Robert Terrell. *The River of No Return: The Autobiography of a Black Militant and the Life and Death of SNCC*. Jackson: University Press of Mississippi, 1990.

Smyth, William D. "Segregation in Charleston in the 1950s: A Decade of Transition." *South Carolina Historical Magazine* 92.2 (April 1991): 99–123.

U.S. Census Bureau. *U.S. Census of Population: 1950, Vol. II, Characteristics of the Population Part 42, South Carolina*. Washington, D.C.: U.S. Government Printing Office, 1973.

Will the Circle Be Unbroken? An Audio History of the Civil Rights Movement in Five Southern Communities and the Music of Those Times, Episode 2: The Road to Litigation. Narrator, Vertamae Grosvenor; writer and producer, George Kinger; senior producers, Worth Long and Randall Williams. Southern Regional Council, Atlanta, Ga., 1997. Distributed by Public Radio International.

Williams, Cecil. *Out-of-the-Box in Dixie: Cecil Williams' Photography of South Carolina Events That Changed America.* Orangeburg, S.C.: Self-published, 2007.

Legal Cases

Brown v. Baskin, 78 Fed. Supp. 933, 1948.
Buchanan v. Warley, 245 U.S. 60, 1917.
Duval v. Seignious et al., unpub. consent decree, 1944.
Elmore v. Rice, 72 Fed. Supp (EDSC), 1947.
Guinn v. U.S., 238 U.S. 347, 1915.
Pearson v. Cleardon County.
Smith v. Allwright, 321 U.S. 649, 1944.
Thompson v. Gibbs, 60 Fed. Supp 872, 1945.

Interviews

Blackwell (Rackley), Gloria. By Sadye L. M. Logan. Oral history of Isaiah DeQuincey Newman's life and legacy. Newman Institute, Columbia, S.C., summer 2006.
Brown, J. Arthur. By Millicent Brown. Charleston, S.C., August 1987.
Cook, G. Roberts. By Sadye L. M. Logan. Oral history of Isaiah DeQuincey Newman's life and legacy. Newman Institute, Columbia, S.C., fall 2006.
Grant, Karen Ross. By Sadye L. M. Logan. Oral history of Isaiah DeQuincey Newman's life and legacy. Newman Institute, Columbia, S.C., fall 2005.
Hicks, G., Reverend. By Sadye L. M. Logan. Oral history of Isaiah DeQuincey Newman's life 16 and legacy. Newman Institute, Columbia, S.C., fall 2006.
McCray, Carrie Allen. By Sadye L. M. Logan. Oral history of Isaiah DeQuincey Newman's life and legacy. Newman Institute, Columbia, S.C., fall 2006.
Newman, Anne Pauline. By Millicent Brown. Columbia, S.C., August 1987, January 1, 2008.
———. By Sadye L. M. Logan. Oral history of Isaiah DeQuincey Newman's life and legacy. Newman Institute, Columbia, S.C., fall 2005, summer 2006.
Newman, Emily Morris. By Millicent Brown. Columbia, S.C., August 1987.
———. Interviewed by Sadye L. M. Logan, summer 2007, and interviewed by Brown, summer 2007. Oral history of Isaiah DeQuincey Newman's life and legacy. Newman Institute, Columbia, S.C., fall 2006.
Noble, Jerome. By Sadye L. M. Logan. Oral history of Isaiah DeQuincey Newman's life and legacy. Newman Institute, Columbia, S.C., summer 2006.
Rearden, Harrison. By Sadye L. M. Logan. Oral history of Isaiah DeQuincey Newman's life and legacy. Newman Institute, Columbia, S.C., summer 2006.
Sanders, Williams. By Sadye L. M. Logan. Oral history of Isaiah DeQuincey Newman's life and legacy. Newman Institute, Columbia, S.C., fall 2006.
Williams, Isaac. By Sadye L. M. Logan. Oral history of Isaiah DeQuincey Newman's life and legacy. Newman Institute, Columbia, S.C., summer 2006.
Witherspoon, E. N. By Sadye L. M. Logan. Oral history of Isaiah DeQuincey Newman's life and legacy. Newman Institute, Columbia, S.C., fall 2006.

Wright, Wendy, former administrative assistant to Reverend Newman. By Karen Ross Grant. Columbia, S.C., February and May 2007.

Secondary Sources

Published Sources and Internet Articles

Adeboyejo, Betsy. "NAACP Archive Is the Largest at the Library of Congress." *Crisis*, January–February 2004.

Anderson, James D. *The Education of Blacks in the South, 1860–1935*. Chapel Hill: University of North Carolina Press, 1988.

Bass, Jack, and Jack Nelson. *The Orangeburg Massacre*. 2nd ed. Macon, Ga.: Mercer University Press, 2002.

Bass, Jack, and W. Scott Poole. *The Palmetto State: The Making of Modern South Carolina*. Columbia: University of South Carolina Press, 2009.

Bass, Jack, and Marilyn W. Thompson. *Ol' Strom: An Unauthorized Biography of Strom Thurmond*. Atlanta, Ga.: Longstreet, 1998.

Beck, E. M., and Stewart E. Tolnay. "The Killing Fields of the Deep South: The Market for Cotton and the Lynching of Blacks, 1882–1930." *American Sociological Review* 55 (August 1990): 526–39.

Bigger, Margaret G., ed. *The Great Depression: How We Coped, Worked and Played: Life Experience Stories from the Carolinas' Piedmont*. Charlotte, N.C.: A. Borough Books, 2001.

Billingsley, Andrew. *Mighty Like a River: The Black Church and Social Reform*. New York: Oxford University Press, 1999.

"Billion Dollar Bug War: Boll Weevil Entrenched for Greatest Damage on Cotton Crop—New Battle Line to Check Worst Enemy of Department of Agriculture's Experts." *New York Times*, April 2, 1922.

Blackman, Douglas A. *Slavery by Another Name: The Re-Enslavement of Black People in America from the Civil War to World War II*. New York: Doubleday, 2008.

Blicck, David G. "'Beyond the Politics of Color': Opposition to South Carolina's 1952 Constitutional Amendment to Abolish the Public School System." *Proceedings of the South Carolina Historical Association* (1995): 21–30.

Bontemps, Arna, and Jack Conroy. *They Seek a City*. New York: Doubleday, Doran, 1945.

Boozer, Michael A., Alan B. Krueger, and Shan Wolkon. "Race and School Quality since *Brown v. Board of Education*." *Brookings Papers on Economic Activity: Microeconomics* (1992): 269–338.

Botsch, Robert E. *The NAACP in South Carolina*. 1999. http://www.usca.sc.edu/aasc/naacp.htm. Accessed August 5, 2006.

Brinson, Claudia Smith. "Quiet Man Helped Change a Nation," (Columbia, S.C.) *State*, 2003, D1–2, McCain Collection, Caroliniana Library, University of South Carolina, Columbia.

———. "The Reverend Mr. Newman: A Long Way from Police Streets to Golden Anniversary Celebration." (Columbia, S.C.) *State*, June 18, 1979, B2: 9.

Burton, Orville Vernon. "The Black Squint of the Law: Racism in South Carolina." In David R. Chesnutt and Clyde N. Wilson, eds., *The Meaning of South Carolina History: Essays in Honor of George C Rogers*, 161–85. Columbia: University of South Carolina Press, 1991.

Byrnes, James E. *All in One Lifetime*. New York: Harper, 1958.

Clyburn.house.gov/index2.ctm. Official Web site of Congressman James E. Clyburn, South Carolina Sixth Congressional District.

Cohodas, Nadine. *Strom Thurmond and the Politics of Southern Change*. Macon, Ga.: Mercer University Press, 1993.

Corbett, Michael, and Julia M. Corbett. *Politics and Religion in the United States*. New York: Garland, 1998.

Crawford, Vickie, Jacqueline A. Rouse, and Barbara A. Woods, eds. *Women in the Civil Rights Movement: Trailblazers and Torchbearers, 1941–1965*. Brooklyn, N.Y.: Carlson, 1990.

Curry, John W. *Passionate Journey: History of the 1886 South Carolina Annual Conference*. St. Matthews, S.C.: Bill Wise Printers, 1980.

Davies, Gareth, and Martha Derthick. "Race and Social Welfare Policy: The Social Security Act of 1935." *Political Science Quarterly* 112 (Summer 1997): 217–35.

DeLaine, Joseph A. *Briggs v. Elliott: Clarendon County's Quest for Equality*. Pine Brook, N.J.: O. Gona Press, 2002.

Donohue, John J., and Jones Heckman. "Continuous versus Episodic Change: The Impact of Civil Rights Policy on the Economic Status of Blacks." *Journal of Economic Literature* 29 (December 1991): 1603–43.

Du Bois, William Edward Burghardt. "The Talented Tenth." In Booker T. Washington, ed., *The Negro Problem*, 31–75. Amherst, N.Y.: James Pott & Co., 1903.

Edgar, Walter. *South Carolina: A History*. Columbia: University of South Carolina Press, 2000.

Edgar, Walter, ed. *The South Carolina Encyclopedia*. Columbia: University of South Carolina Press, 2006.

Egerton, John. "The End of the South as an American Problem." In Larry J. Griffin and Don H. Doyle, eds., *The South as an American Problem*, 259–74. Athens: University of Georgia Press, 1995.

———. *Speak Now against the Day: The Generation before the Civil Rights Movement in the South*. New York: Knopf, 1994.

Fairclough, Adam. *Race and Democracy: The Civil Rights Struggle in Louisiana 1915–1972*. Athens: University of Georgia Press, 1995.

Ferillo, Bud. *Corridor of Shame: The Neglect of South Carolina Rural Schools*. DVD, directed by Lonnie Wehunt, Columbia, S.C., 2006.

Fladung, Thom. "Senator I. DeQuincey Newman Dies: Minister Was in the Forefront of S.C.'s Civil Rights Movement." (Columbia, S.C.) *State*, October 21, 1985, A1.

Fowler, Donald L. "Democratic Party." In Walter Edgar, ed., *The South Carolina Encyclopedia*, 257. Columbia: University of South Carolina Press, 2006.

Fowler, Robert, Allen D. Hertzkem, Laura R. Olson, and Kevin R. denDulk. *Religion and Politics in America: Faith, Culture and Strategic Choices.* 4th ed. Boulder, Colo.: Westview Press, 2010.

Franklin, John Hope, and Alfred A. Moss, Jr. *From Slavery to Freedom: A History of African Americans.* 8th ed. New York: McGraw-Hill, 2006.

Frazier, Franklin E. *The Negro Church in America.* New York: Schoken Books, 1964.

Frazier, Herb. "McCray, John Henry." In Walter Edgar, ed., *The South Carolina Encyclopedia,* 609. Columbia: University of South Carolina Press, 2006.

Frederickson, Kari. "'The Slowest State' and 'Most Backward Community': Racial Violence in South Carolina and Federal Civil Rights Legislation, 1946–1948." *South Carolina Historical Magazine* 98 (April 1997): 177–202.

Freeman, Richard B. "Political Power, Desegregation, and Employment of Black Schoolteachers." *Journal of Political Economy* 85 (April 1977): 299–322.

Gower, Calvin W. "The Struggle of Blacks for Leadership Positions in the Civilian Conservation Corps: 1933–1942." *Journal of Negro History* 61.2 (April 1976): 123–35.

Gregg, Howard D. *History of the AME Church: The Black Church in Action.* Nashville, Tenn.: African Methodist Episcopal Church, 1990.

Grose, Philip. "Activist Spirit Still Burns in Rev. Newman." (Columbia, S.C.) *State,* October 1984, B13, col.1.

———. *South Carolina at the Brink: Robert McNair and the Politics of Civil Rights.* Columbia: University of South Carolina Press, 2006.

Hamilton, Charles Horace. "The Negro Leaves the South." *Demography* 1 (January 1964): 273–95.

Harris, Fredrick C. *Something Within: Religion in African American Political Activism.* New York: Oxford Press, 1999.

Harris, Walter. "Rural Developments: The Crisis Facing Rural South Carolina." *SCRDC Newsletter* 1.8 (Summer 2008): 1, 3.

Hartsook, Herbert, Jr. "West, John Carl." In Walter Edgar, ed., *The South Carolina Encyclopedia,* 1014. Columbia: University of South Carolina Press, 2006.

Heard, Alexander. "Democracy Frontiers." *Journal of Human Relations* 2 (Spring 1954): 63–71.

———. *A Two-Party South?* Chapel Hill: University of North Carolina Press, 1952.

Heckman, James J., and Brook S. Payner. "Determining the Impact of Federal Antidiscrimination Policy on the Economic Status of Blacks: A Study of South Carolina." *American Economic Review* 79 (March 1989): 138–77.

Hine, William C. "Civil Rights and Campus Wrongs: South Carolina State College Students Protest, 1955–1968." *South Carolina Historical Magazine* 97 (October 1996): 310–31.

Hoffman, Edward D. "The Genesis of the Modern Movement for Equal Rights in South Carolina, 1930–1939." *Journal of Negro History* 44 (October 1959): 346–69.

Hollings, Ernest Frederick. *The Case against Hunger: A Demand for a National Policy.* New York: Cowles Book Company, 1968.

Hutchinson, Eric O. *Betrayed: A History of Presidential Failure to Protect Black Lives.* Boulder, Colo.: Westview Press, 1996.

Johnson, Charles S. "How Much of the Migration Was a Flight from Persecution?" *Opportunity* 1 (September 1923): 272–74.

Johnson, Rosamond F. *The Development of Negro Religion.* Chesapeake, N.Y.: ECA Association, 1991.

Johnston, Joyce. "Communism vs. Segregation: Evolution of the Committee to Investigate Communist Activities in South Carolina." *Proceedings of the South Carolina Historical Association* (1993): 19–29.

Johnstone, Ronald L. "Negro Preachers Take Sides." *Review of Religion Research* 11 (Fall 1969): 81–89.

Kern, David F. "S.C. Mourns Activist Era's Calm Diplomat." (Columbia, S.C.) *State,* October 22, 1985, A1, A7.

Key, Valdimer Orlando. *Southern Politics in State and Nation.* Knoxville: University of Tennessee Press, 2000.

Kirby, Jack Temple. "The Southern Exodus, 1910–1960: A Primer for Historians." *Journal of Southern History* 49 (November 1983): 585–600.

Kirk, W. Astor. *Desegregation of the Methodist Church Polity: Reform Movements That Ended Racial Segregation.* Pittsburgh, Pa.: Rosedog Books, 2005.

Kluger, Richard. *Simple Justice.* 1976; reprinted, New York: Vintage, 1997.

Lachicotte, Albert M. *Rebel Senator: Strom Thurmond of South Carolina.* New York: Devin Adair, 1966.

Lamis, Alexander Peter. "The Disruption of a Solidly Democratic State: Civil Rights and South Carolina Electoral Change, 1948–1972." *Journal of Political Science* 6 (Fall 1977): 55–72.

Lee, Joseph Edward. "Timmerman, George Bell, Jr." In Walter Edgar, ed., *The South Carolina Encyclopedia,* 464–65. Columbia: University of South Carolina Press, 2006.

Leemhuis, Roger P. "Olin D. Johnston Runs for the Senate, 1938–1962." *Proceedings of the South Carolina Historical Association* (1986): 57–69.

Lemann, Nicholas. *The Promised Land: The Great Black Migration and How It Changed America.* New York: Knopf, 1991.

Lewis , David Levering. *W. E. B. Du Bois: The Fight for Equality and the American Century, 1919–1963.* New York: Henry Holt, 2000.

Lincoln, Charles Eric, and Lawrence H. Mamiya. *The Black Church in African American Experience.* Durham, N.C.: Duke University Press, 1999.

Liu, Ben-chieh, Thomas Mulvey, and Chang-Tzeh Hsieh. "Effects of Educational Expenditures on Regional Inequality in the Social Quality of Life." *American Journal of Economics and Sociology* 45 (February 1986): 131–44.

Lochbaum, Julie Magruder. *The Word Made Flesh: The Desegregation Leadership of the Rev. J. A. DeLaine.* Pinebrook, N.J.: O. Gona Press, 1999.

Lofton, Paul S., Jr. "Calm and Exemplary: Desegregation in Columbia, South Carolina." In Elizabeth Jacoway and David R. Colburn, eds., *Southern Businessmen and Desegregation,* 72, 75. Baton Rouge: Louisiana State University Press, 1982.

Logan, Sadye L. M. "Social Justice, Political Activism, and Systems Change Related to Black Families and Communities." In E. Freeman and S. L. Logan, eds., *Reconceptualizing the Strengths and Common Heritage of Black Family Practice, Research, and Policy Issues,* 266–80. Springfield, Ill.: Charles C. Thomas, 2004.

Longfellow, Henry Wadsworth. *The Psalm of Life.* Kindle ed. Chennai, India: Nadu Press, 2011.

Margo, Robert Andrew, and T. Aldrich Finegan. "The Decline in Black Teenage Labor-Force Participation in the South, 1900–1970: The Role of Schooling." *American Economic Review* 83 (March 1993): 234–47.

Martin, John Bartlow. *The Deep South Says "Never."* New York: Ballantine, 1957.

Marx, Gary. "Religion: Opiate or Inspiration of Civil Rights Militancy among Negroes." *American Sociological Review* 32 (February 1969): 64–72.

McCray, John. "The Way It Was." *Charleston Chronicle,* November 29, 1980.

McMillian, George. "Integration with Dignity." In Ernest M. Lander and Robert K. Ackerman, eds., *Perspectives in South Carolina History: The First Three Hundred Years,* 382–91. Columbia: University of South Carolina Press, 1993.

Meier, August. "Epilogue: Toward a Synthesis of Civil Rights Activism." In Armstead L. Robinson and Patricia Sullivan, eds., *New Directions in Civil Rights Studies,* 221. Charlottesville: University Press of Virginia, 1991.

———. *Negro Thought in America, 1880–1915: Racial Ideologies in the Age of Booker T. Washington.* Ann Arbor: University of Michigan Press, 1993.

Minuchin, Salvador, Michael P. Nicholas, and Wai Yung Lee. *Assessing Couples and Families: From Symptom to System.* Boston: Allyn and Bacon, 2007.

Moore, William V. "Republican Party." In Walter Edgar, ed., *The South Carolina Encyclopedia,* 785–86. Columbia: University of South Carolina Press, 2006.

Moore, Winfred B., and Orville V. Burton, eds. *Toward the Meeting of the Waters: Currents in the Civil Rights Movements of South Carolina during the Twentieth Century.* Columbia: University of South Carolina Press, 2008.

Nantambu, Kwame. *Role of the Black Church during Slavery.* http://www.trinicenter.com/kwame/2007/0811.htm. Accessed February 15, 2008.

Newby, Idus A. *Black Carolinians: A History of Blacks in South Carolina from 1895 to 1968.* Tercentennial Studies no. 6, published for the South Carolina Tercentennial Commission. Columbia: University of South Carolina Press, 1973.

O'Neil, Stephen. "To Endure, but Not Accept: The *News and Courier* and School Segregation." *Proceedings of the South Carolina Historical Association* (1990): 87–94.

Page, Levona. "New Role for Newman: He Works within the Establishment for Civil Rights." (Columbia, S.C.) *State,* October 15, 1972.

Payne, Charles M. *I've Got the Rights of Freedom: The Ongoing Tradition and the Mississippi Struggle.* Berkeley: University of California Press, 1995.

Quint, Howard H. *Profile in Black and White: A Frank Portrait of South Carolina.* Westport, Conn.: Greenwood Press, 1958.

Richards, Miles S. "Progressive Democratic Party." In Walter Edgar, ed., *The South Carolina Encyclopedia,* 759–60. Columbia: University of South Carolina Press, 2006.

Richey, Russell E., Kenneth E. Rowe, and Jean Miller Schmidt, eds. *The Methodist Experience in America: A Sourcebook*. Nashville, Tenn.: Abingdon Press, 2000.

Robinson, William, Sr. "Democracy's Frontiers." *Journal of Human Relations* 2 (Spring 1954): 63–71.

Roefs, Wim. "Leading the Civil Rights Vanguard in South Carolina: John McCray and the *Lighthouse and Informer*, 1939–1954." In Charles M. Payne and Adam Green, eds., *Times Longer than Rope: A Century of African American Activism*, 462–91. New York: New York University Press, 2003.

Ruef, Martin, and Ben Fletcher. "Legacies of American Slavery: Status Attainment among Southern Blacks after Emancipation." *Social Forces* 82 (December 2003): 445–80.

Salmand, John A. *The Civilian Conservation Corps, 1933–1942: A New Deal Case Study*. Durham, N.C.: Duke University Press, 1967.

Shawki, Ahmed. *Black Liberation and Socialism*. Chicago: Haymarket Books, 2006.

Sherrill, Robert. *Gothic Politics in the Deep South: Start of the New Confederacy*. New York: Grossman, 1968.

Shin, Eui-Hang. "Effects of Migration on the Educational Levels of the Black Resident Population and the Origin and Destination, 1955–1960 and 1965–1970." *Demography* 15 (January 1978): 41–56.

Sitkoff, Harvard. *A New Deal for Blacks*. New York: Oxford University Press, 1978.

Smith, J. Clay, Jr. *Emancipation: The Making of the Black Lawyer, 1844–1944*. Philadelphia: University of Pennsylvania Press, 1993.

Smith, James P., and Finis R. Welch. "Black Economic Progress after Myrdal." *Journal of Economic Literature* 27 (June 1989): 519–64.

Southern, David W. "Beyond Jim Crow Liberalism: Judge Waring's Fights against Segregation in South Carolina, 1942–1952." *Journal of Negro History* 66.3 (Fall 1981): 209–27.

Sproat, John G. "Firm Flexibility: Perspectives on Desegregation in South Carolina." In R. H. Abzug and S. E. Maizlish, eds., *New Perspectives on Race and Slavery in Honor of Kenneth M. Stampp*, 164–84. Lexington: University Press of Kentucky, 1986.

———. "Newman, Isaiah DeQuincey (1911–1985)." In Walter Edgar, ed., *The South Carolina Encyclopedia*, 670. Columbia: University of South Carolina Press, 2006.

Stucker, Jan Collins. "Did You Know I. D. Newman Kept You Safe during Desegregation?" (Columbia, S.C.) *State* magazine, March 25, 1984, 10.

Sullivan, Patricia. *Days of Hope: Race and Democracy in the New Deal Era*. Chapel Hill: University of North Carolina Press, 1996.

Swinton, David. "The Economic Impact on African Americans after Brown." In Fred R. Sheheen, ed., ". . . And Miles to Go before I Sleep." Columbia: University of South Carolina Institute for Public Service and Policy Research, 2004. http://ipspr.sc.edu/brown/And Miles to go.pdf. Accessed April 2011.

Synnott, Marcia G. "Desegregation in South Carolina, 1950–1963: Sometime between 'Now' and 'Never.'" In Winfred B. Moore and Joseph F. Tripp, eds.,

Looking South: Chapters in the Story of an American Region. New York: Greenwood Press, 1989.

Thomas, James S. *Methodism's Racial Dilemma: The Story of the Central Jurisdiction.* Nashville, Tenn.: Abingdon Press, 1992.

Thompson, Thomas E. "Equal Education Opportunity." In Fred R. Sheheen, ed., " . . . And Miles to Go before I Sleep." Columbia: University of South Carolina Institute for Public Service and Policy Research, 2004. http://ipspr.sc.edu/brown/And Miles togo.pdf. Accessed April 2011.

Walton, Hanes, Jr. "Black Political Parties": A Historical and Political Analysis. New York: Free Press, 1972.

Weaver, Robert. "The NAACP Today." *Journal of Negro Education* 29 (Autumn 1960): 421–25.

Welch, Finis. "Catching Up: Wages of Black Men." *American Economic Review* 93 (March 2003): 320–25.

Wickenberg, Charles H., Jr. "Simkins Leaves Legacy of Civil Rights." (Columbia, S.C.) *State*, April 6, 1992, A1, A5.

Wolley, Deb. "Newman Provided a Cool Head When Tempers Ran Hot." (Columbia, S.C.) *State*, October 21, 1985, A5.

Woods, Barbara. "Modjeska Simkins and the South Carolina Conference of the NAACP, 1939–1957." In Vickie L. Crawford, Jacqueline Ann Rouse, and Barbara Woods, eds., *Women in the Civil Rights Movement: Trailblazers and Torchbearers*, 115–16. Brooklyn, N.Y.: Carlson, 1990.

———. "South Carolina Conference of NAACP: Origin and Major Accomplishments, 1939–1954." *Proceedings of the South Carolina Historical Association* (1981): 3.

Wright, Gavin. "The Civil Rights Revolution as Economic History." *Journal of Economic History* 59 (June 1999): 267–89.

———. "The Economic Revolution in the American South." *Journal of Economic Perspectives* 1.1 (Summer 1987): 161–78.

Yarbrough, Tinsley E. *A Passion for Justice: J. Waties Waring and Civil Rights.* New York: Oxford University Press, 1987.

Theses and Dissertations

Baker, R. Scott. "Ambiguous Legacies: Campaign against Segregation in Charleston, S.C., 1935–1975." Ph.D. diss., Columbia University, 1993.

Banks, James G. "Strom Thurmond and Revolt against Modernity." Ph.D. diss., Kent State University, 1970.

Brown, Millicent E. "Civil Rights Activism in Charleston, S.C., 1940–1970." Ph.D. diss., Florida State University, 1997.

Cox, Maxie Myron. "1963—the Year of Decision: Desegregation in South Carolina." Ph.D. diss., University of South Carolina, 1996.

Ellenburg, Henry Cooper. "The Congress of Industrial Organization in South Carolina." Master's thesis, University of South Carolina, 1951.

Faggart, Luther Brady. "Defending the Faith: The 1950 U.S. Senate Race in South Carolina." Master's thesis, University of South Carolina, 1992.

Farmer, James O., Jr. "The End of the White Primary in South Carolina: A Southern State's Fight to Keep Its Politics White." Master's thesis, University of South Carolina, 1969.

Johnson, Thomas I. "James McBride Dabbs: A Life Story." Ph.D. diss., University of South Carolina, 1980.

Lau, Peter F. "Freedom Territory: The Politics of Civil Rights Struggle in South Carolina during the Jim Crow Era." Ph.D. diss., Rutgers University, 2002.

Lochbaum, Julie Magruder, "The Word Made Flesh: The Desegregation Leadership of the Rev. J. A. DeLaine." Ph.D diss., University of South Carolina, 1993.

Martin, Dora Thomas. "The Attitude of the Spartanburg, South Carolina Press toward the 1954 Supreme Court Decision, 1954–1959." Master's thesis, Atlanta University, 1961.

Porter, Kristie. "The Legal Committee of South Carolina NAACP and the Struggle for Civil Rights in the 1960s." B.A. thesis, University of South Carolina, 1990.

Richards, Miles. "Osceola E. McKaine and the Struggle for Black Civil Rights, 1917–1946." Ph.D. diss., University of South Carolina, 1994.

Secrest, Andrew McDowd. "Black and White Press Opinion and Race Relations in South Carolina 1954–1964." Ph.D. diss., Duke University, 1972.

Terry, Robert Lewis. "J. Waties Waring: Spokesman for Racial Justice in the New South." Ph.D. diss., University of Utah, 1970.

Woods Aba-Mecha, Barbara. "Black Woman Activist in Twentieth Century South Carolina: Modjeska Monteith Simkins." Ph.D. diss., Emory University, 1978.

Contributors

Gloria Blackwell (Rackley) was an educator and civil rights activist. Inspired by the *Brown v. Board of Education* decision, she began to participate in and lead numerous nonviolent demonstrations to desegregate the schools, hospitals, and other public accommodations during the 1960s. She retired in 1993 after two decades of teaching at Clark College (now Clark Atlanta University) in Atlanta.

Tanya S. Brice is an associate professor in the School of Social Work at Baylor University in Waco, Texas. Her research interests include social welfare history, program evaluation, and adolescent sexual decision-making. Several of her published works are based on the historical method of research.

Millicent E. Brown is an associate professor of history at Claflin University in Orangeburg, South Carolina. She has published and written extensively about civil rights. She served as chief plaintiff in the 1963 Brown v. School Board District 20 case (Charleston, South Carolina), the first public school desegregation case in the state. Her most recent research interests include being project director of "Somebody Had to Do It," an effort to document all of the children involved in school desegregation nationwide.

Wallace Brown, Sr., is a community activist and former executive assistant to the president of Benedict College in Columbia, South Carolina. He is a former executive director and chief executive officer (CEO) of Richland community health care. He was a protégé and employee of Reverend Newman and is currently a consultant with Unison Health Plan.

James E. Clyburn is a congressman representing the 6th District of South Carolina and majority whip in the 110th Congress.

G. Robert Cook, a graduate of the University of South Carolina, is a retired state government grant coordinator and adjunct professor at Coker College. He was a longtime friend, coworker, and business partner of Reverend Newman.

Carrie Crawford Washington is a native of Rock Hill, South Carolina, and a graduate of South Carolina State University. She was hired by Reverend Newman while in graduate school and continued to work for him after graduating. She is currently a retired state government program manager.

Donald L. Fowler is president of Fowler Communications, Inc., and an adjunct professor in the Department of Government and International Studies at the University of South Carolina.

Karen Ross Grant, a retired state government project administrator, was a protégée and employee of Reverend Newman. After graduating from Winthrop College (now University), she worked in the 1970s with Reverend Newman as a research analyst in rural development across South Carolina. She has been an active member of and contributor to the community and the I. DeQuincey Newman United Methodist Church. Currently she is an active member of Trinity United Methodist Church in Orangeburg, South Carolina.

Sadye L. M. Logan is a professor and director of the I. DeQuincey Newman Institute for Peace and Social Justice, College of Social Work, the University of South Carolina. She is an accomplished scholar and editor of several books, including most recently *Mental Health Care in the African American Community* (2007).

Robert E. McNair served as governor of South Carolina during the height of the civil rights movement, from 1965 to 1971.

Josephine A. McRant, a freelance writer and private consultant, has a master of arts degree in management. She is a charter member of I. DeQuincey Newman United Methodist Church.

Jerome Noble was an active student participant in the civil rights movement and a protégé of Reverend Newman. He is currently director for the Fulton County Department of Purchasing, Atlanta, Georgia.

Matthew J. Perry, Jr., the first African American to be appointed to the federal branch of the U.S. District Court in South Carolina, was senior chief counsel for the South Carolina NAACP for twenty years. He is currently a senior U.S. District Court judge of South Carolina in Columbia.

Harrison Reardon, a civil rights activist, was deputy director of the South Carolina Department of Social Services from 1975 to 1995. He serves as chairperson and commissioner of Richland-Lexington Airport District (1992–present).

Richard W. Riley is former governor of South Carolina (1979–87) and former secretary of education (1993–2001). He is currently a senior partner of Nelson Mullins Riley and Scarborough, LLP, and resident in both the firm's Columbia and Atlanta offices, counseling clients on business, governance, and financial matters.

Wim Roefs is a historian and a freelance writer as well as an art dealer, consultant, and curator. He did doctoral work in American history at the University of South Carolina and has published several historical accounts and perspectives on American history. Currently he is the owner of ART Gallery in Columbia, South Carolina.

Alex Sanders, a graduate of the University of South Carolina and the University of Virginia, has been a lawyer, a legislator, a judge, a teacher, and a college president. He is now president emeritus of the College of Charleston and chairman of the board of the Charleston School of Law.

William "Bill" Saunders was commissioner of the Public Service Commission from 1994 to 2004. He is currently chief executive officer (CEO) of COBRA, a human service agency, and Gullah/Geechee Cultural Heritage Corridor commissioner (S.C.).

Hiram Spain, Jr., a graduate of South Carolina State College (now University), is a community activist, a local pastor at Saint Mark Baptist Church, and executive secretary of the Baptist Educational and Missionary Convention of South Carolina.

James S. Thomas, a resident of Atlanta, Georgia, is a retired bishop of the United Methodist Church.

Isaac "Ike" W. Williams, a former protégé of Reverend Newman, is a forty-year veteran of South Carolina politics. He served as South Carolina's chairman of the Youth Work Committee (1966–76), as South Carolina state field director for the NAACP (1969–83), and as chief district liaison for Congressman James E. Clyburn (1992 2008).

Esther Nell Knuckles Glymph Witherspoon, a lifetime member of the I. DeQuincey Newman United Methodist Church, is a community activist and retired cataloger and librarian at Allen University in Columbia, South Carolina.

Index

Page numbers in italics refers to photographs.